PECULIAR HONOR

Peculiar Honor

*A History of the
28th Texas Cavalry
1862–1865*

M. JANE JOHANSSON

THE UNIVERSITY OF ARKANSAS PRESS

FAYETTEVILLE   1998

06   05   04   03   02   5   4   3   2

Designed by Alice Gail Carter

☉   The paper used in this publication meets
the minimum requirements of the American
National Standard for Permanence of Paper for
Printed Library Materials   Z39.48-1984.

Library of Congress Cataloging-in-Publication Data

Johansson, M. Jane, 1963–
    Peculiar honor : a history of the 28th Texas Cavalry, 1862–1865 /
M. Jane Johansson.
        p.   cm.
    Includes bibliographical references (p.   ) and index.
    ISBN 1-55728-504-7 (pbk. : alk. paper)
    1. Confederate States of America. Army. Texas Cavalry
Regiment, 28th.   2. United States—History—Civil War,
1861–1865—Regimental histories.   3. Texas—History—Civil
War, 1861–1865—Regimental histories.   4. Southwest, Old—
History—Civil War, 1861–1865—Campaigns.   5. United
States—History—Civil War, 1861–1865—Campaigns.   I. Title.
E580.6 28th.J64   1998
973.7'464—dc21   98-10997
                                    CIP

To my parents
Lloyd Jack Harris
and
Belle (Standifer) Harris

TABLE OF CONTENTS

List of Illustrations

LIST OF TABLES

Introduction

*I hope the history of every Texas regiment and brigade
in the Confederate States army will be written. . . .
We have given too many Texas regiments and brigades
to the late Confederate States service, to let their
history sink into obscurity; besides, their bravery and
services are of such a nature as to cause a glow of pride
to tingle through every Texan heart.*

—Joseph P. Blessington, private,
16th Texas Infantry, Walker's division

When Joseph P. Blessington wrote these words in 1875, he believed
Walker's division had achieved a noteworthy place in history. If
Blessington were alive today, he would be disappointed that no full-length
work on any regiment of Walker's division has been written up until now,
surprised that so little has been penned about the Texas regiments which
served so gallantly in the Army of Tennessee and perhaps nonplused at the
many works on Hood's Texas Brigade. This work is an attempt to tell the
story of one regiment in Walker's Texas division, the 28th Texas Cavalry
(dismounted), a regiment with moments of glory and, like most Civil War
regiments, moments of shame also.

By choosing the 28th Texas Cavalry, I hope to highlight a division
only rarely written about, but with a worthy story to share. Walker's
"Greyhounds" fought in only five significant engagements—Milliken's
Bend, Bayou Bourbeau (only part of the division participated in these
two engagements), Mansfield, Pleasant Hill, and Jenkins' Ferry—but the

division campaigned extensively by marching and floating throughout Arkansas and Louisiana with minimal rest during the war. The men of Walker's division were proud soldiers who claimed victory in all of their engagements and succeeded in their primary goal: keeping the Union army out of Texas and, in the process, safeguarding their families and farmlands. Fortunately, one of the division's privates, Joseph P. Blessington, an Irish immigrant in the 16th Texas Infantry, wrote an indispensable history of the division soon after the war. Were it not for Blessington's history, the division would be virtually unknown. In spite of his book, the division's history still remains obscure, and no one, until now, has written a full-length regimental history of any of the units of Walker's division.[1]

I also intend to highlight the Trans-Mississippi Department and the role of Walker's Texas division in it. Traditionally, most Civil War historians have viewed the Trans-Mississippi as merely a footnote to the more "important" part of the war, the campaigns east of the Mississippi River. There is some justification for slighting the Trans-Mississippi part of the war. For the military historian, there were only a few large battles such as Wilson's Creek, Pea Ridge, Prairie Grove, and Westport to justify great interest. Not surprisingly, a casual glance at the literature of the Civil War reveals an abundance of histories on the war east of the Mississippi. A bibliography of the works about Gettysburg alone fills a good-sized volume. In recent years, historians have written fine new studies about such battles as Shiloh, Cedar Mountain, Second Manassas, Antietam, Murfreesboro, Chickamauga, the Atlanta campaign, and Bentonville. In all of these, writers draw upon a number of published and unpublished primary sources, including memoirs, letters, and also a number of regimental histories written by veterans or produced by modern writers.[2]

In contrast, there are few published sources for a Trans-Mississippi historian to utilize (especially one writing about the Confederate side). Regimental or other unit histories about Confederate Trans-Mississippi units are unusual. Fortunately, there is a sizable body of primary material for the historian to mine in regard to Walker's division. Some important primary sources regarding the 28th Texas were located to bolster the narrative portions of this account. These sources include the letters of Dr. Edward W. Cade, regimental surgeon and later brigade surgeon (John Q. Anderson published an edited version of these letters); the extensive correspondence of Capt. Theophilus Perry and his wife Harriet (unpublished); a short book about Pvt. Horace Bishop; a letter written by Capt. Pat H. Martin (unpublished); a letter written by Pvt. William F. Mills after the battles of Mansfield and Pleasant Hill; and a letter written by Maj. Henry G. Hall after the battle of Jenkins' Ferry. Still, a number of gaps in the history of the 28th remained. Additional sources, written by other members of Walker's division, were used to help fill the holes. These include the letters of Pvt. J. H. Armstrong of the 14th Texas Infantry (unpublished); the letters of Pvt. S. W. Farrow of the 19th Texas Infantry (unpublished); the memoirs of Robert S. Gould, commander of Gould's Battalion of Randal's brigade (unpublished); the reminiscences of Pvt. John C. Porter of the 18th Texas Infantry (unpublished); the wartime correspondence of hospital steward David M. Ray of the 16th Texas Cavalry dismounted (unpublished); the published letters of Capt. Elijah P. Petty of the 17th Texas Infantry as edited by Norman D. Brown; and the letters of Pvt. John Simmons of the 22nd Texas Infantry (unpublished).[3]

This history blends two distinct techniques in historical methods: the traditional narrative regimental history and the newer quantitative approach to historical subjects. Veterans wishing to memorialize their regiments or brigades published the first Civil War unit histories soon after the conflict ended. Although this interesting genre eventually reached a considerable size, most historians initially ignored these unit histories. Readers and scholars gave preference to works with a broader scope. Eventually, such writers as Bell I. Wiley and Bruce Catton used regimental and other unit accounts extensively in their rich histories. A fine, new generation of unit studies soon appeared. John Keegan's work, *The Face of Battle* (1976), spurred interest in common soldiers in general by calling for a new approach to military history, one that emphasized the common soldier's point of view.[4]

This "new" military history was soon reflected in Civil War literature. Recently a number of writers have studied various aspects of a regiment by using quantitative methods in an effort to learn even more about the common Civil War soldier. Historians began to use this nontraditional approach in the study of Civil War regiments to answer basic queries about occupation and age patterns of soldiers.[5]

To supplement traditional sources, compiled service records, muster rolls, census schedules, tax records, and casualty lists were used to construct a large database containing a record for each soldier who served in the 28th Texas Cavalry (dismounted) for analysis. This collective-biography approach yielded much information about ages, birthplaces, occupations, family connections, and a wealth of other data. The connection between wealthholding (which encompasses slaveholding, taxable income, value of personal estate, and value of real estate) and rank was closely examined. Some other questions posed included the following: How did original enlistees and later enlistees differ? Were officers and enlisted men dissimilar? Were companies different from one another?

To close, acknowledgments must be made to the helpful and patient staff of the Center for American History at the University of Texas at Austin, Peggy Fox at the Confederate Research Center at Hillsboro, Texas, and Michael R. Green at the Texas State Archives who alerted me to the Brigade Correspondence records. Correspondence with Duke University, the Huntington Library, Mansfield State Commemorative Area, Tulane University, and the United States Military Academy proved helpful. The University of North Texas Interlibrary Loan department, under the direction of fellow Civil War buff Mark Dolive, operated efficiently in filling all of my requests for material while I was a graduate student. The interlibrary loan department of Rogers University at Claremore, Oklahoma, performed the same service in my final frantic days of revising this manuscript.

On a more personal note, I would like to thank my parents, Mr. and Mrs. L. J. Harris of Shawnee, Oklahoma, for fostering my interest in Civil War history by taking me to battlefields, libraries, and museums. This in spite of my mom's insistence that "once you've seen one cannon you've seen them all." My advisor at the University of North Texas in Denton, Dr. Richard G. Lowe, asked probing questions and, in the process, helped shape the dissertation that this history is based on. In addition, since my graduation he has encouraged me to publish this work and has provided much appreciated advice. My research assistants during archival visits, my husband David and my mom, spent much time photocopying documents and taking notes. In addition, David made some important discoveries of materials on his own, listened patiently to my discussions of the 28th, visited battlefields, and critiqued my work even though his interest in history is "low-level." Much thanks goes also to former graduate student, Don Allon Hinton, who spent much time developing the database and support programs for the statistical part of this work, and in the process saved me a good deal of effort.

PECULIAR HONOR

CHAPTER 1

The Organization of the Regiment

A position in this regiment will be one of peculiar honor.
—Texas Republican, 15 March 1862

Texas cut its ties with the Union in a secession resolution passed on 1 February 1861. Only fifteen days later Texas troops in San Antonio captured the Alamo, a storehouse for Federal military supplies. Formal hostilities between North and South began with the Confederate bombardment of Fort Sumter, South Carolina, in mid-April. The surrender of Fort Sumter unleashed war fever in both sections of the country as thousands of men scrambled to volunteer. Texans were just as enthusiastic as their fellow Southerners. By the end of 1861 out of the state's military population of 95,026, Texas raised 17,338 cavalrymen to fill sixteen regiments and several smaller units in addition to 7,100 infantrymen. This marked preference for cavalry service irritated Gov. Edward Clark who set up special infantry training camps that would, in theory, illustrate the glories of infantry life. Most Texans were unimpressed and continued to enlist in the cavalry.[1]

Although thousands of Texans enlisted in the early days of the war, many more Texans held back and bided their time for various reasons. One of these was Theophilus Perry, a twenty-eight-year-old attorney residing in Marshall, Texas. A native of North Carolina, Theophilus was part of a well-to-do family able to provide a college education for him at the University of North Carolina. His father, Levin, immigrated to Texas in the late 1840s with several relatives and began to carve out a plantation in Harrison County in northeast Texas. In 1854 Theophilus returned to Texas as a college graduate and began to study for the bar examination. Two years later Theophilus was a practicing attorney in Marshall, the county seat, and possessed land and slaves given to him by his father. In 1859 Theophilus traveled to North Carolina to court his cousin Harriet Eliza Person, three years younger and of delicate health. The couple married on 9 February 1860 and set up housekeeping in Marshall.[2]

When the presidential election of 1860 occurred and the subsequent secession crisis, Theophilus Perry had definite opinions, but they were opinions he apparently failed to share publicly. Perry, like a number of other Texans, possessed conservative viewpoints and opposed secession. Not surprisingly Perry did not rush to volunteer: in addition to his views on secession, Theophilus doted on his first child, his daughter, Martha, born in the summer of 1861. As time passed though, Theophilus apparently felt increasing pressure to enlist. His younger brother, Hugh, enlisted in North Carolina, and four cousins in Harrison County took up arms. Serious reverses at Fort Donelson, Tennessee, and at Pea Ridge in Arkansas showed that the war would continue and apparently encouraged many to enlist in the Trans-Mississippi. As one young man in the north Texas town of Decatur explained "the idea of the Yankees heading for Texas soil to despoil our fair homes, insult our women and eat up the substance of the people was just a little more than we proposed to submit to." On a springtime day in 1862, Theophilus Perry enlisted in a newly forming company that became part of the 28th Texas Cavalry.[3]

In early 1862 several important changes occurred that affected Texas greatly—increased organization of the Trans-Mississippi region, passage of the first conscription act, the removal of thousands of troops from the Trans-Mississippi, and the raising of a new force including the 28th Texas Cavalry. On 10 January 1862 the Trans-Mississippi area received its first regional commander, Maj. Gen. Earl Van Dorn, who encouraged reenlistments, stiffened discipline, and recruited new units. A bill passed by the Confederate Congress on 27 January 1862 attempted to monitor the raising of cavalry. The bill sought to establish an increased level of organization in the raising of new cavalry troops by stating that only men holding commissions from the War Department were allowed to raise cavalry units. In early March 1862 Federals mauled Van Dorn's army at Pea Ridge in the woods of northwestern Arkansas. Following this defeat, from March to May 1862, approximately twenty-two thousand troops from the Trans-Mississippi were transferred across the Mississippi River to reinforce Confederate armies east of the river. Authorities had stripped the region of troops, and the Confederacy needed a new army for the defense of the Trans-Mississippi.[4]

The Confederacy's first conscription act aided in the raising of this new force. Conscription served as an impetus to enlistment in Texas and probably encouraged enlistment in the 28th Texas Cavalry. Passed on 16 April 1862, the law subjected every white man between the ages of eighteen to thirty-five to military service. The Confederate conscription act and the later Northern conscription laws were both controversial, partly because they allowed the practice of substitution (i.e., a drafted man could hire a substitute not of draft age to serve in his place). The Confederate government fashioned this conscription act to keep the twelve-month men in the service and to force more men into the military. Little more than a month after the passage of the conscription act, the Confederate government sent Maj. Gen. Thomas C. Hindman to the Trans-Mississippi with authority to raise an army and to conscript men. Hindman divided the area into districts and authorized the conscription of men who refused to enlist voluntarily. Thousands of men enlisted in Texas and requested cavalry service to escape the twin disgraces of being drafted and perhaps placed in another branch of the service. By mid-September 1862 Hindman had raised an army. In Texas alone nearly twenty-thousand men enlisted in the cavalry, most of whom remained in the Trans-Mississippi. Among the regiments raised in this great cavalry surge was the 28th Texas Cavalry, primarily organized by Horace Randal, a young professional soldier.[5]

Born on 1 January 1833 in Tennessee, Randal immigrated to Texas with his family after the Texas Revolution. His father, Leonard Randal, who would become one of the regiment's surgeons, served in the Texas Republic's Sixth and Seventh Congresses and then as an assistant surgeon

Horace Randal and His Wife

Photo courtesy of the Henry E. Huntington Library and Art Gallery

during part of the Mexican War. Leonard solicited a place for Horace at the United States Military Academy by writing to Secretary of War William L. Marcy in 1849. In the letter Leonard described his son as "sprightly, healthy, and sound in every respect," standing a slight five feet, four inches tall and weighing 120 pounds. The letter was apparently referred to Randal's congressman, David S. Kaufman, who recommended young Randal's appointment in February 1849, and Horace accepted the appointment in April 1849. Horace Randal entered the United States Military Academy in the summer of 1850 at the age of sixteen with only a limited educational background. Instructors at West Point found him deficient in English and mathematics, and he repeated his first year. Due partially at least to his educational background and his average standing in demerits, Randal was graduated forty-fifth out of forty-six members in the class of 1854. Because of his low class standing, the War Department appointed him to the infantry rather than to the elite engineering branch. His class included a number of graduates who became well known during the Civil War—Oliver Otis Howard, George Washington Custis Lee, Stephen Dill Lee, John Pegram, and James Ewell Brown Stuart. Perhaps some of these graduates or even the academy's superintendent, Robert E. Lee, had a favorable influence on Randal's development.[6]

By the time of the Civil War, Randal had gained experience in the infantry, the dragoons, and supply offices and had been in combat. After his graduation the War Department assigned him to the 8th U.S. Infantry as a brevet second lieutenant. Nearly a year later he was assigned as a second lieutenant in the 1st Dragoons on 3 March 1855. As a member of the 1st Dragoons, Randal took part in several Indian skirmishes on the Texas and New Mexican frontiers and at some point served as a quartermaster and commissary officer. In addition, Randal married Julia S. Bassett on 2 June 1858, in New London, Connecticut. Julia traveled with him to the southwestern frontier but died in the fall of 1860. When Texas seceded in 1861, young Randal traveled to Washington, D.C., where the *Texas Republican* (published in Marshall) later noted, that he settled his accounts and was offered command of a party of dragoons in Abraham Lincoln's inauguration parade. Angrily, Randal refused to take part in the inauguration and instead forcefully noted that "he was ready to take up arms with the South, and drive the traitors who had usurped the power of the government from the national capitol." He resigned his commission on 27 February 1861.[7]

Following his resignation Randal served in the quartermaster corps at Pensacola, Florida, and later became Gen. Gustavus Woodson Smith's inspector general in Virginia. In the fall of 1861 John Cheves Haskell also served on Smith's staff and in a postwar memoir described Randal as a "most diffident, modest man in speaking of himself." Yet Haskell, who went on to meet most of the important generals of the Army of Northern Virginia, also noted that Randal was

> in some respects the most remarkable man I met during the war. He was, when I first met him, a year or two under thirty, of a handsome carriage, and a most remarkable horseman. He never spared his horse, but rode always at half speed, day or night. I have seen his horse go down with him many times, but he was always up as soon as the horse was, on him and off again in the time that most men would take to pick themselves up. He was a classmate of Stuart at West Point, but had more physical dash than Stuart. His other classmates, Hood among them, always predicted that he would be the cavalry leader of the war if he got a chance.

Randal then was a "remarkable" man and an ambitious one also. While serving in Virginia, Randal requested a commission as captain from President Jefferson Davis. Although denied a captaincy at that time, the War Department eventually gave him permission to raise a regiment of Texas troops. Randal coordinated efforts to organize his regiment by traveling first to Marshall, Texas, in the spring of 1862 where he announced his plans to raise a cavalry regiment. Next he traveled to Austin, met with Gov. Francis Richard Lubbock, and then sent a letter to the *Texas Republican* in late March announcing Lubbock's approval of a proposed regiment under his call for fifteen regiments to serve for the duration of the war. The new unit was to be armed with "one of the most formidable weapons of modern warfare," the lance. More practically, the men expected to be equipped with pistols and "breech loading carbine[s]."[8]

The soldiers of the future 28th Texas Cavalry came almost entirely from east Texas, a region stretching from Bowie County in the extreme northeast, down the Louisiana-Texas border to Newton County, westward through Polk, Trinity, Houston, and Leon Counties, then northward through Freestone, Anderson, and Henderson Counties and continuing northeast to Red River County. Three-fourths of the regiment's soldiers were from six counties: Anderson, Cherokee, Freestone, Houston, Panola, and Shelby. In all, twenty-six different counties of residence and at least one other state (Louisiana) were represented in the ranks of the 28th Texas Cavalry.[9]

This area has been described as "a relatively homogeneous region of small and middling farms and plantations peopled mainly by Southern-born Protestants." Most east Texans were indeed Southern in origin, and many were part of the great migration to Texas in the 1850s that caused the state's population to nearly triple from 212,592 in 1850 to 604,215 in 1860. Their ancestors had emigrated from the Carolinas and Georgia, then into Tennessee or Alabama and had continued westward into Texas. In the early years of Texas independence many families entering east Texas came from Tennessee, but by the 1850s more and more families were emigrating from Alabama. These Southern emigrants, many of whom were farmers, soon began to till the soil of east Texas. The raising of livestock, particularly milch cows and other cattle, became increasingly important as did dairy products and crops of Indian corn, wheat, and cotton.[10]

In matters of religion, Protestantism dominated east Texas, with Methodist, Baptist, and Presbyterian churches being particularly prominent. In Cherokee County, for example, there were sixteen Methodist congregations totaling 9,600 members and ten Baptist congregations with 2,150 members in a total 1860 population of 12,098. Other counties were also heavily Protestant. Anderson County included nineteen Baptist, two Christian, one Episcopal, ten Methodist, five Presbyterian, and four Cumberland Presbyterian churches. Only one east-Texas county, Nacogdoches, listed a Roman Catholic church in the 1860 census.[11]

East Texas lacked many of the rudiments of what today would be considered "civilization." No towns in east Texas included as many residents as Houston (4,845), Galveston (7,307), San Antonio (8,235), or Austin (3,494) in the coastal and south-central regions. The Harrison County town of Marshall reached a population of "two to three thousand by 1860." Fairfield, in Freestone County, had a total population of 609 almost evenly divided between 301 whites and 308 slaves. Jefferson, in Marion County, listed 722 whites and 266 slaves for a total of 988, and the bustling town of Tyler in Smith County had a total population of 1,024. These cities were the major population centers in east Texas.[12]

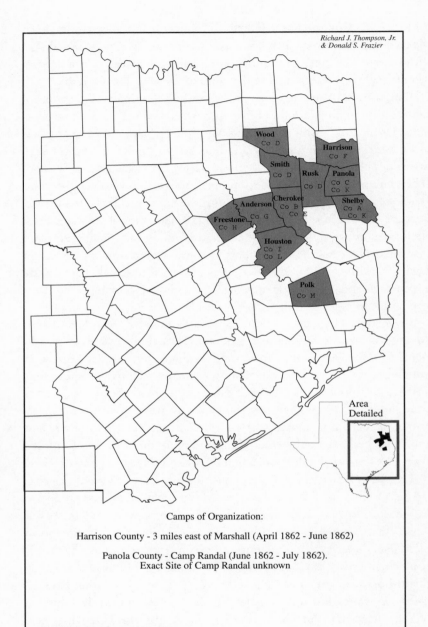

Richard J. Thompson, Jr.
& Donald S. Frazier

Area
Detailed

Camps of Organization:

Harrison County - 3 miles east of Marshall (April 1862 - June 1862)

Panola County - Camp Randal (June 1862 - July 1862).
Exact Site of Camp Randal unknown

Texas Counties
of Recruitment and Organization

An inadequate transportation system served the region, but in this it differed little from the rest of the state. By 1860 there were only six operating railroads in Texas, with a total of 306 miles of track. The Southern Pacific, an unremarkable twenty-seven miles long, was the only railroad in east Texas, and it served Harrison County primarily. Unlike many other counties in the region, Harrison was accessible to New Orleans via a waterway from Caddo Lake, to the Red River, and on to the Mississippi River. Those counties further inland relied on stagecoaches, saddle horses, and ox wagons.[13]

Manufacturing establishments were scarce and unevenly distributed in the region, conditions explained partly by the inadequate transportation system. Rusk County possessed the most manufacturing establishments in the area with eighty-five. Harrison and Smith Counties, which had two of the larger towns in the area, had thirty-two and fifty-seven manufacturing establishments respectively. These businesses were generally small and included blacksmithing, cotton ginning, shoemaking, carpentering, furniture making, wagon making, and distilling establishments. Some counties had even fewer manufacturers. Freestone, Panola, and Anderson Counties contained thirteen each, Houston County had twenty-two, and Shelby had five. In short, most of the men of the 28th came from an agricultural area with few transportation facilities or manufacturing establishments.[14]

Horace Randal organized the 28th Texas to be a typical Civil War cavalry regiment with twelve companies to consist of 115 men each. Each company's line officer contingent consisted of a captain, one first lieutenant, and two second lieutenants (one was referred to as a junior second lieutenant). In theory the regiment was to number 1,380 men, but the regiment achieved a strength of only 1,021 before leaving Texas.[15]

The new soldiers rendezvoused three miles east of Marshall. The first companies rode to this encampment where they were mustered into the 28th Texas Cavalry. During the week of 20 April 1862, two companies of "fine looking men" traveled through Marshall to the encampment. Interest was high in the new regiment, and a reporter soon made his way to the encampment to comment on progress. The first companies at the rendezvous were Companies B and E from Cherokee County, approximately 100 miles southwest of Marshall.

TABLE I

28th Texas Cavalry, Officers and Men on Original Roll

1 FEBRUARY–30 JULY 1862

CO.	NO. ON ORIGINAL ROLL	FOUND ON CENSUS NO.	%	MEAN AGE IN 1860	DOLLAR VALUE OF MEAN WEALTH ALL HOUSEHOLDS	PERCENT OF SLAVEHOLDING HOUSEHOLDS
A	98	58	64.4	26.5	9,496	35.6
B	102	66	64.7	27.9	2,501	28.8
C	88	52	59.1	27.8	3,413	30.8
D	81	55	67.9	27.5	2,073	23.2
E	84	39	46.4	21.3	8,834	38.5
F	75	26	34.7	30.1	8,072	37.0
G	72	43	59.7	27.1	5,303	32.6
H	100	65	65.0	25.4	4,337	32.3
I	91	53	58.2	24.6	1,332	11.1
K	91	47	51.6	26.2	3,482	25.5
L	86	45	52.3	25.5	2,563	13.0
M	53	26	49.1	25.6	7,216	46.2
Regt.	1,021	575	56.3	26.3	4,532	28.7

Company B formed in March 1862 under the command of Capt. Patrick Henry and began service as Company I of a unit later designated as the 17th Texas Cavalry. The reasons for Henry's company leaving the 17th are obscure, but according to surviving documents, Henry believed they would not "be received" by the 17th, perhaps reflecting interunit politics. Accordingly, Henry's company offered themselves to Horace Randal and later rode to the Marshall encampment where they arrived in April with about seventy-five men. Latecomers were added, and by the time the regiment left for Louisiana in July, Company B numbered ninety-eight men. Capt. Orlands M. Doty's Company E began its organization in early 1862 and grew slowly from thirty-four men in early February to forty-eight men in early April. By the time of their mustering into the 28th Texas Cavalry, Company E, bolstered by several enlistments in late spring, numbered eighty-one soldiers.[16]

On Tuesday, 6 May, a large company numbering about 125 men rode into the Marshall encampment and joined Companies B and E. The reporter from the *Texas Republican* remarked enthusiastically that the three companies were made up from the flower of Texas chivalry, are superbly mounted and equipped, and are commanded by men who will prove themselves, in the field, worthy of the positions assigned them. . . . Col. Randal's regiment will be perhaps the finest cavalry regiment that has ever been sent from Texas to the seat of war. The history and reputation of the Colonel for ability and gallantry has drawn towards him the best material in the State.

Capt. Alfred M. Truitt commanded the newly arrived company. Sixteen-year-old James W. Truitt, the company's bugler, perhaps rode near his father. Eventually designated "A," the company came primarily from Shelby County along the Louisiana-Texas border.[17]

By 17 May four other companies (C, D, F, and G) had joined Companies A, B, and E, and the camp now bustled with hundreds of new soldiers. Neighboring Panola County provided most of the men for Company C commanded by A. W. DeBerry. Eighty-one men of Company D, eventually commanded by Capt. Martin V. Smith, joined the 28th Texas from Rusk, Smith, and Wood counties. The "Harrison County Lancers" (Company F) began to form in February and March 1862 when a young grocer named Phil Brown advertised for cavalry recruits in the *Texas Republican.* Recruits were to supply their horses, although Brown offered to supply a horse to any who did not own one. Soon after Brown began advertising, Eli H. Baxter Jr. began recruiting his own company. Eventually the efforts of Brown and Baxter merged, and Company F was the result of their work. When Company G, commanded by Capt. William H. Tucker, arrived from Anderson County, about 115 miles southwest of Marshall, in May 1862, it was only partially organized; many of its men enlisted a month later.[18]

On 17 May the seven companies in camp elected their company officers and Horace Randal as colonel, Eli H. Baxter Jr. as lieutenant colonel, and Henry Gerard Hall as major. Both Baxter and Hall showed promise of being capable leaders. Baxter, a native Georgian, attended the United States Military Academy in 1853 when he was sixteen years old but resigned because he desired "a profession more peaceful in its avocations, and far more genial to his nature and impulses." This explanation obscured his indifference as a cadet. After examinations in January 1854, Baxter's instructors found him deficient in both mathematics and English and recommended his discharge. School officials accepted Baxter's resignation on 17 January 1854. While at the academy, Baxter accrued demerits for tardiness to meals, to reveille, and to parade; failed to clean his belongings properly; and socialized while on sentry duty. After his resignation he attended law school at the University of Virginia in 1856 and 1857 and obtained a law license. After receiving his law license, Baxter immigrated to Harrison County, Texas, and settled in Marshall in March 1858. In 1859 Baxter supported Sam Houston's gubernatorial campaign and quickly established himself as a stump speaker. Voters elected Baxter to the state legislature "by a triumphant majority." In spite of his recent support of Houston, who proved to be a firm unionist, Baxter, in a speech in Austin, showed clearly that he was a secessionist. When the war began, Baxter enlisted in the "Marshall Guards," a company organized in Harrison County as part of the 1st Texas Infantry. After spending several months in Virginia, he returned to Texas and helped raise Company F of the 28th Texas Cavalry. Henry G. Hall, a native South Carolinian, enlisted as a mere private in Company A at the age of twenty-nine. Hall, though, was no ordinary private soldier. He was a graduate of Princeton University and an established attorney with total holdings of six thousand dollars that included one slave. Thus, the three top officers of the 28th Texas Cavalry had all attended college, were professionals in their chosen fields, and were well qualified to provide leadership.[19]

In its first encampments, the men of the 28th Texas Cavalry began the transition from civilian to military life. The regiment engaged in a variety of activities at its first encampment near Marshall and later at Camp Randal in nearby Panola County. The enlisted men served on a number of details. At least some of these details related to the acquisition of weapons. A report that weapons awaited them in Little Rock, Arkansas, proved false, and the men were forced to impress arms. First Lt. Edward W. Cade of Company D sent out two detachments to Smith County near the end of June for this purpose. This business entailed many difficulties, as attested by Cade's report of these two detachments. "They pressed two from old Peter Marsh. The men were obliged to take them out of his hands by force. They also pressed a gun from old man Butler near Starrville. He cursed like a trooper." The regiment obtained other weapons by more peaceful means than impressment. Col. Horace Randal placed a call in the *Texas Republican* for arms for Company F and noted that the regiment would pay for the weapons. Besides weapons, the unit also lacked tents and other equipment. Near the end of June wagons left for the state penitentiary at Huntsville,

Texas, to pick up material for the tents. Even so, the men realized it would take about three weeks to receive the cloth, and then the tents had to be constructed from the raw material. Officers and presumably enlisted men petitioned their families for uniforms. Young Lieutenant Cade asked his wife for braid and two dozen brass army buttons.[20]

At Camp Randal in Panola County many of the soldiers first experienced homesickness. First Lt. Cade and his wife Allie, who was expecting the couple's second child, felt the pain of separation. In one letter to Allie, Cade wrote of his duty to the Confederate cause and said he felt fortunate that his family was not destitute. There was still much sadness though, and he wrote, "could I only be with you in our little home today how pleasantly would the time pass. Darling we have never felt as we should the happiness of our condition until forced to be separated." Cade noted that "the married men of the company are at me constantly for furloughs to go home to see their wives and I cannot find it in my heart to refuse them." Cade reported that only about thirty men were left in camp. The men knew of the impending movement to Little Rock in July and were taking the opportunity to visit family and friends, perhaps for the last time. Those who remained in camp heard Capt. Martin V. Smith's preaching that always drew a considerable audience. The officers socialized and sang with "numbers of young ladies." Cade, a physician by profession, particularly noted the fitness of his company and the healthy location of the camp but expressed fears that if disease struck, the men would "suffer tremendously."[21]

On 20 June, several weeks after the election of officers, a new company commanded by Capt. Patrick H. Martin was formed at Camp Randal by the surplus of the first seven companies. Companies A and C supplied the greatest number of surplus men for Company K. The new company was composed primarily of men from Panola and Shelby counties and an additional twenty men from DeSoto Parish, Louisiana, situated directly east of Panola County.[22]

Soon after Company K formed, Colonel Randal received an order from Brig. Gen. Henry Eustace McCulloch, commander of the Eastern District of Texas, directing him to move his regiment quickly to Little Rock, Arkansas. The regiment lingered in the encampment, though, waiting for the other companies to arrive.[23]

In early July, Company I and Company M arrived at Camp Randal from Houston County and Polk County respectively. Company I, organized in early June, was commanded by John A. McLemore. Capt. L. B. Wood's Company M joined the encampment with about fifty-three men.[24]

On 5 July, soon after the arrival of Company I and Company M, the *Texas Republican* reported that Colonel Randal had ordered the regiment to leave for Little Rock at 6:00 A.M. on 10 July. There was a flurry of activity as men returned to the encampment, and officers attempted to organize the move. The more diligent officers, particularly those with no military experience, attempted to school themselves in the complicated tactics of the nineteenth century. Many men, though, were engaged in departure ceremonies typical of Civil War units. The colonel himself was involved in an important last-minute ceremony. On Tuesday, 8 July, Colonel Randal married Nannie Taylor in Marshall. His bride traveled with him to Arkansas and stayed with him often during the war. At least two flag presentations took place before the regiment left Texas. The citizens of Starrville in Smith County presented Company D with "a battle flag" and then treated their guests to "a good dinner." Cora Sims presented a banner made by several Harrison County ladies to Company F. Speaking in front of the Marshall courthouse, Miss Sims impressed her audience with "her faultless pronunciation and the clearness of her enunciation." First Lt. Theophilus Perry of Company F accepted the flag with "an appropriate speech." Before leaving for Arkansas, eight companies of the regiment "paraded through [Marshall], presenting an imposing sight." The *Texas Republican* asked Chaplain Frank J. Patillo, one of the cofounders of the newspaper, to write to them on occasion and essentially serve as their correspondent. With the promise of another hot day, the regiment left Marshall and rode east toward Shreveport, Louisiana.[25]

The remaining two companies (H and L) joined the regiment on its ride to Shreveport. Though enlisting primarily in March, the one-hundred "Freestone Freemen" of Company H lingered for some undocumented reason in their home county before joining the 28th. Capt. J. C. Means led Company H of Freestone County throughout the war. Company L, the "Crockett Boys," formed near the end of June. Its captain, David A. Nunn, brought eighty-six men with him to join the 28th Texas.[26]

As all twelve companies, 1,021 strong, rode toward Shreveport a careful observer would have noted some general characteristics of this east-Texas regiment. Were the men of the 28th characteristic of their region? Were the men of the 28th typical of other Civil War regiments?

The men of the 28th Texas Cavalry were older than those in other regiments scholars have studied. The generally older age of the soldiers in the 28th was probably due to the passage of the Confederacy's first conscription act on 16 April 1862 that may have forced "older men into the army" as it did in Northern armies. The mean enlistment age for 553 men was 27.1, and the median was 27. In the 28th Texas Cavalry teenagers numbered eighty-nine (or 16.1 percent), almost half of the men (47.6 percent) were in their twenties, a substantial number were in the thirty to thirty-four age bracket (24.5 percent), and finally sixty-five men (or 11.7 percent) were thirty-five years or older. By comparison, in Sibley's Texas brigade (raised in 1861), teenagers accounted for 25.6 percent, 61.2 percent of the men were in their twenties, 9.1 percent were in the thirty to thirty-four age bracket, and only 4.1 percent were over thirty-five years. Conscription, then, was probably an important factor in explaining the regiment's older mean age. A wide age range existed in the 28th Texas Cavalry in spite of conscription. Fifteen-year-old Oscar F. Hall, a brother of Lt. Col. Henry G. Hall, qualified as one of the unit's youngest soldiers. Other youthful soldiers included William Cannon of Company A, who enlisted at age sixteen, and W. S. Eubanks, age sixteen of Company E, who served throughout the war. Dr. Leonard Randal, the father of Col. Horace Randal, enlisted at age sixty-two and was the oldest man in the regiment. Other "oldsters" included George R. Rains, age fifty, Alfred M. Truitt, a "retired merchant" from Shelby County who enlisted at age forty-five, and H. L. Givins, age forty-six.[27]

High percentages of married men, heads of households, and men with separate residences from their parents in the 28th Texas are probably connected to the conscription act. Most of the men identified in the census were heads of households (354 or 61.6 percent of those located in the census). These numbers corresponded exactly with married men (354 or 61.6 percent) and unmarried men (221 or 38.4 percent). The latter characteristics distinguish the regiment from other Civil War units at first glance. In the 3rd Texas Cavalry, a unit formed in 1861 and, like the 28th Texas Cavalry, recruited primarily in east Texas, only 22 percent of the men were heads of households (a number that implies most of the men were unmarried). In addition, the Civil War historian, Bell Irvin Wiley, noted in his landmark work, *The Life of Johnny Reb,* that the typical Confederate soldier was "more than likely unmarried." Wiley, though, commented on Civil War soldiers *as a whole* and did not compare soldiers who enlisted early in the war with those who enlisted after the conscription act in April 1862. Another scholar, Martin Crawford, has suggested that conscription encouraged a different type of man to enlist in order to escape the stigma of being a draftee. Crawford's case study of Ashe County, North Carolina, suggests that conscription accounted for an increased enrollment of married men in 1862 and may help explain the high percentage of married men in the 28th Texas Cavalry.[28]

Southern origins dominated among the men in the regiment. The individuals for whom birthplaces can be determined were predominantly from the lower South (with 392 [or 68.4 percent] born in that region), while 170 (or 29.7 percent) were born in the upper South. In contrast, only six (or 1 percent) were from the old Northwest, two (.4 percent) were from other parts of the country, and three (.5 percent) were foreign born. Nearly three-fourths of the men were born in four states: Alabama (160 or 27.9 percent), Tennessee (121 or 21.1 percent), Georgia (96 or 16.8 percent), and Texas (36 or 6.3 percent), but every slave state except for Delaware and Maryland was represented. Altogether, seventeen different states and two foreign nations were represented among original enlistees. As seen above, few men were from the North or foreign countries. Among those born in the North were E. W. Cade from Ohio, who later became regimental surgeon; Orlands M. Doty from New York; C. E. Ford from Connecticut; and several from Illinois, including John J. Gregg, G. N. Hancock, Alfred A. Kennedy, and Perry Starr. The few foreigners included Capt. Phil Brown of Company F, apparently born in the German states, and James Devine of Company D, an Irishman. In a large sample population of antebellum Texans drawn for a study conducted by Randolph B. Campbell and Richard G. Lowe, lower Southerners made up 51.6 percent of east-Texas heads of households, and upper Southerners composed 41.1 percent. In the 28th Texas Cavalry, 63 percent of heads of households were from the lower South, and 34.7 percent were from the upper South. Strong Southern origins, particularly with respect to the lower South, characterized the regiment and probably marked other east-Texas regiments as well. Approximately 60 percent of the 3rd Texas Cavalry, another regiment recruited primarily in east Texas, were from the lower South, about "a third from the upper South, and only 4.5 percent from the North."[29]

The men also shared a number of similar occupations. Farmers, farm laborers, overseers, and other agricultural occupations dominated all others in this regiment, with 75.3 percent of those located in the census (393 of 522) placed in this grouping. The next four categories in descending order were professionals, such as physicians, attorneys, and teachers (32 men or 6.1 percent); skilled workers including wagon makers, blacksmiths, and carpenters (31 or 5.9 percent); unskilled workers like clerks, wagoners, and barkeepers (27 or 5.2 percent); and those working in commerce including merchants, traders, and grocers (26 or 5 percent). The minor categories were manufacturers (7 or 1.3 percent), miscellaneous (5 or 1 percent), and public officials (1 or .2 percent). The most common occupation was farmer (339 or 64.9 percent), followed by farm laborer (39 or 7.5 percent), and merchant (18 or 3.4 percent). Other well-represented categories were physicians (14 or 2.7 percent), overseers (14 or 2.7 percent), lawyers (10 or 1.9 percent), and carpenters (10 or 1.9 percent). Despite the fact that most men engaged in agricultural pursuits, a number of different occupations were represented in the regiment. These included a grocer (Phil Brown, Company F), a furniture maker (W. J. Foster, Company L), a sheriff (William A. Jameson, Company B), a druggist (Leonard Randal Jr., Company F), a master cabinetmaker (H. P. Daviss, Company H), a lumber dealer (L. G. Suggs, Company G), a stable keeper (W. J. Averyt, Company G), and a contractor (J. W. Johnson, Company B). In effect, the regiment resembled a self-sustaining community and was about the size of Tyler, one of the largest towns in east Texas.[30]

The demographics of 28th Texas Cavalry closely resembled the region's with only small differences in professional and unskilled occupations. Interestingly, the younger and wealthier 3rd Texas Cavalry, although recruited primarily in east Texas, deviated markedly from the regional occupation patterns. In regard to wealth, a analysis of heads of households in the 28th shows no such deviation. The men of the 3rd Texas Cavalry were also much wealthier than the norm for the region as a whole.[31]

Speaking of the regiment in general terms obscures some of the diversity among the individual companies. The troopers of Company E collectively were the youngest of the regiment with an average enlistment age of 24.2 and 21.3 percent (19) of all the teenagers in the regiment. Many of these young men were scions of prosperous families, such as nineteen-year-old 2nd Lt. S. G. Wolfe, whose father owned forty-nine slaves and had a total wealth of $99,397. On the other hand, the soldiers of Company B had an average enlistment age of nearly thirty and had several members who were in their forties including Pvt. S. W. Aston, a forty-seven year old farmer and 2nd Lt. J. Matthew Newman, a forty-nine year old farmer.[32]

In all of the companies the majority of the men were engaged in agricultural pursuits. Company D, though, had the smallest proportion of those with agricultural occupations (52.1 percent) of any of the regiment's companies. Primarily from Rusk, Smith, and Wood Counties, Company D had one-fourth of all the professionals in the regiment (including four of the ten physicians in the 28th) and 29 percent of all the skilled workers in the unit. This pattern is explained in large part by the company's home counties, particularly in regard to skilled workers. Of the nine skilled workers in Company D, seven were from either Rusk or Smith County. These counties had more manufacturing establishments (85 and 57 respectively) than any other east-Texas counties, so it is not surprising that this company contained a higher proportion of skilled workers.[33]

The final distinction among the companies is in regard to wealth. Most of the companies in the unit reflected the economic circumstances of their home counties. The men of Company I possessed an average of $1,332 per man compared to $9,496 per man in the wealthiest company of the regiment, Company A. Company I was primarily from Houston County, a county that had already provided about 900 men to the Confederate army out of a total male population (ages 15 to 39) of 1,131 in 1860. The manpower of the county was nearly depleted by June 1862 when the company was formed. Although Houston County was relatively prosperous, the company was composed primarily of those owning small farms and no slaves. Nearly 60 percent were married men, and most had families. Conscriptions laws may have encouraged these men to enlist. Company A came primarily from Shelby County along the Louisiana-Texas border. Shelby County had a well-developed plantation economy even though it had one of the lower percentages of slaves (27.5 percent) in the region. The men in Company A reflected such an economy with their higher economic status: 35.6 percent of the men owned slaves, one of the higher proportions in the 28th Texas Cavalry. These figures pale in contrast to those of Company E of the 3rd Texas Cavalry, recruited primarily in Shelby and San Augustine counties. Their average wealth was $28,430, and 65 percent of them owned slaves.[34]

Like many Confederate regiments, the 28th Texas Cavalry included numerous soldiers tied by kinship bonds. Family connections were particularly conspicuous in the companies just discussed, A and I. In Company

A, Pvt. Alfred W. Wheeler, a farmer born in Tennessee, rode to war with two sons: Anderson, age 18, Henry, age 16, and a nephew Monroe, age 19. Enlisting soon after was Leonadus Wheeler , age 26, who was, perhaps, a third son of Alfred W. Wheeler. At least two of the officers were also related. Capt. Alfred M. Truitt's younger brother, Levi M., a thirty-two-year-old merchant, became the company's first lieutenant. After the captain's quick promotion to regimental quartermaster, the men elected Levi to the captaincy. Company I left for the war with a seven-man contingent of the Hallmark family as well as four Vaughn family members, four members of the Turner family, and three men from the Sikes [Sykes] family. Finally, Col. Horace Randal rode to war with his younger brother, Leonard Jr., who served on his personal staff and his father, Leonard, who was the regiment's first surgeon.[35]

The captains elected to lead the companies were a varied lot with little military experience. No background information is known for Capt. Patrick H. Martin of Company K. At least three of the twelve captains were veterans. Capt. Alfred M. Truitt of Company A served in the Mexican War while Capt. Orlands M. Doty of Company E and Capt. David A. Nunn of Company L had recently served in other Texas units. As a former member of the 3rd Texas Cavalry, Doty was already a veteran of actions in the Indian Territory and at Wilson's Creek, Missouri. Twenty-three-year-old Doty proved one of the most dependable officers in the 28th, and by the end of the war he was one of only three remaining original company commanders in the regiment. Captain Nunn, an attorney and former mayor of Crockett, was only twenty-five years old. In spite of his age, Nunn had already raised one company, Company I of the 4th Texas Mounted Volunteers, and participated in the New Mexico campaign. Nunn's original company, though, disliked him, and he resigned soon after the battle of Valverde, New Mexico, in February 1862. Returning home to Crockett, he raised Company L.[36]

Two captains, thirty-seven year old Patrick Henry of Company B and William H. Tucker of Company G engaged in agricultural pursuits like many of their men. Captain Tucker arrived in Shelby County, Texas, in 1841 with several brothers. When his brothers enlisted for the Mexican War, they reportedly left him in charge of the farm even though he was only nineteen years old. Tucker moved to Anderson County in 1856 and quickly established himself in politics as an alternate delegate to the Democratic convention that year. Though selected as a delegate to the 1860 Democratic convention, he declined attending because his support of Stephen A. Douglas rendered Tucker "obnoxious to the Texas delegation." Tucker was devoted to duty and known as "a born aristocrat . . . [who] was fastidious in personal habits."[37]

The remaining six captains engaged in either business or professional occupations. A. W. DeBerry of Company C, like Captain Nunn, practiced law. Company D had the services of twenty-five-year-old Martin V. Smith, a minister since the age of nineteen. Phil Brown (Company F), J. C. Means (Company H), John A. McLemore (Company I), L. B. Wood (Company M) and the young veteran, Orlands M. Doty, were all businessmen. Although three captains were veterans, the majority of the captains were ignorant of war matters and had much to learn about their new profession.[38]

Officers in the 28th Texas Cavalry were older, wealthier, and had more diverse occupations than the enlisted men (see Table 2). A sizable proportion (22.9 percent) of the officers had more than $10,000 in total wealth holdings. Additionally, a greater proportion of officers were married (71.4 percent compared to 60.8 percent for enlisted men), and more were heads of households (69 percent compared to 61 percent). In regard to occupations, officers were less likely to work in an agricultural occupation (43.9 percent compared to 78 percent for enlisted men) and much more likely to be in commerce or a professional occupation (53.6 percent) than the enlisted men (7.5 percent).

TABLE 2
A Comparison of Officers and Enlisted Men
ORIGINAL ROLL

	OFFICERS	ENLISTED MEN
Average enlistment age	31.9	26.8
Real estate (in dollars)	7050	1207
Personal estate (in dollars)	9221	2393
Wealth (combined real and personal estate, in dollars)	16,270	3603
Taxable property (in dollars)	7441	2090
Proportion of slaveholders (in percentages)	59.5	26.0
Average total acres	937	313
Value of farm (in dollars)	7906	1361

Why were officers wealthier and more occupationally diverse than the enlisted men? The regiment was a reflection of Southern society at that time. Although there were certainly wealthy enlisted men and poor officers, still Texans were more likely to elect officers who were preeminent in civilian life in some way. Often this meant electing men who were dominant economically or professionally. This was the case in the 3rd Texas Cavalry where company commanders and staff were "drawn from the economic and political elite of east Texas" and in Hood's Texas Brigade, and it was also the case in Ashe County, North Carolina, as noted in a case study by Martin Crawford. It was possible to be elected an officer even if one had little economic means, but other attributes such as character, occupation, or war experience came into play in such cases. Although Capt. Orlands M. Doty of Company E had no wealth listed in the census, he was a merchant and already had combat experience. Capt. David Nunn of Company L had little wealth in comparison to the other officers, but he had already raised one other company and was a lawyer and a former mayor. Both Doty and Nunn, though poorer, seemed to have promising leadership capabilities.[39]

As the 28th Texas Cavalry traveled along the dusty road to Shreveport, an observer, then, would have noticed that the 28th was perhaps little different than other Confederate units raised in the spring and summer of 1862. Older men and married men predominated in the regiment, family connections were apparent, and most of the soldiers were natives of the South. In many ways, the 28th Texas Cavalry reflected their east-Texas society closely with many Protestants, men of moderate means in the ranks, and men accustomed to working with the soil. Although these east Texans were now officially considered "soldiers" by the War Department, the enlisted men and their officers had much to learn about the military on the road to Shreveport and beyond.

CHAPTER 2

From Texas to Arkansas

We are all mighty green.
—LT. THEOPHILUS PERRY, COMPANY F, 28TH TEXAS CAVALRY

By 12 July the 28th arrived near Shreveport and set up a camp. The camp was uncomfortable owing to the extreme heat and the clouds of dust that seemed to cover everything. Lieutenant Perry found the conditions "disagreeable" and fought to keep clean by taking some form of sponge bath at night. The stay at Shreveport was not disagreeable to everyone, however. Many of the officers traveled into town, and at least one staff officer, Commissary Sgt. Rene Fitzpatrick Jr., returned to camp drunk. On 13 July, a Sunday night, Lieutenant Perry, serving as regimental provost, went into Shreveport, accompanied by sixteen enlisted men and three other lieutenants, and "scour[ed] the town out." They brought back a long line of soldiers from the assorted brothels of Shreveport. Perry informed his wife, Harriet, that on this expedition "he had to go to some places, a gentleman ought never to be caught at, and take them [the soldiers] out of the presence of their amours." In addition to the latter duty, Perry also visited guards placed around the city and made sure they were checking for passes properly. He admitted to his wife, though, that he hardly knew his duties and confessed that "we are all mighty green."[1]

The unit busied itself with other activities as well. The soldiers shoed the horses and repaired wagons. Some of the officers tried to shop in Shreveport for items to send home, but the stores had little stock. The regiment still lacked important supplies, and there were still no tents, not even for the staff. The unit remained healthy, however. Perry attributed the regiment's good health to the lack of tents, for he had noticed that the companies in Col. George Washington Carter's brigade that slept out of their tents were healthier than other companies. A few cases of measles erupted in the 28th Texas Cavalry, though. When one of the enlisted men of Company F became ill, Perry offered to pay his bill so he could stay at a hotel. The appearance of measles worried Perry who had his personal servant, Norflet, with him, and he was concerned that Norflet may not have had the measles. Perhaps this was also a concern of two others Perry knew, Nathan P. Ward and 2nd Lt. James S. Wagnon who each had a personal servant.[2]

Randal's regiment left Shreveport on 18 July after the colonel received orders urging him on to Little Rock, Arkansas. They could leave no earlier because Colonel Carter's brigade had kept the farrier shops busy, and there was a delay in the 28th for horseshoeing. On the 18th the regiment traveled northward seven miles toward Arkansas and then camped. The rumor was that the enemy had entered the White River country in Arkansas. Meanwhile, Lieutenant Cade and a detachment of men were sent ahead of the regiment to establish advance campgrounds for the unit. On 21 July Cade wrote from a point approximately twenty-five miles south of Arkadelphia, Arkansas, on the Little Missouri River and stated that the regiment was four days late. He attributed the unit's tardiness to the order he had heard to dismount (i.e., to change the regiment from cavalry to infantry).[3]

The order to dismount was not officially issued until 28 September 1862. It is apparent that by late July rumors of an impending order to dismount were already circulating. The *Texas Republican* of 26 July reported that cavalry regiments moving to Arkansas would be ordered to dismount. The 28th Texas Cavalry apparently remained mounted until at least early September when a detail returned the regiment's horses to Texas. Although some units were threatened with dismounting as a punishment, this was usually confined to the later stages of the war and did not include the 28th

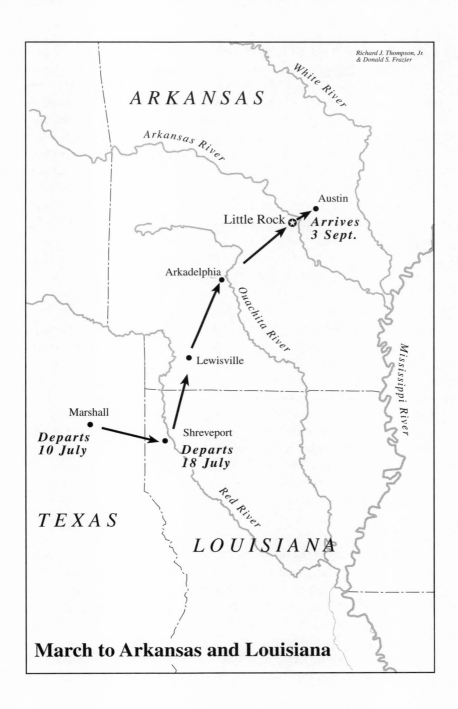

Richard J. Thompson, Jr.
& Donald S. Frazier

March to Arkansas and Louisiana

Texas. Nor was the order to dismount due to a shortage of horses. The Trans-Mississippi Department had many problems, but it never had a lack of horses, because Texas had a surplus of mounts throughout the war. Rather, authorities ordered several cavalry regiments dismounted because of a shortage of infantry and a lack of forage for the horses in Arkansas. Lieutenant Cade, who was required to gather supplies for the 28th Texas Cavalry at the advance camps, noted the difficulty of obtaining forage for the animals. He estimated that it took "250 bushels of corn and 9000# fodder to do them [the regiment] of a night."[4]

It is not known how the men of the 28th reacted to the news of dismounting. Other cavalry regiments in similar circumstances reacted with anger, bitterness, and a sense that they had been betrayed by the military. Texans were known for their decided preference for cavalry service. Dismounted units, including the 28th, refused to call themselves infantry, instead preferring the label "dismounted cavalry" as though it were a temporary condition. The immediate effect of dismounting was a loss of morale and occasional discharges and resignations of men who were clearly unable to stand the stress of marching. An example of the latter was the case of 2nd Lt. John N. Garner of Company I, who enlisted in the 28th because it was a cavalry regiment. Constant marching so inflamed an old ax injury on Garner's foot that it led to a bone fracture and then a chronic ulcer. Garner resigned in August 1863 after being unable to put on a boot, or even walk, for two months. Men such as this were eventually weeded out by the conversion of the regiment to infantry.[5]

Progress was slow as the regiment traveled, probably still by horse, from Shreveport to Lewisville, Arkansas, a town approximately twenty-five miles east of Texarkana. Lack of regular meals for the men, the near absence of fodder, and the inexperience of the regiment were all factors in the slow journey. Finally by 5 August, the regiment was encamped at Lewisville. Rumors flew about the camp as men speculated on their next movements. At least at Lewisville there were sufficient supplies for the regiment despite the fact that the country appeared ravished, probably because of the other military units that had passed through the area. Perry stated that "the poor people live as poorly as Job's Turkey," and Cade noted in a letter near Lewisville that the inhabitants were rough but good hearted. Cade saw many women without shoes, and if they owned shoes, they often lacked stockings. Lieutenant Perry saw more redeeming features. He told his wife that the women were "kind and attentive" and that he would "never forget the hospitality of these people."[6]

The men grumbled a great deal in camp, a situation that Lieutenant Perry believed was typical in large gatherings of people. Probably the news of dismounting and the demoralizing presence of one hundred sick men from the 18th Texas Infantry recovering from the measles caused much of the complaining. Then too, the men may have been getting used to camp life. Perry noted that men became indifferent to cleanliness quickly in camp. He personally reported changing clothes several times a week and washing each night, but still he was dirty. The 28th probably spent several days in Lewisville and then continued their trek northeast toward Little Rock. On 3 September 1862 the regiment arrived in camp two miles from Austin, Arkansas, a town about twenty miles northeast of Little Rock.[7]

Soon the various regiments at Austin, Arkansas, were organized into brigades. By 17 September the regiment was part of a brigade commanded by their former colonel, Horace Randal, and composed of Col. Oran M. Robert's 11th Texas Infantry, Col. Edward Clark's 14th Texas Infantry, Col. John W. Speight's 15th Texas Infantry, and Maj. Robert S. Gould's dismounted 6th Texas Cavalry Battalion. Like the 28th Texas, all of the units in the brigade were organized in 1862. The 11th Texas and the 14th Texas were primarily east-Texas units like the 28th Texas. The band of counties northwest of Houston (Freestone, Leon, Madison, and Walker) contributed heavily to the composition of Gould's Battalion. Colonel Speight and his 15th Texas left the brigade sometime in late 1862 or early 1863 and campaigned for a time in the Indian Territory. The 15th Texas eventually returned to the division and was assigned to a different brigade. In September 1862, Randal's brigade was reported to number three thousand in effective strength, an average of about six hundred per unit, although Gould's battalion numbered about four hundred men. During this time, Companies L and M were removed from the 28th Texas Cavalry. Company L, commanded by Capt. David A. Nunn of Houston County, remained mounted and became part of Lt. Col. Charles L. Morgan's cavalry regiment. Company M remained in Randal's brigade, becoming Company K of the 14th Texas Infantry. The division, composed at that time of Randal's and Col. Overton Young's brigades, was commanded by Brig. Gen. Henry E. McCulloch. By December the division was augmented by a third brigade commanded by Col. George Flournoy. The division was composed entirely of troops recruited in Texas.[8]

The transition from civilian to soldier was undoubtedly difficult for most of the men of the 28th as well as the other volunteer regiments near Austin, Arkansas. Robert S. Gould, the commander of Gould's Battalion in Randal's brigade, highlighted some of the problems by stating that his battalion was "armed with double-barreled shotguns and rifles, dissatisfied and dispirited at being dismounted, thinned by the measles and other diseases." It was hoped that eventually one company in each regiment would be armed with Enfield rifles to "act as skirmishers." At that time, though, soldiers were mostly thinking about their daily routine, a rigorous schedule typical of most Civil War camps. A typical day at Camp Holmes, according to Lieutenant Cade, included the following activities:

5:00 A.M.	Reveille beat and roll called
5:30 A.M.	Surgeon's call for the sick
7:00 A.M.	Guard mounting
7:00–8:00 A.M.	Officer's drill
8:00–10:00 A.M.	Company drill
NOON	Dinner
2:00–5:00 P.M.	Battalion drill
6:00 P.M.	Dress parade
8:00 P.M.	Tatoo; preparation for bed
9:30 P.M.	Taps beat and lights off

The days were so long and fatiguing that they could wear out a unit. On the day Lieutenant Cade described above, his Company D numbered only fourteen men present for duty; the rest were either sick or on detached service.[9]

In spite of the work, there were some high points in camp. Some of the pastimes that the soldiers engaged in when not drilling were attending revivals and playing cards. The regiment's chaplain, Frank Patillo, organized a camp meeting that proved to be popular among the homesick men who "would listen to anything in order to mitigate anxiety." Soon the revival lasted until midnight, a time inconsistent with military life, and Colonel Randal ordered an end to the meetings. When Patillo refused to stop he was "ordered home" thus sparking "an insurrection in camp." Colonel Randal became unpopular as a result of this action but quickly restored his reputation until his men "would not give him up as Col if they could help themselves." When not drilling or attending religious meetings, many members of the 28th played cards, an activity they held in common with most Confederate soldiers. In the 28th the many variations of poker were the most popular with one called "freeze-out" being perhaps the most played. To play freeze-out, five or six men obtained something good to eat like a watermelon or a pig. The participants played the game with kernels of corn representing money. The man who ended up with all the kernels was the winner and thus claimed the prize. The winner then had the choice to share the prize with his opponents or freeze them out by eating it alone. Most soldiers shared their prize rather than risk the label of thief.[10]

Other soldiers carefully observed camp life. Lieutenant Cade enjoyed the "7 or 8 good Brass Bands in the regiment and we hear some fine music on dress parade and at the different calls during the day." Lieutenant Perry seemed to take pride in the regulation encampment of the regiment, especially the recently arrived tents laid out in precise rows according to company. David Ray of the 16th Texas Cavalry (dismounted) enjoyed the artillery drill and declared it "a right pretty sight." In spite of these things, the soldiers' appearance undoubtedly was uninspiring.[11]

The units encamped around Austin were plagued with a lack of clothing, a problem that persisted throughout the war years. By the winter of 1862 the army was in dire need of clothes. The men were "dependent almost entirely upon local and domestic manufactures." Regiments generally sent their quartermaster or another representative to Texas to gather clothing donations. As early as October 1862, notices appeared in the *Texas Republican* for clothing and other necessities for Capt. Phil Brown's Company F. Small parties of men were detached from the regiment to collect clothing and assist in other duties in Texas throughout the war. These Trans-Mississippi troops were destined to spend the war in inferior and shoddy clothing. Even officers had difficulties with clothing as attested in the Perry correspondence. Harriet warned Theophilus to "*not let* Norflet abuse your clothes. Make him take time to wash them well."[12]

The search for food seemed to be easier, at least during the initial stages of the encampment. The gathering of provisions involved a number of wagons pulled by either horses or mules. At least one six-horse wagon was allowed to each company, and each regiment was allowed a medical, an ordnance, and two staff wagons. A commissary train of twelve four-horse wagons was allowed each brigade. Randal's brigade alone required approximately eighty wagons and at least 350 horses or mules. Finding forage for the animals did not present a problem in September, but even at that comparatively early date, beef was becoming scarce for the troops. Five hundred bushels of meal were required each week for the brigade. Details often traveled fifteen miles in September to acquire the meal. By November soldiers were traveling twenty-five miles to obtain corn. In addition, large numbers of men were required to keep the wagons in good repair and the mules and horses shod. The number of men detailed for special or extra duty varied from company to company, dependent partially on the number of healthy men available for service. Company A reported twelve men detached for special duty in late 1862. Company D reported eighteen detached men, and Company H, fifteen detached soldiers. Many of these men were detailed as teamsters, but some served as either blacksmiths or nurses. In addition, constant rumors about impending movements made it difficult to keep the brigade in order. Lieutenant Perry reported that as acting brigade quartermaster he was instructed to be ready to move "at a moments warning." Still, there were perquisites for staff officers—Perry and his tentmates had a wagon, a tent, and two slaves.[13]

When Colonel Randal began his new duties as brigade commander, Lt. Col. Eli H. Baxter Jr. became the new commander of the regiment. Lieutenant Cade politicked for regimental commissary, and Lieutenant Perry hoped for an appointment as regimental quartermaster but refused to ask for the position. Throughout his military career, Perry remained critical of Baxter, commenting on his political ambitions and convinced that Baxter made friends with those who would become his political supporters someday. In Perry's opinion, Baxter was a demagogue. Others whom Perry disliked included George T. Howard, the adjutant, and Rene Fitzpatrick, second lieutenant in Company F. He believed that Baxter and the latter two were "inclined to dissipate . . . it is doubtful whether men of moral sensibilities like either of them have can be true friends to any body." Such tensions among ambitious men made it difficult for the regiment to become a team.[14]

There were also rivalries among the brigade officers, with colonels debating the question of seniority. In mid-September Maj. Gen. Theophilus Hunter Holmes, the department commander, traveled to Austin to settle the question. While subordinate officers looked on curiously and deferentially, General Holmes gathered all the brigade colonels around him and stated that his decisions must be obeyed and that he would crush out any discontent. Opposition to the youthful Randal surfaced during this time. Holmes, though, sided with Randal by complimenting him on his enthusiasm and capabilities. The general did state, however, that Randal was young and not conciliatory enough. Warming to his topic, Holmes continued by advising Randal to gain "the esteem and love of his Men, and officers." The issue was settled for the time being, but within a few months Randal would meet opposition by another colonel in his brigade.[15]

In spite of the arduous schedule and officer rivalries, rumors still flew through the encampment. Some of the most interesting, for those regiments recruited in north Texas, revolved around the Unionist movement in Cooke County. Others reflected on a possible march north to Missouri where the soldiers would recruit and "make the Federals smell brimstone." Occasionally, Federal prisoners were brought through camp. The sight of them filled Lieutenant Perry "with hatred and vindictiveness." The soldiers longed to fight, and a number of the Texas regiments, including Baxter's, complained of the lack of military operations. Others, though, longed for peace. Cade hoped that rumors of Confederate victories in the east would bring an early peace. The soldiers did not move, though, and the drilling continued. First Lieutenant Cade did not receive the commissary position, but he did pass an examination before the Medical Examining Board and became a surgeon. On the morning of 22 September a special order concerning Cade's resignation as first lieutenant and appointment as surgeon was read during dress parade in front of the entire brigade. Colonel Randal gave Cade the special order which the proud surgeon sent home to his wife to be "preserved *always* to show what sort of a Soldier I made my Country."[16]

By midautumn, disease had infected the regiments camped at Camp Nelson near Austin, filling the newspapers back home with morbid lists of those struck down by germs rather than enemy bullets. Hundreds of soldiers died that winter at Camp Nelson, a situation unfortunately common during the Civil War. Indeed, disease killed two soldiers for each man who died in battle. Typically, as at Camp Nelson, the first wave of infection, consisting of measles and mumps, sickened hundreds of men. Next, the second wave of infection, including dysentery and various fevers, swept through the camp. This second wave often proved to be the deadliest a regiment would experience during the war. These diseases were generally most deadly in those regiments recruited from rural areas, where the likelihood of prior exposure was low. The 28th Texas Cavalry was struck particularly hard by disease during this period, probably because of the overwhelmingly rural background of the men. At Camp Nelson the army's condition was apparently weakened by its "cornbread and beef" diet, insufficient clothing, and the weather. The worst seemed to strike in early November following a brief snow storm in late October and freezes every night. Cade reported the "Army dying up like rotten sheep," with the 28th reporting only 150 men well enough for duty and the rest either sick or recovering. The number of ill men was appalling. In November 1862, during the worst time, Companies A, D, and H reported respectively thirty-three, twenty-four, and twenty-seven sick men. These figures were little different from those for other companies.[17]

Companies were nearly incapacitated by the large numbers of sick, dead, and detached soldiers. Company I had the highest death rate by 19 December 1862 with fifteen dead men; Company A had fourteen. Miraculously, Company C reported no deaths at that time. Among the sick was Dr. Cade who became ill with dysentery after his appointment to St. John's Hospital in Little Rock. Cade recovered at a private home near camp with the help of a nurse assigned from Company D. Some of the other soldiers were also boarded in private homes near the camp, sometimes nursed by a brother or good friend from the regiment. Camp life was depressing, with volleys being fired nearly every hour "over the graves of poor fellows who have died far away from friends and relatives." In the 28th Texas Cavalry, seventy-eight men had died and forty-six men had been discharged by 19 December. Most of the deaths and discharges occurred in November or early December. Death was no respecter of rank. Included in the toll was Capt. Pat H. Martin, commander of Company K. By 1 January 1863 seventy-seven men had died in the 14th Texas Infantry, also in Randal's brigade. Near the height of the sickness, furloughs were limited and resignations were examined more carefully. Cade claimed that "a man must be near the point of death before they will grant either."[18]

Morale plummeted as a result of this policy and the spread of disease. In February 1863 the *Texas Republican* published a list of stragglers and deserters from the Arkansas army. Included in the list were thirty-six supposed stragglers or deserters from the 28th Texas Cavalry, ten from the 14th Texas Infantry, five from the 11th Texas Infantry, thirteen from Gould's Battalion, and fifteen from Capt. Horace Haldeman's battery, attached to

Randal's brigade. Few of the men included in the total for Baxter's regiment were actual deserters, for all but a handful returned to the regiment. Rather, many were recovering from illness or perhaps had become so demoralized that they simply went home for a visit.[19]

Like other Civil War soldiers, the men camped around Austin, Arkansas, became somewhat callous to death as measles, mumps, and other diseases swept through regiments recruited from rural areas. Lieutenant Perry related one instance where a company from another regiment went out to dig a grave for one of their comrades. When they carried the corpse out to the freshly dug grave, they discovered that another man had already been buried in it. This started the joke that a dead man's grave had been stolen. A soldier in the 16th Texas Cavalry (dismounted), later camped near Little Rock, wrote his sister in August 1862 that "men become accustomed to anything here, they will even play cards while perhaps a man is dying in the next tent." Cade echoed this sentiment when he complained that men became selfish and would not even help their friends and relatives when they were ill.[20]

In late November the remnants of the 28th Texas Cavalry embarked on their first campaign. By this time the previously naive boys and men in the regiment had learned the basics of drill and through other experiences were becoming soldiers. As in other Civil War regiments, disease, camp life, drilling, and marching had served to weed out the old, the weak, and the injured in a process dubbed "'simmering down.'" The horrifying power of disease shocked most Civil War soldiers, even though they were perhaps initially more familiar with death than Americans are today. This experience, coupled with the strangeness of camp life, helped harden the men to suffering. In the space of only a few months, soldiers in the 28th had nearly completed the transition from civilian to soldier.[21]

CHAPTER 3

The Vicksburg Campaign

It may be strategy, but it looks to me like confusion.
—LT. THEOPHILUS PERRY, 28TH TEXAS CAVALRY,
14 DECEMBER 1862

S oon after the initial "simmering down" process, the regiment left on its first campaign: an effort to relieve the beleaguered Post of Arkansas on the Arkansas River. This campaign involved the regiment and the rest of Walker's division for the first time in the Vicksburg campaign. Union forces under Maj. Gen. Ulysses S. Grant and Maj. Gen. John A. McClernand began their movements toward Vicksburg, Mississippi, a Confederate stronghold along the Mississippi River, in November 1862. In July 1863 Vicksburg finally surrendered, after months of maneuvering and fighting between the opposing sides in every state that bordered Mississippi. Caught up in this huge struggle, the 28th Texas Cavalry and other Confederate Trans-Mississippi forces played bit parts that culminated in failure because of a faulty intelligence system, Maj. Gen. Richard Taylor's strategic miscues during the Milliken's Bend campaign, and the unwieldy departmental system of the Confederate military. In spite of the failure of the Trans-Mississippi Department to relieve Vicksburg, the difficult campaign transformed the men of the 28th into soldiers.

On 23 or 24 November 1862, Brig. Gen. Henry Eustace McCulloch's division left Camp Nelson and marched about eight miles southward toward a new campground along Bayou Meto. The entire march took three days to cover eighteen miles and was slowed by the work of corduroying (essentially paving the roads with logs) the soft roads to ease the passage of the wagons. David M. Ray of the 16th Texas Cavalry (dismounted), impressed by this march, exclaimed "an army marching over the prairie, extending as far as the eye can reach is quite a grand sight to one not accustomed to such sights." Officers quickly reestablished the usual military routine, and a division review took place on a parade ground near camp on 27 November, followed the next day by orders for "company drills four hours each day." Camp was moved on 1 December a few miles further up the bayou, and on the fourth it snowed two inches.[1]

On the 10th, Lt. Gen. Theophilus H. Holmes, the commander of the Trans-Mississippi Department, ordered General McCulloch and his division to march toward Vicksburg, Mississippi. Holmes, though, countermanded the order and instead directed the men to the Post of Arkansas, a Confederate stronghold 117 miles down the Arkansas River from Little Rock and twenty-five miles above the juncture of the Arkansas and Mississippi Rivers. Confederate engineers had designed the fortifications at the Post of Arkansas to defend the Arkansas River, one of the principal waterways of the state, and to serve as a launching point for attacks against Federal shipping on the Mississippi River. The next day Col. Horace Randal's brigade, followed later by the rest of the division, started down the south bank of the Arkansas River to reinforce Arkansas Post. Reportedly, morale was high in anticipation of tangling with the enemy, and most believed "that the most good can be done on the Mississippi." After a march of eighteen miles the order was countermanded, and the soldiers believed they would proceed to Van Buren, Arkansas, near Fort Smith. Instead, the men marched back to Little Rock and arrived there by Christmas. The men were confused by such maneuvering. Because of the defeat of Maj. Gen. Thomas C. Hindman's army at Prairie Grove in northwestern Arkansas on 7 December, McCulloch's men were spared crossing the Mississippi since they were needed in Arkansas.[2]

The soldiers of McCulloch's division spent Christmas in Little Rock. Christmas dinner for the common soldiers consisted of cornbread and "blue beef" (i.e. spoiled meat). Some of the soldiers obtained passes and toured Little Rock with some able to buy a meal in a restaurant and others visiting gambling saloons. Meanwhile, still as acting brigade quartermaster, Lt. Theophilus Perry was ordered to the mouth of Cadron Creek about thirty miles above Little Rock. His orders were to collect provisions for the division, and he estimated that 100,000 bushels of corn would be purchased if it could be found. The corn could then be shipped up or down the Arkansas River as needed. On the twenty-sixth, the men crossed the Arkansas River and camped three miles south of Little Rock on the road to Pine Bluff, Arkansas. That evening officers read Special Order No. 121 to the division that announced the assignment of Maj. Gen. John G. Walker as the new commander of the division. McCulloch was reassigned as commander of the third brigade. Pvt. John C. Porter of the 18th Texas Infantry recalled that Walker reviewed the division upon taking command and met each company commander. Porter went on to describe Walker as "a small man, weight about 140 lbs., height about 5 ft., 10 in., auburn hair, very large blue eyes, long bunch of beard upon his chin, and a mustache; in all a handsome man."[3]

Walker, a native of Missouri, was forty-one years old when appointed commander of the division. Although not a West Pointer, he had served in the regular army during the Mexican War and eventually rose to the rank of captain. He had resigned in July 1861, and the Confederate government commissioned him as colonel of the 2nd Virginia Infantry. He was soon promoted to brigadier general and assigned to the eastern theater. In September 1862 he joined the Army of Northern Virginia, and, commanding a division of two brigades, he performed capably in the capture of Harper's Ferry, Virginia, and in the battle of Antietam. Because of his performance in the Antietam campaign, he earned promotion to major general on 8 November 1862 and was transferred to the Trans-Mississippi Department, where he took command of McCulloch's former division. He commanded this division until June 1864 and won a great deal of respect from his Texas soldiers. Pvt. Joseph P. Blessington wrote in later years that Walker "was always hailed with the wildest enthusiasm by both officers and soldiers."[4]

The Texans had little time to become acquainted with their new commander, for on the twenty-seventh they continued their march to Pine

John G. Walker

*Photo courtesy of the Louisiana Historical Association Collection,
Manuscripts Department, Tulane University Library*

Bluff, about thirty miles southeast of Little Rock. After arriving in Pine Bluff, the division was ordered back to Little Rock but soon began marching again to Pine Bluff on 5 January 1863. Such activities, taking place in chilly weather, annoyed the soldiers and led to the belief "that General Holmes was advised by the Medical Board to give Walker's Division enough of exercise." On the eighth the soldiers arrived again in Pine Bluff and camped west of town where the division drummed three men from McCulloch's brigade out of camp for stealing hogs. The entire division observed the proceedings, and hearty laughter at the expense of the unfortunates filled the camp. Three days later the division marched twenty-five miles toward the Post of Arkansas in an attempt to reinforce the now seriously threatened post. The next day, the twelfth, they learned of the surrender of the post the day before. Included among the 4,791 Confederates surrendered to General McClernand's force were seven Texas regiments and two companies of Texas cavalry. Compounding the gloom, a snow and sleet storm hit the region the next day, snow fell to a depth of six inches, and a cold north wind blew through the encampment. Sleet covered the tents, and the tents became so stiff the soldiers could not fold or roll them. At 2:00 A.M. officers awakened the men and told them the wagon trains would leave soon with the division's supplies. The soldiers dragged their shelters to the riverbanks where boats picked them up. The men huddled under one or two blankets each for the remainder of the frigid night and nicknamed this place "Camp Freeze Out." Walker's division, fearing the advance of Federal gunboats, began constructing defensive works along the Arkansas River with details of twenty men from each regiment. Three days later it snowed again, and on the seventeenth the division discontinued construction because the Federals had left the river. Two days later the division marched twelve miles along muddy roads churned up by "hundreds of waggons" and the next day arrived at Pine Bluff.[5]

Ordered into a winter encampment after this fatiguing campaign, the men stayed at Camp Mills, approximately four miles northwest of Pine Bluff, until 22 February. There, the soldiers camped in a pine forest with convenient supplies of wood and water. Rainy weather turned the roads into mud and transformed the camp into a swamp, adding to the discomfort of the soldiers and playing a role in the moving of the camp.[6]

In spite of the wet weather, the health of the army steadily improved, perhaps as a result of better food supplies. Dr. Cade mentioned approvingly to his wife the improved commissary and noted that he could purchase potatoes on occasion. The camp had no vegetable stall, though, and coffee remained a luxury. In spite of these favorable comments by men in the 28th Texas Cavalry, food supplies were apparently unevenly distributed, perhaps resulting from the differing abilities of individual regimental commissaries. Another regiment, the 17th Texas Infantry in McCulloch's brigade, complained of bad beef and a tiresome abundance of cornbread. The enlisted men in the 17th were reportedly spending as much as half of their pay in an effort to supplement their diet. In the 28th Texas Cavalry, reported rates of illness dropped from highs of 150 a day in November and December to only twenty-six sick on 30 January 1863. Many more soldiers in the 28th, though, feigned illness in hopes of a discharge or a furlough. At sick call each morning at 6:00 A.M., the orderly sergeants presented the sick men to Dr. Cade. Each morning Dr. Cade ordered about twenty men who were pretending sickness back to duty.[7]

An overwhelming homesickness was a factor in much of the feigned illness. One of those afflicted with homesickness, young Dr. Cade longed for peace so he could return home, and he sent a poem to his wife that read in part:

> I send you *dearest wife* a kiss
> A kiss of love and joy tis true
> And dearest when you're reading this
> Think *that I'm kissing* you.

Although homesickness was acute on the part of some, the general morale of the soldiers seemed higher than in autumn. Special work details occupied the time of some of the men. Lt. Theophilus Perry commanded a detail of fifty men who upgraded the road between Pine Bluff and White Sulphur Spring, about six miles west of Pine Bluff. Upon completion of this project, seventy thousand bushels of corn were transferred from Pine Bluff to White Sulphur Spring. Morale increased after the troops drew two months' pay in early February. Additionally, the men's brigade commander, Col. Horace Randal, remained popular with the men.[8]

Union desertion and a new departmental commander also boosted morale. Confederate troops in the area picked up a number of Union deserters. Estimates of their numbers varied from hundreds to four thousand. David Ray of the 16th Texas Cavalry (dismounted) reported that Union soldiers explained they were deserting because of President Abraham Lincoln's Emancipation Proclamation. This led to high hopes among Confederate soldiers that the proclamation would cause many desertions, thus forcing the North into accepting peace terms. A further source of satisfaction to the men in the 28th and other regiments in the division was the arrival of Lt. Gen. Edmund Kirby Smith as the new departmental commander. General Holmes was reassigned as commander of the District of Arkansas, and the soldiers were heartily glad of the change. Capt. Elijah P. Petty of the 17th Texas Infantry reflected, "I am truly glad of [the change]. I look upon Genl H[olmes] as a dilapidated old Granny and a drunkard besides."[9]

Kirby Smith, a native Floridian born in 1824, attended the United States Military Academy and was graduated twenty-fifth out of a class of forty-one in 1845. He served in the Mexican War and was cited for gallantry at the battle of Cerro Gordo. In 1855 he became a captain in the elite 2nd United States Cavalry regiment with such later noteworthies as Robert E. Lee, Albert Sidney Johnston, John Bell Hood, and George H. Thomas. Smith received a commission as brigadier general following Florida's secession from the Union and became one of the Confederacy's heroes at the battle of First Manassas. Later he commanded one of the two Confederate columns that invaded Kentucky in the autumn of 1862. The soldiers welcomed Smith to the Trans-Mississippi Department and viewed him as an improvement over General Holmes.[10]

Meanwhile the heavy rainfall turned Camp Mills into a quagmire, forcing Walker's division to move its camp about 22 February. The new site, located on the Arkansas River approximately four miles north of Pine Bluff, was named Camp Wright. Here the division remained until 24 April. The soldiers remembered Camp Wright as a beautiful and singularly comfortable camp. The fields along the river filled with tents, the regiments drilled often, and the bands played martial tunes. In later life, Pvt. Joseph P. Blessington of the 16th Texas Infantry fondly remembered smoking and playing poker by a "well-shaded" lamp after the lights out call. Perhaps the men of the 28th Texas amused themselves in similar fashion.[11]

The steadily improving health of the soldiers, more furloughs, and the relatively abundant food supplies also contributed to the happy memories of Camp Wright. In the 28th Texas the number of ill men dropped to between eight and sixteen each day. The rather free granting of furloughs in February and March enabled many of the Texans to visit their families. Food supplies were good in the regiment, and the men were supplied with apparently abundant quantities of pork, cornmeal, sugar, and molasses. To the regret of the soldiers, coffee remained scarce. Occasional fishing expeditions along the Arkansas River no doubt supplemented food supplies. The 16th Texas Infantry reported such added delicacies as butter, eggs, and honey, items that the 28th possibly had also. The soldiers purchased some of these additional foodstuffs, but the prices were considered rather high. Lieutenant Perry reported chickens selling for $1.50 each, eggs for $1.00 per dozen, and milk for $.50 a quart.[12]

In spite of the troops' satisfaction at Camp Wright, desertion was a problem. At least two men deserted from the 28th Texas at this time: W. M. Manuel of Company F and H. G. McGwire of Company H. Both men served as teamsters and may have encouraged Lieutenant Perry's personal servant, Norflet, to run away also. Norflet had become steadily dissatisfied while cooking for Colonel Randal and his wife, because Norflet did "not like Mrs. Randol at all . . . [believing] she is too particular and hard to please." Homesickness and boredom probably were the underlying causes for the desertions of the soldiers. Dr. Cade mentioned numerous "poor emaciated men suffering such mental anxiety" about their families and claimed he suggested twice the number of furloughs recommended by any other surgeon in the division. Such a liberal policy on Dr. Cade's part may have lowered the number of deserters from the regiment.[13]

Desertion was dealt with as in other armies during the Civil War. A handful of deserters were selected as examples and executed publicly. Witnesses were greatly affected by these executions and often wrote about them in letters home. On 12 March the entire division witnessed the execution of two men from Capt. Horace Haldeman's battery. Walker's division stood at attention forming three sides of a square as the prisoners, accompanied by the music of the "dead march," were escorted to the site. A wagon containing coffins followed the prisoners. Graves were already prepared in the center of the square, and the prisoners knelt down by the graves. A firing squad riddled the prisoners, one a married man with a family and the other a teenager. Mercifully, they died almost immediately. Although many of the men understood the importance of maintaining discipline, they still revolted "at the idea of sending two souls young and flushed in the prime of life into eternity," as Dr. Cade reflected.[14]

The general monotony of camp life seemed to fuel increased tensions among officers. In the spring of 1863 a rather long-standing claim of seniority over Col. Horace Randal by Col. Oran M. Roberts of the 11th Texas Infantry was concluded. Roberts, a stickler for justice, had previously lost a claim of seniority over Col. Richard B. Hubbard in the summer of 1862. Arriving in the Arkansas army in October 1862, Roberts quickly asked General McCulloch to settle the issue of seniority of rank between him and Randal. General McCulloch believed Roberts should serve as senior colonel of the brigade but referred the question to General Holmes who ruled in favor of Randal. Holmes offered to submit the question to the secretary of war if Roberts agreed to accept his opinion, however—an offer Roberts readily accepted. To aid in preparing his case, Roberts interviewed John A. Harris of the 28th to garner various facts. Roberts based his argument on the fact that Randal's commission of 12 February 1862 contained a stipulation that his commission would be deemed void if his regiment was not raised, organized, and ready for duty in four months. As Roberts showed, not all of the regiment's companies arrived at the rendezvous within four months. The secretary of war's opinion in favor of Randal ended the matter quietly. Randal survived one final attempt on his position, this time by Brig. Gen. Paul Octave Hébert in March 1863, who, according to Dr. Cade, arrived to command Randal's brigade. Details are vague, but Hébert soon returned to Texas.[15]

On a much lower level, Dr. Cade eventually fended off a claim of a Dr. Jones that he was senior surgeon of the brigade. Jones was, interestingly enough, of Colonel Roberts's regiment. Cade firmly believed that Randal would support him in his claims. Randal apparently maintained a keen interest in the 28th and kept abreast of matters to the point of expressing concern that "Captain [Martin V.] Smith did not appear to be getting on very rapidly." [16]

The men of Walker's division began their springtime campaigning in response to Union threats along the Mississippi River. Both the armies of General Grant and Maj. Gen. Nathaniel P. Banks were threatening, and Walker's men were ordered to Monroe, Louisiana, via Camden, Arkansas. At Monroe they could presumably counter moves from either Union army. Although Grant's army was in the process of moving down the west side of the Mississippi, Banks's army was perceived as the more immediate threat. This army of fifteen thousand men had forced its way across Berwick Bay in southern Louisiana and pushed Maj. Gen. Richard Taylor's smaller army back northward to Opelousas. Kirby Smith reiterated his instructions for Walker's division to move to Monroe, anticipating that they would aid Taylor if he retreated to Alexandria. During dress parade on the evening of 23 April, each regiment of Walker's division heard General Holmes's order directing them to Monroe. In the meantime, General Smith requested help from Lt. Gen. John Clifford Pemberton at Vicksburg, the commander of the Department of Mississippi and East Louisiana. Pemberton refused to send troops and instead asked Smith to act against Grant's army.[17]

Neither general cooperated nor coordinated efforts against Union forces. Much of this was due to President Jefferson Davis's and the War Department's decision that the Mississippi River formed the boundary between Smith's Trans-Mississippi Department and Pemberton's department. Both men were more concerned with protecting their own departments than coordinating a defense against Union forces. Such an awkward arrangement also meant questions regarding cooperation between the two departments were referred to the War Department in Richmond, Virginia. The resulting time lag seriously impeded efforts in forestalling the enemy advance. Knowing little of such matters, the men in the ranks optimistically believed they could defeat the enemy. The soldiers hastily prepared for departure and left on the morning of 24 April in high spirits, marching "to the sound of music." The ranks of every unit buzzed with speculation regarding the march, and such thoughts were not confined to enlisted men. Colonel Randal believed the men would cross the Mississippi River, while others were certain that Alexandria, Louisiana, was the ultimate destination. All expected fighting and eagerly expected to strike an enemy reportedly committing atrocities along the St. Francis River.[18]

The 28th Texas left Arkansas by passing southward through the towns of Monticello, Lacy, Fountain Hill, and Hamburg, a route roughly paralleling present-day state highway 81. The marches averaged twelve miles a day owing to the poor condition of the roads. Soldiers corduroyed the roads to allow the heavy baggage and subsistence trains to pass. In addition, laborers constructed several bridges to replace those washed away by floods. As was typical for Civil War soldiers on their first major campaign, the men discarded a certain amount of superfluous baggage along the rural roadway.

Pvt. S. W. Farrow of the 19th Texas Infantry discarded some clothing after explaining to his wife that the wagons transported only fourteen pounds of baggage per man. He could not possibly carry everything else, he ruefully declared. Enthusiastic greetings from civilians, particularly in Drew County, Arkansas, characterized the march. Women gathered in crowds, waved handkerchiefs, and threw flowers to the passing soldiers. In Monticello the welcome was exceptionally hearty, and the soldiers responded by cheering so much that their voices became hoarse. In addition to this greeting, there were several social activities for the soldiers along the route. A minstrel show and a ball occurred near Hamburg as the social-minded Capt. Elijah P. Petty of the 17th Texas Infantry happily reported. On 1 May, after a march of eight days, Walker's division crossed into Louisiana.[19]

The 28th and the other units marched along Bayou Bartholomew as it flowed to the southwest, then left the bayou and marched to Ouachita City on the Ouachita River. From here the division moved southward and intercepted Bayou Bartholomew, this time at its mouth. At this point the soldiers boarded transports and sailed about fifteen miles to Trenton, a struggling town only three miles north of Monroe on the Ouachita River. Monroe, in the northeast part of the state, was a transportation center serving as the western terminus of the Vicksburg, Shreveport, and Texas Railroad and as a port on the Ouachita River, a major north/south water-way that emptied into the Red River. The men stayed at Monroe for several days and while there reflected on probable destinations. Lieutenant Perry and others hoped to go to Shreveport, in the northwest corner of Louisiana, a location closer to their families, but instead, officers ordered the men to cook two days of rations in preparation for departing for Alexandria in the central part of the state. The morale of the 28th remained high, and the men hoped to destroy the enemy. The morning of 7 May was busy as the men prepared to leave and the wagon trains rolled out of camp. Pvt. S. W. Farrow probably reflected others' thoughts as he confessed to his wife that "everything in such a stir I can hardly think of anything this morning."[20]

On the morning of 9 May the division filled fourteen steamboats at Trenton and chugged down the Ouachita River. The movement turned into a spectacle as ladies lined the riverbank near Monroe waving hand-kerchiefs, bands played, and men cheered. The entertainment was abruptly cut short after seventy miles when General Walker received a dispatch that Taylor's army had evacuated Alexandria. In all probability, Union gunboats

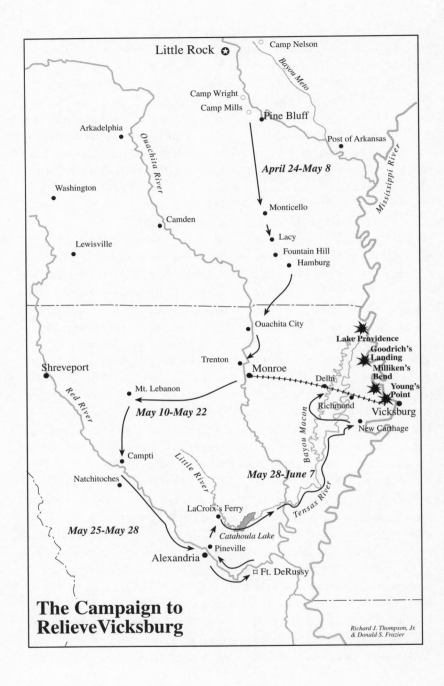

Little Rock ✪   ○ Camp Nelson

Camp Wright ○
Camp Mills ○
                ● Pine Bluff

Arkadelphia ●   ● Post of Arkansas

                                    April 24-May 8

Washington ●

                Camden ●   ● Monticello

Lewisville ●   ● Lacy

                                ● Fountain Hill
                                ● Hamburg

                            ● Ouachita City

                                                    ✦ Lake Providence
                                                    ✦ Goodrich's
                                                      Landing
Shreveport ●   Trenton ●   Milliken's
                            ● Monroe   Delhi ●   ✦ Bend
                                                    ✦ Young's
            Mt. Lebanon ●   Point
                                        Richmond ●   Vicksburg
        May 10-May 22

                                                ● New Carthage

        Campti ●

    Natchitoches ●   *May 28-June 7*

                    LaCroix's Ferry ●
    May 25-May 28   ▨ Catahoula Lake

                        ● Pineville
            Alexandria ●
                            ▢ Ft. DeRussy

The Campaign to
Relieve Vicksburg

Richard J. Thompson, Jr.
& Donald S. Frazier

were already probing the Ouachita River, and Walker ordered a return to Monroe. Nervously, soldiers scanned the horizon for telltale signs of smoke, loaded their guns, and discussed the situation with their comrades. Allegedly, Lt. Col. Benjamin A. Phillpot of the 12th Texas Infantry offered "his services to the pilot to help turn his wheel, which, when rejected, he mounted the chicken coop on the hurricane deck with his spurs to urge the boat forward." The division returned to the Monroe area about 2:00 A.M. on 10 May, having luckily missed the dreaded gunboats by only hours. The strategic situation had altered quickly as Taylor retreated from Alexandria northwest about forty-five miles to Natchitoches and Grant's army crossed to the east side of the Mississippi River. As the month progressed, the Federal presence began diminishing steadily on the western side of the Mississippi.[21]

General Kirby Smith remained unaware of the changing strategic situation and ordered Walker's division to Natchitoches as reinforcements for Taylor's army rather than attempting to delay Grant's progress. For most of May 1863 the 28th Texas marched toward Natchitoches and then moved toward Alexandria to counter the swiftly diminishing threat of Banks's army. General Walker dispatched Randal's and Brig. Gen. James M. Hawes's brigades to Natchitoches, while he and McCulloch's brigade remained in Trenton to guard the area against gunboats. The two brigades left on 10 May only a few hours after the aborted trip on the Ouachita.[22]

The weather during this march was hot and dusty. A number of men in the 28th and in other units became ill or footsore. Dr. Cade helped the sick and tired each day by guiding the men into wagons and ambulances. Most of the ill were victims of impure water that produced diarrhea. Other men were afflicted by chills, probably associated with malaria or typhoid fever and probably also connected to poor water supplies or the bites of mosquitoes. In spite of these debilitating diseases, the men remained eager, even anxious, to meet the enemy and prove themselves. Dr. Cade in particular declared himself eager for a fight, but for an unusual reason, as he declared, "I am tired of prescribing for nothing but diarrheas and chills." The soldiers were in part encouraged onward by the continuing support of civilians practically everywhere they traveled. As they left Monroe at the beginning of the march, children sitting on top of fences greeted the units of Walker's division by offering buckets of water and gourds for dipping the liquid.

In Mount Lebanon, Louisiana, about forty-five miles west of Monroe, women guided the sick and lame of the 28th into their homes and gave them dinner. Girls and young ladies in this same village greeted Lieutenant Perry and staff officer William A. Tarlton by offering bread and cakes to the weary Confederates.[23]

Soon after this excited greeting Mrs. Randal left the regiment to return to Texas after traveling with her husband for much of the time since their marriage in July 1862. Additionally, Tarlton left for Shreveport, transporting baggage and Perry's quartermaster papers. Perry warned his wife, Harriet, that the quartermaster papers would be entrusted to her for safekeeping. Apparently officials designated no site for the protection of such documents. Perry also took a moment to request a newer uniform and some white shirts from his wife. Throughout his service, Perry took great care with his clothing, believing that an officer had a duty to "make as good appearance as possible."[24]

The two brigades arrived near Campti, about ten miles north of Natchitoches on the north bank of the Red River, on 22 May and remained there until 25 May. Here, the Texans of Walker's division first came under the immediate command of the remarkable Maj. Gen. Richard Taylor, the commander of the District of West Louisiana. The only son of former president and general Zachary Taylor, Taylor graduated from Yale University in 1845 with fair grades. In the years before the outbreak of the Civil War, he lived in Louisiana as a sugar planter and served in the Louisiana State Senate. With no military experience Taylor became commander of the 9th Louisiana Infantry in July 1861 and traveled with his regiment to Virginia. Taylor exhibited a rare talent for warfare while serving under Maj. Gen. Thomas J. "Stonewall" Jackson in the famed Valley Campaign of 1862. By the time the Confederate government transferred Taylor to the Trans-Mississippi in July 1862, Taylor was a major general. Until the Vicksburg campaign, Taylor with a small army operated in southern Louisiana.[25]

As the soldiers rested, McCulloch's brigade also marched to Campti, and the generals discussed future plans. The dialogue between General Smith and General Taylor revolved around the fact that Banks's army was rapidly withdrawing from the Red River valley, and a letter from General Pemberton outlining his troubles, including a request that Grant's supply line be broken. General Smith believed the time was ripe for striking at Grant while Banks was withdrawing. Taylor, though, believed threatening Federal-occupied New Orleans would force Banks to withdraw pressure on Port Hudson, a Confederate stronghold on the Mississippi twenty miles north of Baton Rouge, thus allowing the Confederates at Port Hudson to march to Vicksburg's aid. Smith insisted on a move to cut Grant's supply line, believed to extend from Milliken's Bend, twenty miles north of Vicksburg on the west bank of the Mississippi River, south through Young's Point and continuing through Warrenton and New Carthage, eight miles and twenty-five miles south of Vicksburg respectively. Grant's army, however, had already crossed the Mississippi River, and Grant's supply line had shifted so that Grand Gulf, Mississippi, was the supply center for the Union army. In reality, Grant's force had abandoned the supply line segment from Milliken's Bend to Young's Point, but a line extending from Young's Point to Bowers' Landing, on the west bank of the Mississippi River opposite Warrenton, remained operational throughout the siege. Neither Smith, Taylor, nor the common soldiers knew that Federal forces had abandoned the supply line between Milliken's Bend and Young's Point, so the upcoming attack on Milliken's Bend, no longer part of the supply line, and Young's Point at the northern end of the line would be a fruitless exercise.[26]

From Campti the 28th marched to the vicinity of Alexandria, arriving there on 25 May and camping on the north side of the Red River. Thankfully, there was a good supply of spring water at this site. Two days later Randal's brigade went on a special mission down the Red River in an attempt to capture Banks's stragglers and perhaps learn more of the enemy's movements. Cottonclads escorted the brigade as they sailed down the river to Fort DeRussy, about thirty miles downstream from Alexandria. No stragglers were captured, no great excitement occurred, and the brigade returned to Alexandria on 28 May. When they returned, the men quickly prepared for their next march, one that they knew was designed to cut supply or communication lines of the enemy. After so much marching and other maneuvering, the division was extremely eager to fight. Captain Petty of the 17th Texas believed, though, that "one fight will sober them." The men, now familiar with campaigning, lightened their loads further. Enlisted men generally took only the clothing on their backs, their weapons and accouterments, a blanket, and perhaps some cooking supplies. Officers could manage to take more. Lieutenant Perry carried a change of underclothes, two blankets, an oilcloth, and two shirts. Many wagons containing additional baggage of the soldiers and some artillery were left at Pineville opposite Alexandria so that the division could move quickly. The army, by purging itself of extra baggage and some artillery, signaled that the march would be a rapid one, as if they were cavalry.[27]

At dusk on 28 May the division marched northward from Pineville toward LaCroix's Ferry on Little River. The next day the men arrived at the ferry after a march of about twenty miles. Before embarking, the troops cooked two days' rations over fires made of fence rails or branches. The men cooked their meals hastily like any other Civil War soldiers by placing their bacon or beef on a stick and roasting it over fires. Embarkation began as the men finished cooking, and the division completed the neat operation by 2:00 P.M. Soldiers placed artillery pieces in the bow of each boat, and each regiment posted men for lookout duty to evade ambushes. McCulloch's brigade took the lead down the river, followed by Randal's men, and then by Hawes's troops. The journey down Little River, through Catahoula Lake, into Little River once again, and finally up the Tensas River was uneventful except for the accidental drowning of a man from Capt. William Edgar's battery.[28]

The regiment journeyed for approximately 120 miles before debarking about 3:00 A.M. on 31 May near the mouth of Bayou DuRosset, a point ten miles slightly southwest of New Carthage. The small town of New Carthage sat on the west bank of the Mississippi about halfway between Vicksburg to the north and Grand Gulf to the south. McCulloch's brigade had disembarked several hours earlier and after midnight marched toward the camp of the 60th Indiana Infantry near Somerset plantation, about two miles below New Carthage. Meanwhile, Randal's brigade followed behind McCulloch's from a distance of about five to six miles. By the time the 28th arrived near New Carthage, McCulloch's men had attacked the deserted encampment of the 60th Indiana, which had been warned of the approaching Confederates. McCulloch's brigade accompanied by Edgar's battery then started a nearly bloodless duel with the Union gunboat *Carondelet*. The *Carondelet* and Edgar's overmatched section of two guns exchanged thirty to forty shots, resulting in the death of a member of McCulloch's staff. At 11:00 A.M. Generals Taylor and Walker accompanied Randal's brigade as it marched within earshot of the firing, but the uneven duel soon ended when Taylor ordered Edgar to cease fire. Evidently the men of McCulloch's and Randal's brigades soon mingled and discussed this gunboat encounter, and McCulloch's men confessed that they felt "very strangely" under fire. By sundown of 31 May the men of these two brigades had returned to their disembarkation point.[29]

For the next week, Walker's division went on a series of marches that culminated in attacks on Lake Providence, Milliken's Bend, and Young's Point. Following the attempted attack near New Carthage, Walker's division moved northward to jockey into position for another lunge at the supposed Union supply lines. On 1 June the soldiers ferried across the Tensas, and the next day Randal's and Hawes's brigades marched through swampland to Bayou Macon. The men on this day and the next few marched through an eerily desolated and depopulated countryside. In the distance the soldiers heard the sound of cannonading from the direction of Vicksburg. The men passed plantations abandoned by their white owners and under the caretakership in some cases of black women. As the men marched under the hot sun, plagued by mosquitoes, they periodically paused to drink bayou water, water sometimes so foul that horses refused to drink it. As they marched, they relished the rumor that Grant had been mortally wounded. On 4 and 5 June the soldiers trudged northward along the west bank of Bayou Macon and halted near the Vicksburg, Shreveport, and Texas Railroad east of Delhi. Here rations were welcomed from the recently stocked commissary depot at Delhi, a railroad town about thirty miles east of Monroe. From this point, the division marched on 6 June fifteen miles east to Richmond, prepared two days' rations, and rested for a few hours.[30]

To avoid the heat of the day the soldiers pulled out of camp, crossed Roundaway Bayou near Richmond, and marched northeast toward Milliken's Bend. General Taylor had devised an attack plan based on erroneous intelligence gained by a small force of Louisiana cavalrymen. This information underestimated the number of Union troops at Young's Point and failed to detect a continuing supply line from Young's Point to Bowers' Landing. Taylor decided to attack three points simultaneously: Lake Providence, Milliken's Bend, about thirty miles south of Lake Providence, and Young's Point, situated about ten miles south of Milliken's Bend. McCulloch and Hawes were to assail Milliken's Bend and Young's Point respectively while a force composed of the 13th Louisiana Cavalry and the 13th Texas Cavalry (dismounted, of Hawes's brigade) were to attack Lake Providence. Randal's brigade and the artillery of the division would remain in reserve at a fork in the road leading between Milliken's Bend and Young's

Point so they could aid either McCulloch or Hawes. McCulloch's brigade led the march and by 3:00 A.M. were about a mile and a half from Milliken's Bend. By daybreak Randal's brigade reached the fork, a site about four miles from Richmond, perhaps two miles from Milliken's Bend, and approximately seven miles from Young's Point.[31]

As the men of Randal's brigade reached the fork in the road, they heard firing from Milliken's Bend. Near dawn McCulloch's brigade attacked Milliken's Bend, garrisoned by four raw and half-trained black regiments (the 9th, 11th, and 13th Louisiana [African descent], and the 1st Mississippi [African descent]), who were reinforced by the 23rd Iowa and a portion of the 10th Illinois Cavalry. Advancing through obstacles of abatis, hedgerows, and ditches, McCulloch's brigade at first was successful, mauling and driving the enemy from the first defense line. Resistance by the Union troops, though, was stiff, with black soldiers using the bayonet when they found they did not know how to reload their guns. In addition, the ironclad *Choctaw* and later the *Lexington* opened fire, and one-hundred-pound shells began exploding over the battlefield. At this point Randal's brigade marched onto the battlefield, accompanied by General Walker, after listening to gunfire for about an hour. Randal's brigade formed into line of battle amid shells bursting and whizzing through the air. In spite of this, no one in the brigade was injured, and the men soon withdrew with McCulloch's thirsty, tired, and somewhat demoralized brigade. Lieutenant Perry confided to his wife his belief that McCulloch had been whipped. McCulloch's brigade suffered casualties of 44 killed, 131 wounded, and 10 missing out of approximately 1,500 engaged, and inflicted casualties of 101 killed, 285 wounded, and 266 missing out of 1,061 Union troops engaged. Hawes failed to attack Young's Point after sighting a heavier force than expected, and the Lake Providence attack accomplished nothing of importance. Bitterly disappointed, Taylor believed a lack of vigor and a fear of gunboats led to the unraveling of his plans. Of course, he devised his plans based on erroneous information and spread his troops too thinly instead of concentrating on one site. Furthermore, no infantry troops could stand against naval fire for long. Following these engagements the division returned to Richmond.[32]

Reports that Confederate soldiers had murdered black troops and their white officers followed the battle of Milliken's Bend. Approximately 35 percent of the black troops engaged were either killed or wounded, an appallingly high rate. One of the white regiments engaged, the 23rd Iowa Infantry, had casualties of twenty-three killed, thirty-nine wounded, and one missing. Although the 23rd Iowa did not suffer losses as severe as the black troops, its ratio of killed to wounded (more than one to two) was unusually high. Clearly, the fighting at Milliken's Bend was severe and desperate, perhaps ranking as one of the most vicious small engagements of the war. It is difficult to state with certainty whether or not the men of McCulloch's brigade were guilty of atrocities at Milliken's Bend. However, several circumstances at least point to the possibility that so-called atrocities occurred. Most Confederate soldiers felt a deep hatred toward black soldiers, and there were several occasions during the war when blacks were killed after they surrendered. The after-action report of General Taylor expressed regret that any of the black soldiers were captured, an attitude that could be reflective of a great hostility. Possibly, though, Taylor feared the political problems associated with the capture of black troops. Finally, black soldiers at Milliken's Bend fought with great obstinacy, using the bayonet and fighting hand-to-hand with McCulloch's men. Such stubbornness, coupled with the Texans' probable hatred of black troops, perhaps led to instances in which wounded men were killed or men were shot after they surrendered.[33]

The battle of Milliken's Bend marked one of the first occasions of the use of black troops in combat during the war. Lieutenant Perry heard many of McCulloch's soldiers state that the black soldiers fought bravely and stubbornly. A lesser number commented that the blacks did not stand fire well. Perry, though, concluded, "I think it is conceded that they fought as well as the whites." Some civilians could scarcely believe the news that black soldiers fought bravely against white troops. At least one Louisiana civilian, Kate Stone, reported hearing of the brave defense by the black soldiers, but she wrote, "we cannot believe that. We know from long experience that they are cowards."[34]

For the next month, the division continued marching through northeast Louisiana. Taylor decided to shift Walker's division south of the Red River for a move to relieve Port Hudson on the Mississippi. Randal's brigade on 11 June rode the railroad to Monroe and the next day boarded transports for Alexandria and traveled 120 miles south. At that point the men halted and returned to Monroe on 13 June. Taylor had decided that Walker's division might be needed to harass the enemy if Vicksburg were relieved. By the time the men returned to Monroe, Dr. Cade had calculated they had traveled 1,170 miles in forty-nine days, an average of 24 miles a day. Shortly after, a Union brigade threatened Walker's other two brigades, and Walker ordered a retreat because he erroneously believed the enemy heavily outnumbered his troops. Federal troops burned the town of Richmond following Walker's retreat. Randal and Brig. Gen. James C. Tappan's brigade of Arkansas conscripts moved to Delhi and met the rest of the division by 17 June. Here sickness increased daily, and the regiment sent Pvt. Henry Grandberry of Company F to Shreveport to pick up medical supplies. Meanwhile the weary soldiers washed their tattered clothing. Some of the men had not changed clothing in over a month, and many were naked as they gently washed their garments. The 28th and other regiments in Randal's brigade left many men in Monroe who were shoe-less, and Lieutenant Perry estimated that others would remain in Delhi for the same reason. Perry himself, like others, had holes in his shoes.[35]

In spite of the worsening condition of his command, Walker decided to strike the enemy again. From 22 to 29 June the division, with Tappan's brigade and Col. William Henry Parsons's Texas cavalry brigade, marched northeast toward Lake Providence to attack Union-controlled cotton plan-tations that were raising cotton for the United States Treasury Department. Parsons's Texas cavalry brigade, supported by Walker's division, captured about 2,000 blacks employed on the cotton plantations. The cavalry-men shot resisting blacks and torched cotton, cotton gins, and houses. Apparently, the Confederates looted the plantations as Union soldiers later reported seeing roadsides strewn with stolen goods, even including a piano. A detailed account of this expedition implies that Parsons's cavalry brigade caused much of the devastation during this expedition. S. W. Farrow of the 19th Texas Infantry recorded that Parsons's cavalry captured 1,300 blacks, "destroyed a great deal of commissary stores and captured several hundred head of Horses and mules from the Feds." Dr. Cade reported to his wife that the "Cavalry is now in all the Country between this point [Delhi] and the Mississippi river burning all the cotton and corn."[36]

The only real brush with the enemy occurred about three miles from Goodrich's Landing on the Mississippi. Here two companies of the 1st Arkansas Infantry (African descent) had fortified a fifty-foot-high Indian mound in a clearing near a plantation. Parsons's cavalry made a half-hearted charge at the mound before the 28th fell into line of battle with the other units of Randal's brigade plus parts of Tappan's brigade. Dressing their lines carefully in full view of the enemy, the soldiers prepared an advance toward the mound. Before this occurred, the defenders waved white flags of surrender from the little fort, and 113 black soldiers and three white officers surrendered. Apparently, as part of Walker's division escorted the prisoners to camp, about twelve to fifteen of the prisoners were murdered by the infantrymen. By 1 July the expedition returned to Delhi.[37]

Two days later the death of Capt. Phil Brown of Company F, who died as the result of a pistol wound, shook the regiment. Whether he died as a result of an accident, foul play, or suicide is unknown. Lieutenant Perry was promoted to captain of Company F on 5 July. With little time to reflect on this event, the division marched north along Bayou Macon toward Lake Providence on 7 July. This march, partially through a "miserable swamp," was halted by news of Vicksburg's surrender, and the men returned to Delhi. The regiment then moved to Monroe about 11 July, signaling an end for them of the Vicksburg campaign.[38]

When the Vicksburg campaign ended in July, Trans-Mississippi soldiers were tired, many were ill, some were dispirited. Only a few months before, the division had left Arkansas with high morale and relatively few sick men. From May to July the number of men present for duty in Walker's division dropped sharply. In the 11th Texas Infantry of Randal's brigade 447 men were present for duty on 1 May. By 1 June this number had fallen to 348 men, and near the end of the tiring campaign in July only 219 were present for duty. Quite likely a similar plunge occurred in the 28th, and they, like the 11th Texas, had not even suffered any battle casualties.[39]

Walker's division traveled an impressive number of miles from 24 April to 7 July 1863. As mentioned previously, Dr. Cade estimated that a total of 1,170 miles were traveled by 13 June. Probably the division traveled about 1,600 miles during the entire campaign including the smaller marches in November and December involving the Post of Arkansas. The marches in Louisiana followed a pattern if one excludes the abortive movement from Monroe to Alexandria on the Ouachita River. Once arrived in Monroe, the division traveled roughly counterclockwise in a loop westward to Campti, southward to Alexandria, eastward to Milliken's Bend, and eventually back to Monroe. Walker's division visited Monroe on three separate occasions, and Randal's brigade passed through the town two additional times.

In spite of all this movement, these Texans accomplished little of significance during the Vicksburg campaign. Blame should not be attached to the soldiers themselves, for they were eager to come to blows with the enemy and followed orders willingly. Reasons for their lack of success revolved around three factors: the faulty intelligence system attributable to an ironic lack of cavalry and perhaps the flight of white civilians from northeast Louisiana, Taylor's failure to concentrate Walker's division against Milliken's Bend, and the unwieldy departmental system mentioned previously.

In spite of the campaign's failure, steady campaigning molded the men into soldiers and hardened them. The 28th itself continued to change as men were weeded out and as some of the original officers resigned their positions. As the days passed, the men of the 28th Texas became veterans, lacking only the experience of heavy combat.

CHAPTER 4

Soldier Life in the Trans-Mississippi

*The commander of this department has no bed of roses,
nor is it a field in which laurels are to be gained or
reputation made.*
                    —Lt. Gen. Edmund Kirby Smith

Following the Vicksburg campaign, the men of the 28th Texas Cavalry were exhausted, and many were ill as a result of the rigorous campaign. Most of Maj. Gen. John G. Walker's division felt dispirited because of the surrender of Vicksburg, Mississippi, on 4 July 1863. The campaigning had transformed the men into veterans and caused a turnover in the ranks of the officers. Changes also took place outside the rather narrow scope of the regiment as a result of the fall of Vicksburg. Since the Trans-Mississippi Department was now effectively cut off from the government in Richmond, Virginia, it developed parallel structures of its own. Just as significantly, the home front became the most important supplier of certain products to the regiment. During the summer and fall of 1863 the regiment dealt with the effects of campaigning, coped with internal changes such as new officers and recruits, and provided soldiers to work at the many bureaus in the Trans-Mississippi Department.

The fall of Vicksburg elicited a wide range of opinions among the soldiers in Walker's division. Lt. Gen. John C. Pemberton's decision to surrender the town on the revered Fourth of July upset some soldiers. Many men had placed great hope in Gen. Joseph E. Johnston's relief effort and were sorely disappointed at the city's surrender. A number of soldiers felt "low spirited" and believed the war would surely end soon, and not necessarily to the Confederacy's advantage. In spite of this attitude, few soldiers seemed truly willing to give up, and a small core believed that the fall of Vicksburg was not the disaster some made it out to be. Included among the latter category was Volney Ellis of the 12th Texas Infantry, who believed that the men's spirits would improve with rest and the eventual recovery of their health from the recent campaign. Capt. Theophilus Perry, Company F of the 28th, tried to remain optimistic: "I met the news of the fall of Vicksburg with more equanamity than any body I have seen. I have endeavored to cheer up all that are in low spirits. Our armies are yet in the field and they are the hope of the country." The range of attitudes about Vicksburg was wide in the division. One observation everyone agreed on was that the recent campaign had produced large numbers of sick men.[1]

The regiment, along with other units in Walker's division, was almost continually active during the Vicksburg campaign and in the months to follow. Hard campaigning resulted in large numbers of sick men in the division that probably impaired the functioning of the unit. General Walker later claimed that the division's strength dropped from 5,000 effectives at the beginning of the campaign to 1,500 effectives by the end of the campaign. During the period May to August 1863, a total of 233 were sick in the 28th out of approximately 400 men aggregate present. These ill men were unevenly distributed among the unit's companies. Companies B, I, and H had the highest number of sick with 38, 36, and 34 respectively. The smallest number of afflicted soldiers were in Companies F and G, with 9 and 8 respectively. Disease badly afflicted all of the units of Col. Horace Randal's brigade, particularly in May and June during part of the Vicksburg campaign. In mid-July surgeon Edward W. Cade reported "about one-third of them [the command] are sick. I reported the last quarter 799 cases of sickness." On the other hand, the death rate was low, as Cade attested when he stated there were only 2 deaths among the 799 cases mentioned above.

As he proudly told his wife, "that is what I call very successful treatment in the army." Because of these illnesses a large number of men in the brigade were given sick furloughs after Dr. Cade personally examined them. Records indicate that 58 men in the 28th received furloughs and presumably traveled home to recuperate with their families.[2]

Virtually all of the sick men were victims of fevers associated with malaria, typhoid fever, or diarrhea. These illnesses started during the Vicksburg campaign, but the men mentioned the diseases most often in letters written in mid-July after the campaign ended. In the 28th, as in other regiments apparently, there were, "not many violent cases, but much complaint. We have all been debilitated in the swamps. The men look badly."[3]

The causes of these diseases included exposure during campaigning, impure water, and contaminated food. Along the march the scarcity of tents, inadequate clothing and shoes, and the heat weakened soldiers and left them more vulnerable to disease. Dr. Cade pinpointed many of these problems in a passage to his wife:

> Men may sit at home and talk of what soldiers and armies could do or should do but no one can conceive of what a soldier suffers in an arduous and active campaign like ours. Could they see men marching all day through the broiling sun with the thermometer over a hundred degrees carry a load of forty pounds and suffering the intense thirst that is caused by heat, dust, and perspiration and no water to drink for hours at a time and when night comes camped along some stream with water *thick* with insects and warm as water can be made by sun and eat their supper of corn bread and beef, they then would show more sympathy . . . [than] damning them for what they do not accomplish.

The men drank the hot, soupy water under necessity, and the water caused typhoid fever in some instances and, more likely, diarrhea. Diarrhea and dysentery were the most common diseases of the war for both sides. These conditions sometimes lasted only a few days but often persisted for years, causing weakness and fever. The men of the 28th, and probably other regiments as well, were most seriously affected by periodic, or intermittent, fevers that were probably a sign of malaria. This disease had the potential to "damage or destroy the effectiveness of a military unit" since the victims were fatigued and emaciated. Certainly, during parts of the summer of 1863, chills and fevers hindered the division's effectiveness.[4]

For the time, the men apparently received adequate care from physicians and the medical department. The fall of Vicksburg isolated the Trans-Mississippi medical department from the leadership of the Surgeon General's Office in Richmond, Virginia. The Trans-Mississippi medical department reacted to this situation by ordering physicians to collect certain medicinally valuable wild plants, establishing several manufacturing laboratories, centralizing control, and creating general hospitals. These general hospitals admitted patients from any state, unlike some hospitals in other parts of the Confederacy that were organized along state lines. In Little Rock, Niblett's Bluff (Texas), Galveston, Houston, Alexandria, Monroe, and Shreveport medical officials established general hospitals. Branch hospitals to these general hospitals were established as necessary.[5]

During the summer of 1863 the regiment used Alexandria, Monroe, Delhi, and Campti, Louisiana, as recovery areas. "Open air" hospitals apparently associated with the medical facilities already in those towns were used. In the compiled service records of the 28th these hospitals are called "convalescent camps." In late July the one thousand sick men from the division at the Monroe convalescent camp were evacuated to Natchitoches, Louisiana, because of the retreat of the division. Although only "twenty wagons and twelve ambulances" were available for this evacuation, all the sick were moved the one hundred miles in sixteen days. Medical officials shuttled the worst cases in short stages to Natchitoches while the stronger patients marched on their own. Ill men, then, for a time followed the division and composed a semi-mobile force at least partially attended by physicians. General Walker noted that the march improved the health of the convalescents and stated that nine hundred of the one thousand men were ready for duty when they reached Natchitoches.[6]

One important change involving the regiment in 1863 was a partial turnover of officers. By 15 November 1863 seventeen new officers (men who had never served as commissioned officers before) were on the roster and consisted of 35.4 percent of all commissioned officers. Most of these new men were commissioned in the lower ranks, for there were only two new captains, one new first lieutenant, and one new staff officer. On the other hand, there were now thirteen new second lieutenants. Additionally, eleven of the original officers had been promoted to new positions and thus were new to their rank. These included four captains, and seven first lieutenants.[7]

Of the twenty-six original officers who were no longer in the regiment, nineteen had resigned their commissions, three had died, three had been promoted higher than company grade level, and one had been discharged. The primary reason for the departure of an officer was unfitness for duty, a category that included illness, cowardice, or death. Illness proved the major reason for an officer's departure, accounting for fifteen resignations, well over half of those who left. These illnesses were often the result of campaigning. Among these men were 2nd Lt. Samuel C. Heath of Company A, who suffered a disorder of the lungs, and 2nd Lt. James C. Clark (Company B), Capt. William H. Tucker (Company G), and Capt. A. W. DeBerry (Company C), all of whom resigned due to chronic diarrhea. These men were unable to perform their military responsibilities to the extent that Colonel Randal stated, in the case of Clark, "he will be of more service to his country by *remaining at his home.*" Age coupled with disease caused surgeon Leonard Randal to submit a letter of resignation to his son, Horace.[8]

In one instance an officer was forced to resign for the good of the service. First Lt. James H. Clardy (Company A), a physician in civilian life, "disgraced himself by leaving his company when danger was near at hand." After Clardy was tried for cowardice and found guilty, Lt. Gen. Theophilus H. Holmes set the sentence aside. His company, though, was "composed of good and brave soldiers who are not willing to serve under an officer whose heart may *be in the cause* yet his legs have not the strength to carry him into an engagement," as Randal firmly stated. Clardy resigned on 24 August 1863 perhaps because of actions at either Milliken's Bend or Goodrich's Landing.[9]

Occasionally men resigned for personal reasons. Capt. Levi M. Truitt (Company A) cited family circumstances as well as a duty to serve out a contract as a mail carrier in Texas. When Truitt left for the war, he hired a man to serve as mail carrier, but his employee quit and entered the army as a substitute. Capt. Martin V. Smith (Company D), who worked as a minister in civilian life, resigned to become a brigade "missionary." Those who resigned came from no particular occupational group. The wealthiest, or those of certain occupational groups, did not resign at a proportionately greater rate.[10]

Unlike the original group, who were elected by the men, new captains or first lieutenants were appointed or promoted rather than elected and had usually served first as a noncommissioned officer. The enlisted men apparently elected the second lieutenants (who accounted for most of the new group). Five of the new officers had first served as noncommissioned officers. Twice as many enlisted as privates and then jumped directly from private to commissioned officer. Among the new officers was twenty-eight-year-old Capt. Jesse W. Fuller, a native South Carolinian and merchant, who served first as a quartermaster sergeant and then was promoted to a captaincy. He served as Company A's third and last captain. Second Lt. James H. Gee, a thirty-two-year-old farmer in Company G, enlisted as a private then became a third lieutenant and finally a second lieutenant. Twenty-nine-year-old 2nd Lt. Thomas M. Lambright, a farm laborer in civilian life, enlisted as a private in Company A, transferred to Company K when it was formed, then jumped from private to second lieutenant when elected on 5 February 1863.[11]

These new officers were different in several significant ways from the original group (see Table 3).

TABLE 3
A Comparison of Original Officers, New Officers, and Enlisted Men

	ORIGINAL	NEW	ENLISTED MEN
Mean enlistment age	31.9	29.8	26.8
Mean real estate (in dollars)	7050	1117	1207
Mean personal estate (in dollars)	9221	3277	2393
Mean wealth (combined real and personal estate in dollars)	16,270	4394	3603
Mean taxable property (in dollars)	7441	3830	2090
Proportion of slaveholders (in percentages)	59.5	58.3	26.0
Agricultural occupations	43.9	76.9	78.0

Only four of these officers were appointed or promoted to their positions, and thirteen were apparently elected. Interestingly, the enlisted men now elected men much more similar to themselves than the original officers had been. Nevertheless, those who were wealthier than the average enlisted man and owned slaves still tended to be elected at a proportionately greater rate, just as previously. Personal qualities such as bravery and leadership shown during recent campaigning undoubtedly influenced the selection of officers. In contrast, in the 3rd Texas Cavalry, another east-Texas regiment, enlisted men elected officers who were much younger and represented more affluent households than the original officers. Newer officers in the 3rd

Texas were much closer in age to the enlisted men than original officers, but the wealth disparity was now much greater between enlisted men and officers in the 3rd Texas. The reason the men of the 3rd Texas Cavalry and the 28th Texas Cavalry elected such different men to replace original officers may be related to different campaign theaters, amount of campaigning, amount of fighting, pre-draft or post-draft status, or just the simple fact that the composition of the two regiments differed. Perhaps men of the 3rd had different standards for officers from those in the 28th Texas.[12]

In addition to the turnover of officers, the regiment also had to adjust to changes in the Trans-Mississippi Department. When Lt. Gen. Edmund Kirby Smith arrived in the Trans-Mississippi in February 1863, he gained control of a department theoretically covering about 600,000 square miles and including Arizona Territory, Indian Territory, Texas, Louisiana, Arkansas, and Missouri. As was so often the case in the Trans-Mississippi, reality did not match theory. Actually, when General Smith arrived, the Arizona Territory and much of west Texas was under Federal control. Most of Indian Territory and Arkansas functioned as a sort of "no-man's-land," an exiled Confederate government represented Missouri, and west Louisiana "was little more than a single crowded river valley." The population of this primarily rural, agricultural department numbered approximately 2.9 million in 1860 and consisted of about 2.1 million whites, 666,000 slaves, 121,500 Indians, and 9,200 free blacks.[13]

Kirby Smith's power over this paper organization increased after the fall of Vicksburg in July 1863. The Confederate government anticipated that the city's fall and consequent Union control of the Mississippi would disrupt communications between the Trans-Mississippi and the rest of the Confederacy. Accordingly, President Jefferson Davis urged Smith to open talks with civilian authorities, namely the four Trans-Mississippi governors. In addition, Secretary of War James A. Seddon apparently informed Smith that he would be responsible for military operations and probably also civil administration. Smith was directed to build upon existing structures and establish parallel bureaus to the ones in Richmond. By the spring of 1864 the Confederate government treated the Trans-Mississippi almost like "a detached province of the Confederacy." Smith strove to undertake these responsibilities and beginning in August 1863 established bureaus that, by the summer of 1864, numbered seventeen.[14]

Regiments, like the 28th Texas, provided much of the manpower for these bureaus and associated programs. Previously, men had been detached from the regiment to act as teamsters, nurses, and to collect clothing, but by the summer of 1863 men were often detached to work at a facility that later passed under the control of one of the bureaus Smith established. Such bureaus required sizable numbers of men for their operations. The Shreveport Quartermaster Post, for example, employed a total of one hundred soldiers out of the 160 total workers at the site. The soldiers were detailed to the post and included skilled workers like tailors, blacksmiths, wagon makers, and shoemakers plus unskilled workers such as teamsters. For the 28th the most complete records are for the period from May to August 1863, and this time frame provides an idea of the numbers detached and the services they rendered. For this period eighty-six enlisted men and four officers were detached on special duty. Detached men tended to be older, not wealthy, and were more likely to be skilled laborers. Their lack of wealth, reflected in a lower proportion of slaveholders, perhaps connects to their chosen occupations. Those from certain occupational categories like manufacturing and skilled trades no doubt had special skills useful in the various bureaus. Officers in the 28th Texas must have been familiar with the peacetime occupations of their men, and these men were moved to positions where their skills could better be used.[15]

Detached men from the 28th Texas engaged in a number of different tasks. Eight men in the summer of 1863 served in Capt. Horace Haldeman's battery attached to Randal's brigade. Apparently at this time each brigade detached a small number of men from each regiment to strengthen that brigade's battery. Also in the summer of 1863 Capt. J. M. Daniel's battery of Brig. Gen. James M. Hawes's brigade received twenty-three transfers from other regiments in that brigade. In the 28th these were temporary transfers. Several other men such as Monroe Wheeler (Company A), John W. King (Company D), Robert A. L. Morgan (Company I), and William K. Moorman (Company K) worked as nurses. W. L. Harrison (Company D) served as an assistant surgeon at Pine Bluff, Arkansas. Other tasks called for special skills. Charles Cannon (Company B) worked as a clerk in the assistant adjutant general's office. Five men were detached to the Arkadelphia, Arkansas, shoe factory. A. C. Atwood (Company D) made hats in Texas, T. E. Scarbrough, also of Company D, worked as a carpenter in Alexandria, two men worked as blacksmiths, two were detached to the Rusk Armory, and J. C. Prather (Company B) carried mail. William J. Rogers of

Company K worked at the only salt works in Arkansas at a site near Arkadelphia. Some men served as teamsters of the many wagons attached to the brigade or worked as temporary guards. Lt. John N. Garner oversaw the work of a party of slaves at Delhi, Louisiana. Many of the detached soldiers performed important duties in the Trans-Mississippi Department.[16]

Partially compensating for the men who were detached were a number of new enlistees or conscripts who entered the unit after the regiment left Texas. These "later enlistees" would by the end of the war total 151 men; in 1862 28 men joined, followed by 101 in 1863, 15 in 1864, and only 7 in 1865 and were unevenly distributed among the various companies. Company A received the most (27) and Company H the least (4). Perhaps the number each company received depended on the efforts of their officers or men. In early 1864 an order stated that any soldier who obtained a recruit would receive a sixty-day furlough. Some of the men, such as those who joined other family members in the unit, probably volunteered. M. W. Burleson who was fifteen years old in 1860 joined brothers David and Joshua in August 1863 in Company H. James Bralley joined his brother Leroy in Company A in April 1863. There are indications that officers occasionally traveled to Texas to try their hand at recruiting men. In early July 1863 Capt. Martin V. Smith of Company D traveled to Texas where he had a difficult time obtaining recruits.[17]

Theoretically, the process for obtaining conscripts was straightforward. An enrolling officer called for all men of conscription age, who had not already volunteered, to report. Once small squads were enrolled, they were sent to instruction camps. Officials allowed conscripts to choose the branch of the service where they wished to serve, and the raw men were usually assigned to units from their area. Conscription, though, was unpopular, partially owing to the very principle of it but also because of various loopholes that seemingly allowed the wealthy to avoid service. Many conscripts petitioned their congressmen for discharges from the army, while other draftees deserted. In Texas large parties of organized deserters periodically caused problems. Probably some of the later enlistees in the 28th were conscripts since by late 1863 few men were volunteering. It is difficult however to ascertain exactly who among the later enlistees volunteered and who were conscripts. In either case, as far as the records indicate, these later enlistees served adequately. Few of them deserted, and several were casualties. The fact that they made adequate soldiers may be explained by their service with men from the same region and perhaps in some cases from the same neighborhoods.[18]

A general profile of these later enlistees reveals that most were engaged in agricultural occupations, were from counties that had contributed already to the regiment, were less likely to be married men or heads of households, and were poorer than the original enlistees. An analysis of ages also reveals that there was more of a tendency for these men to be considerably older or younger than earlier enlistees. The conscription act was in effect geared toward men like these who were of moderate means and from age groups not drawn from as much earlier.

Like other Trans-Mississippi units, the 28th Texas suffered during the war from an inadequate weapons and accouterment supply. Partially this deficiency was due to the early fall of New Orleans in April 1862, which deprived the Trans-Mississippi Department of "two cannon foundries, two saber and bayonet factories, a large Enfield rifle plant, and the most extensive complex of ammunition laboratories and percussion cap shops in the entire Mississippi basin." The department accordingly relied primarily on two sources for weapons supplies: captured arms and small gun factories. Small gun works were established in Tyler, Lancaster, Marshall, San Antonio, Austin, Rusk County, and Columbia, Texas, during the conflict. Unfortunately for Confederate troops, the production from all of the Trans-Mississippi factories totaled only about eight hundred weapons a month, and demand was much higher than that. In late 1862 Gov. Francis R. Lubbock of Texas complained that his state's troops needed an additional fifteen thousand arms.[19]

As a result, Trans-Mississippi regiments often possessed a bewildering variety of guns though they seemed to have adequate ammunition supplies throughout the war. An example of the variety of weapons carried by Walker's men may be found in a report from 8 August 1863, when the division was chiefly armed with 2,697 .69-caliber muskets (percussion) distributed among the brigades as follows: Hawes's (1,440), McCulloch's (273), and Randal's (984). Enfield rifles counted for 1,485, distributed among Hawes's (288), McCulloch's (939), and Randal's (258) brigades. Additionally, Randal's troops possessed nine rifled muskets, and Hawes's brigade had forty-three Colt repeating rifles.[20]

Unlike Confederates in other areas who were mostly armed with rifles by 1863, Walker's division was armed chiefly with smoothbore muskets until the spring of 1864. Because Trans-Mississippi factories could not meet the demand for weapons, the Confederates there probably relied on the enemy for supplies of rifles. McCulloch's men probably obtained their rifles during the Vicksburg campaign when they bore the brunt of the fighting at Milliken's Bend. In November 1863 three regiments of Walker's division with several units of Texas cavalry scored a triumph at Bayou Bourbeau and captured over five hundred Union soldiers along with "a large quantity of improved small-arms." However, until the spring of 1864, most of Walker's men had seen little combat, and so had fewer opportunities to rearm as compared to many Confederates in other areas of the war. By the conclusion of the Red River campaign, the division reported a total of 848 muskets and 2,353 Enfields. Presumably the division rearmed itself mostly during this campaign, most likely at Mansfield, Louisiana, the site of its major victory. Ironically, the 28th Texas Cavalry, in addition to many other units in Walker's division, was probably well-equipped in arms after their only major combat experiences of the war.[21]

The Enfield rifle "was perhaps the most popular gun in Confederate service." The use of the .69-caliber muskets was especially prevalent during the beginning of the war and, as in Walker's division, were loaded with either a single ball or buck and ball. At close range (less than one hundred yards) the weapon was exceedingly dangerous but beyond that, nearly worthless. Enfields, in contrast, were effective practically up to seven hundred yards. How Walker's division obtained the small number of repeating rifles is unknown, but there were occasional Confederate companies who obtained the weapons at the beginning of the war. Though capable of greater firepower than the smoothbore muskets and the Enfields and though used effectively by some units during the war, the Colt had a defect in that all the cylinders tended at times to fire at once resulting in blown off fingers or even hands. Walker's division in theory was capable of packing quite a punch at close range. The Enfield rifles were assigned to certain companies which were "to act as skirmishers" as planned by General Holmes in the autumn of 1862. For example, Col. Oran M. Roberts commanded the infantry at the battle of Bayou Bourbeau, and he reported that Company C of the 11th Texas Infantry and Companies A and F of the 15th Texas Infantry were armed with rifles and so were assigned as skirmishers.[22]

In spite of this improvement in quality of weapons by June 1864, the division still suffered from shortages of weapons and also accouterments.

Sometime in 1864 the 11th Texas Infantry of Randal's brigade reported a shortage of 210 Enfields and 58 .67-caliber rifles. The regiment's ledger book reported that only 112 new guns would be supplied, leaving, presumably, a number of men without weapons. There were also shortages of cartridge boxes (165), cap boxes (179), bayonets (349), shoulder belts (380), and waist belts (258) in the 11th Texas. Such severe deficiencies, with the exception of the bayonets, undoubtedly were part of the problems the Trans-Mississippi Department had during the war of supplying leather goods.[23]

Just as severe were the clothing shortages among the Trans-Mississippi troops. Again the fall of New Orleans, with its important textile mills and shoe factory, proved crucial. An important complex of textile works was established at the Huntsville, Texas, state penitentiary. The prisoners at the penitentiary attempted to fill both military and civilian clothing needs and by 1 August 1862 had produced one million yards of cloth. Production declined after that because the state was unable to repair broken machinery. As a consequence of a clothing shortage, there was little uniformity in the clothing worn by soldiers. A vivid depiction of Walker's division was written by Joseph P. Blessington:

> It is impossible to paint the variety our division presented. Here would be a fellow dressed in homespun pants, with the knees out of them; on his head might be stuck the remnant of a straw hat, while a faded Texas penitentiary cloth jacket would perhaps complete his outfit. His neighbor, very likely, was arrayed in breeches made out of some castoff blanket, with a dyed shirt as black as the ace of spades, and no hat at all. Then would come a man with a woolen hat made like a pyramid, sitting jauntily upon his head, while, to introduce his style of hat, he had it covered over with assorted buttons; and, to top the climax, had a red tassel sewed on top. Notwithstanding his gaudy hat, a part of a shirt, and occasional fragments only of what had once been a pair of military pantaloons, made up the rest of his attire.[24]

There were different ways to obtain clothing, and most men relied on the home front. Commonly, units sent soldiers, often officers, to Texas to ask for donations. Col. Oran M. Roberts of the 11th Texas Infantry believed donations were the main source of clothing for soldiers in the Trans-Mississippi. In the summer of 1863, a time of particular need, Capt. Patrick Henry traveled to Texas for the specific purpose of collecting clothing for the ragged men of the 28th. Apparently, all the units in the division lacked clothing. Sam Farrow explained to his wife that many of the soldiers were "nearly naked" and that many of the clothes left in storage before the campaign were either stolen or "ruined with mildew." He had a shirt and one pair of pants and both were nearly worn out. A few weeks later the need for clothing was still so dire for Farrow that he told his wife, "if they do not give me clothes I intend coming home after them this fall." Some men simply asked their wives directly for clothing as Dr. Cade did when he asked for an overcoat, although he warned his wife not to deprive herself or the children "of anything to get it for me." Captain Perry occasionally purchased cloth and sent it home to be made into clothing as he did in February 1864 when he obtained six yards "of stout overcoat cloth," fifteen yards of other cloth, six yards of cotton cloth for pants, and even a calico dress for his wife.[25]

The home front was obviously important in meeting supply needs. Women met most of the clothing needs in Texas, and they often established Ladies' Aid Societies. A number of these societies formed in communities throughout the state, such as the Ladies' Volunteer Relief Association established in Marshall in November 1861. Meeting each Tuesday morning in the courthouse at ten o'clock, the ladies decided on their priorities, like making bandages, and perused want lists submitted by captains of companies. Sometimes the products of these societies were purchased by post quartermasters in Texas. Harriet Perry, who lived near Marshall, reported on some of these group activities in the fall of 1862. In one letter Mrs. Perry informed her husband, Capt. Theophilus Perry, that many women were weaving cloth. One woman even had her slaves spinning yarn "till ten and twelve o'clock at night." Her mother-in-law manufactured ninety yards of cloth per week in the fall of 1862 and was assisted by "Aunt Betsy" who prepared the looms for weaving.[26]

Individual efforts were also important. Allie Cade in September 1863 told her husband she was knitting some "nice socks" for him, and Harriet Perry made a "confederate candle" of beeswax for her husband in the fall of 1862. Captain Perry's father also helped in supply efforts by obtaining boots. Visiting soldiers from the regiment often transported these products to the fortunate recipients. In one packet Harriet Perry sent a blue overcoat, pants, three pairs of socks, a comforter, a hat, pepper, and clothes for Norflet, Theophilus's personal servant. Another time Capt. Phil Brown carried coffee, shirts, and "flannel drawers" to Perry. Such efforts on the part of the women on the home front were much appreciated by soldiers.[27]

The veteran soldiers of the 28th Texas coped with a variety of internal changes and external circumstances during the summer of 1863. The unit entered the 1863 fall campaign somewhat weakened by disease and plagued by occasional clothing shortages. Several new commissioned officers and a number of new enlisted men, who served as replacements for detached soldiers, altered the internal structure of the unit. The regiment's experiences during the hard summer of 1863, though, was probably typical of the experiences of other units in Walker's division at that time. In the fall campaign, the soldiers of Walker's division would help repel a Union advance in Louisiana and earn the proud nickname of "Walker's Greyhounds."

CHAPTER 5

Walker's Greyhounds

If the question of war or peace on any terms was
submitted to this army the side of peace would get a
heavy vote. I hate to believe this but am pretty sure it
would be the case although the army is in fine spirits
and would fight an awful fight now. Yet they sigh for
peace, peace, peace, home and family etc etc.
—CAPT. ELIJAH P. PETTY, 17TH TEXAS INFANTRY,
9 JANUARY 1864

Following the end of the Vicksburg campaign, in July 1863, to mid-March 1864, Maj. Gen. John G. Walker's division engaged in a variety of services. These activities included blocking a tentative Federal advance in southern Louisiana, bombarding enemy transports along the Mississippi River, and rebuilding Fort DeRussy along the Red River. Additionally the division survived a serious crisis of morale, and the 28th Texas endured a mutiny. By mid-March 1864, Walker's men, including the 28th Texas, were fairly well prepared to meet the enemy's advances in the forthcoming Red River campaign.

During the closing stages of the Vicksburg campaign, Walker's men campaigned in northeast Louisiana. At the same time, Maj. Gen. Richard Taylor's army moved toward New Orleans. Since at least May 1863, Taylor had hoped to capture Federal-occupied New Orleans and force Maj. Gen. Nathaniel P. Banks to lift his siege of Port Hudson, Louisiana, farther up the Mississippi River. In early July, Taylor's men reached a point only twenty miles from New Orleans before Taylor heard on 10 July of the surrender of Port Hudson the day before. Now Taylor had to abandon the Lafourche country because Banks's larger army was free to move through the region. Taylor believed he owed his failure to capture New Orleans to Lt. Gen. Edmund Kirby Smith's refusal to release Walker's division for service in Taylor's army. Soon after the close of Taylor's campaign, Smith ordered Walker to move from Monroe, Louisiana, to join Taylor in Alexandria, Louisiana. Only small numbers of Confederate cavalrymen and artillerymen were left in northeast Louisiana when Walker's division left the area.[1]

During the march of the division from Monroe to Alexandria, Col. Oran M. Roberts of the 11th Texas Infantry commanded Col. Horace Randal's brigade because Randal was on leave in Texas. The division moved first to Trenton, three miles north of Monroe, on 17 July. By 22 July the men had arrived in Vernon, a storage site for commissary supplies, about twenty-five miles southwest of Monroe. At Vernon, Brig. Gen. Henry E. McCulloch, who had been the division's first commander, and subsequently a brigade commander, left for Texas to take up new duties. Col. George Flournoy took temporary command of McCulloch's old brigade. Six days later the division camped near Campti. The men were exhausted from the dusty march in dry, hot weather, but they had enjoyed the large summer huckleberries all along their route. Not surprisingly, the soldiers remained at Campti for several days. On 3 August the regiments trudged downstream along the river for about four miles until they reached a site opposite Grand Ecore. Here they were ferried across the river and the next day boarded transports for their trip to Alexandria. Walker's division stayed near Alexandria until 10 August when they started marching to Camp Green, twenty-five miles southwest of Alexandria. The men rested at Camp Green from 11 to 31 August when they moved the camp.[2]

In spite of some positive things to reflect on during the movement to

Alexandria, many of Walker's men were demoralized and discontented. Some soldiers in the division and the regiment were perhaps encouraged by conversations with some of the paroled prisoners from Vicksburg. Dr. Edward Cade reported that these Vicksburg parolees were not disheartened at all. In addition, many men believed that Gen. Robert E. Lee's army had won a great victory in Pennsylvania. Many more soldiers, though, were demoralized, and some were dispirited by the fall of Vicksburg. The surrender of Vicksburg, coupled with general war weariness and home-sickness, combined to demoralize men not just in Walker's division but throughout the Trans-Mississippi Department. Particularly hard hit by demoralization was Taylor's small army, whose effectiveness was seriously impaired by heavy desertion. In comparison, Walker's division remained relatively intact, but still there were some problems. Pvt. S. W. Farrow of the 19th Texas Infantry commented, "there is very little encouragement to hold the Army together much longer though bright hopes may spring up before to lead us on."[3]

Many soldiers simply were tired of war and the routine of army life. In the 28th Texas Cavalry, "the constant contact of rough and obscene men" sickened Dr. Cade. Private Farrow was "tired of the war" and hoped it would end soon. Even the usually optimistic Capt. Theophilus Perry of the 28th commented to his wife about his "miserable" life in Company F. Army routine wearied many soldiers, and in particular the infrequent issuance of passes to leave camp irritated many men. Enlisted men found passes difficult to obtain, and the penalties for leaving camp without authorization were humiliating. In the 19th Texas Infantry the punishment for being caught without a pass outside of camp required the transgressor to carry a log or pole on his back for two hours while marching in a circle in camp.[4]

More commonly, homesickness plagued the men, making them ill at ease because they saw no real prospect of obtaining a furlough. During the summer of 1863, and well into wintertime, officers granted furloughs only to sick men. In some units, like the 19th Texas Infantry, men were promised furloughs after a year of service. These promised furloughs were denied in the 19th Texas Infantry and caused some desertions in that regiment. Home-sickness, combined with the difficulty of obtaining a leave, led to much dissatisfaction and unhappiness. Captain Perry wrote his wife forlornly, "I can not tell when I shall ever see you. I am sick at heart to be with you, but the longer the war continues the more the prospect for going home diminishes." In such cases the relatively recent invention of photography aided homesick soldiers. Dr. Cade always carried a photograph of his wife with him, and Captain Perry carried photographs of his wife and daughter in his coat pocket and even slept "with my head on them at night."[5]

Discontent in Walker's division caused some desertions and more commonly emotional turmoil. Even though a total of ten men deserted from the 28th Texas in the summer of 1863, despondency and even anger were more typical responses during that period. Captain Perry grew quite angry that summer at civilians who eagerly encouraged others to enlist while they stayed at home and speculated on the war's outcome. Perry aimed his particular wrath at secessionists "who denounced all persons that differed from him" and then did not enlist. In the midst of his anger, Perry drafted his will and wrote his wife, Harriet, long letters that "were very sad." In July 1863 all was gloom for Perry.[6]

Desertion became a serious problem in the division from about 10 August to 10 September, when three hundred soldiers deserted according to Dr. Cade. Deserters from Randal's brigade accounted for only a fraction of the three hundred. Four men from the 28th Texas deserted during this period. Cade attributed the low rate of desertion in Randal's brigade to a heightened sense of an "'esprit de corps'" compared to the other brigades of the division. Proudly, Cade wrote his wife that "Genls Taylor and Walker both say that [Randal's] is the best Brigade west of the Mississippi River." Desertion, though, reached a serious level in other brigades, and perhaps more in Randal's than Cade perceived. Deserters often left with their guns, and as they passed other units boldly "hallowed for all men who wanted to go to Texas to fall in." At just this stage, and perhaps partially because of the desertions, a series of religious revivals began in Walker's division.[7]

Although most Southerners were religious, religion did not thrive in Southern armies during the first two years of the war. To many soldiers, going off to war was viewed as a great adventure. To soldiers from rural areas, a large part of the 28th, going off to war seemed like an exciting visit to a city. These men, for the most part, "wanted to have a fling at gambling, drinking and swearing, and they did not wish to be bothered with preachers." As in many Civil War regiments, profanity and card playing was common. Many of the units' soldiers were also tempted by women. Soon after leaving Texas in July 1862, a number of the regiment's men visited Shreveport brothels. Later in the war, Dr. Cade noted that "the married men of the army are about as constant in their attentions to the fair as the single ones."[8]

Revivalism reached a peak in the winter of 1863–1864 in Walker's division, the Army of Northern Virginia, and the Army of Tennessee. There were several reasons for the rather sudden interest in religion by the soldiers of the Confederacy. Preachers made a greater effort to speak to soldiers, and religious workers distributed a great amount of tract literature by the middle of the war. In Walker's division preachers occasionally visited, as did a minister from New Orleans in early September 1863. Another factor in the rise of religion was the church background of many of the soldiers. In the 28th Texas most of the men came from east Texas, an area heavily influenced by Protestant denominations that relied on revivals as a tool for reaching sinners. Defeats on the battlefield, and the corresponding demoralization, led to a belief in many that God would not allow a Southern triumph until the South did penance. In Walker's division the recent loss of Vicksburg and Port Hudson, as previously discussed, led to a certain despondency and perhaps set the stage for revivals. In addition, the "increasing prospect of death" drew some to religion.[9]

One of the most important revivalists in the division was originally a member of the 28th Texas, Capt. Martin V. Smith of Company D. Smith, a native South Carolinian, was born in 1837 and arrived in Texas in 1850. He became a Baptist minister at age nineteen and was Dr. Cade's brother-in-law. Enlisted men elected Smith captain of Company D when that company formed in the spring of 1862. The steps leading up to Smith's resignation and subsequent position as brigade "missionary" are interesting. Smith included with his resignation two petitions—one from a committee of the Eastern Baptist Convention of Texas and one signed by a number of commissioned officers in Randal's brigade. The document from the Baptist Convention petitioned Smith to perform the duties of a missionary in the brigade. The petition from the officers was longer and more detailed. This document explained that Randal's brigade was from an area of Texas where churches were common and observed that preaching "will satisfy the desire of the religious part of the Command and have a good effect in restraining *many* from vile practices which soldiers are liable to engage in. . . ." Smith could also aid the sick and travel to obtain medical supplies for the brigade. As a soldier, Smith would know better than a civilian the particular spiritual needs of soldiers. Ten officers of the 28th Texas, ten from the 14th Texas, twelve in the 11th Texas, and five from Gould's

Battalion signed this petition. Smith's resignation, submitted on 17 August, contained many of the ideas in the officers' petition, but he also noted that his expenses would be paid by people in Texas. He promised to preach often to the brigade and "indevor to counteract those feelings of despondency and disaffection so injurious to the private soldiers." Officials seemingly ignored his first resignation, so Smith resubmitted it on 22 September. Finally, Smith learned of his resignation's acceptance in early November. By that time, Smith was already serving as a missionary to the brigade.[10]

Several other ministers also preached in the division, although Smith was apparently the only person ministering to Randal's men. A chaplain in the 16th Texas Infantry preached regularly to those men, and civilian ministers visited the soldiers. Smith, "a smooth and persuasive speaker," according to one listener, held religious meetings in both Randal's and Hawes's brigades. Smith threw himself into his ministerial duties with fervor and a determination to convert sinners. By October forty men had been converted in Randal's brigade, and twelve men were baptized. Smith also baptized twelve in Hawes's brigade. Although revivals were being held in all the brigades by this time, they were particularly noticeable in Randal's unit. The revivals increased in intensity as autumn progressed, in spite of the fact that the brigade was often on the march during that time. By 3 November, Smith had baptized ninety-two men. The peak, though, came in late November when on a single day Smith baptized twenty-three soldiers. These meetings continued into December when Smith left, as he intended, to obtain medical supplies. At least temporarily, the revivals effected a great moral change in the regiment. Instead of profanity and card playing in the camp of the 28th Texas, the forest was "filled day and night with men praying and singing." As a result of the revivals and the withdrawal of the enemy in the upcoming campaign, morale improved, and apparently the level of desertion dropped in the division.[11]

During the period of demoralization and the religious revivals, the unit was involved in several military movements. Horace Randal's brigade, including the 28th Texas, left the Alexandria area on an expedition sometime on 1 September. Randal's brigade marched out of camp and moved toward Harrisonburg, Louisiana, about forty miles northeast of Alexandria. A Union raid by two brigades led by Brig. Gen. Marcellus M. Crocker from Natchez, Mississippi, to Harrisonburg, twenty-three miles to the northwest, triggered the movement of Randal's men. The Union objective was to destroy Fort Beauregard, situated on the nearly five-hundred-foot-wide Ouachita River at Harrisonburg. Forty men commanded by Lt. Col. George W. Logan garrisoned this small, twelve-gun post situated on a hill in rear of the town. Confederate scouts quickly detected the movement of Crocker's troops sometime on 1 September. By 3 September, Randal's brigade of 1,110 men arrived at Brushy Bridge, "ten miles west of Harrisonburg." East of the bridge the men of the 28th saw the enemy in line of battle with artillery well posted to cover the open fields in front of the Union position. Pickets of both sides spent the night about four hundred yards from each other.[12]

After Randal's men arrived at Brushy Bridge, a courier from Lt. Col. Logan at the fort arrived with a message for Randal. Logan informed Randal of his decision to evacuate the fort because he feared Randal would be unable to reinforce him. At 3:00 A.M. on the morning of 4 September, Logan's men destroyed ammunition, commissary goods, and small arms, and attempted to destroy eight of the fort's cannon. They evacuated the fort and took four cannon with them. Meanwhile, Randal formed his brigade on some hills near the bridge. At dawn on the fourth, enemy skirmishers advanced and were driven in by "sharpshooters" commanded by Capt. J. J. Flinn of the 14th Texas Infantry. The enemy attempted no other advance, and Randal's brigade retreated about ten miles south to Little River. Randal claimed the enemy losses were three men killed, and his brigade suffered no killed or wounded.[13]

Crocker's force had achieved their objective. They captured Fort Beauregard, destroyed six cannon, and took two cannon back to Natchez. Crocker's men also captured twenty Confederates, including privates George W. Nesbith and Charles O'Donohue of Company F of the 28th Texas. These men were confined in Natchez on 6 September and transported to Vicksburg on 23 September. The fate of these prisoners is unknown, as their compiled service records end with their capture. As for Randal's brigade, they were back in the Alexandria vicinity by 13 September. Although unable to reinforce Logan, the men of the 28th knew Randal's skill and coolness had extricated them from a situation in which they would have faced a force almost four times their size.[14]

Soon after the brigade returned to Alexandria, a Union army tentatively attempted to invade Texas by way of Louisiana. By mid-September 1863, General Smith and General Taylor believed Union forces had a master plan to drive the Trans-Mississippi Confederates into Texas. In the space of six days, from 4 September to 10 September, Fort Beauregard fell, Sabine Pass, Texas, was attacked, and Union troops occupied Little Rock, Arkansas. Understandably, Smith and Taylor believed Union armies in Arkansas and Louisiana would soon act in concert against their comparatively tiny force. In reality, the Union forces had devised no coordinated plan for the subjugation of Confederate forces in the Trans-Mississippi. President Abraham Lincoln, however, desired the invasion of Texas in spite of opposition by Maj. Gen. Ulysses S. Grant and General Banks, who both believed Mobile, Alabama, was a more important target than Texas. Lincoln's concerns about Texas centered on "the French monarchy's recent establishment of a military protectorate over Mexico [that] presented the danger of a Confederate-Mexican alliance." Additionally a Confederate supply line that crossed the Rio Grande into Mexico annoyed the Northern government. Many Northerners also believed there were many Unionists in Texas who would welcome an invasion by Lincoln's forces.[15]

Lt. Richard Dowling, a former saloonkeeper, and his forty-three rowdy men humiliated a Union force of four thousand men and four gunboats at Sabine Pass. When this attack was turned away, Banks gave control of an attempt to move overland to Texas to Maj. Gen. William B. Franklin, an exile from the Army of the Potomac. Franklin's force consisted of a large portion of the 13th Corps, veterans of the Vicksburg campaign, and the 19th Corps. This army totaled about thirty thousand men. Taylor's army, consisting of Brig. Gen. Alfred A. Mouton's division (6,971 present for duty) and Walker's division (3,942 present for duty), totaled not quite eleven thousand men. Effective probes, particularly by Mouton and Brig. Gen. Thomas Green, Taylor's cavalry leader, at Morganza on 29 September, revealed that a large enemy force was gathering. The Union army was organizing at Brashear City (present day Morgan City), Louisiana, approximately fifty-five to sixty miles west and a bit south of New Orleans and about ninety miles southeast of Alexandria.[16]

The Union campaign began on 3 October with the occupation of New Iberia, about forty miles northwest of Brashear City, by Union troops. Despite their great advantage in numbers, Franklin's men advanced slowly and indecisively northward while harassed by Green's cavalrymen. (Franklin's route roughly paralleled present-day U.S. Highway 90 to Lafayette and then current U.S. Interstate 49 toward Opelousas.)[17]

Even before Taylor learned with certainty of the size of Franklin's army, Walker's division moved to a location where Taylor could use it more effectively. The division left the Alexandria vicinity on 27 September and two days later arrived near Washington, about five miles north of Opelousas. Opelousas was about forty miles south and a little east of Alexandria. Opelousas, a town of about fifteen hundred population, was the "commercial, judicial and cultural center of a thriving agricultural area." Washington, with about one thousand inhabitants, was an important shipping center due to its location on Bayou Courtableau. During this march Walker's men learned that the Federals had given them the nickname "Walker's Greyhounds." According to Virgil Rabb of the 16th Texas Infantry, his division received this name because "they [the Yankees] said they could hear of us one day perhaps a hundred and fifty miles off and the next day we would be fighting them." Near Washington the men saw some of the enemy, "a pretty savage looking set," whom Green's men had captured near Morganza. Rather than being downcast, these prisoners were confident the South would soon be subdued.[18]

After marching to Washington, Walker's division left on a series of confusing marches, first to the Simmesport area and then back to the vicinity of Opelousas. From 3 October to 5 October the Greyhounds marched to near Simmesport, about thirty miles northeast of Opelousas. Simmesport was located near the junction of the Red and Atchafalaya rivers. About five miles east of Simmesport the newly joined rivers flowed into the Mississippi River. Why Walker was ordered to Simmesport is unclear. Perhaps Taylor believed in the likelihood of Union activity near Simmesport, or perhaps Walker's move was designed to confuse the enemy. There were two enemy movements in the Simmesport area in October. On 7 October the Union navy captured and burned two Confederate steamers near Simmesport, and from 16 to 20 October, a Union expedition moved from Natchez to the mouth of the Red River (near Simmesport). More than likely, Taylor feared a Union thrust that presumably would coincide with movements by Franklin's army. Walker's division stayed only briefly in the Simmesport area, leaving on 6 October. The men believed they were returning to the Opelousas vicinity to reinforce parts of Taylor's cavalry force. By 8 October Walker's men were at Big Cane, "an insignificant place" twelve miles north and a little east of Washington. The Greyhounds spent 10 October to 13 October marching between Big Cane and Evergreen, thirteen miles northwest of Big Cane. By 19 October the men were stationed five miles north of Washington on Bayou Boeuf.[19]

These marches confused the soldiers. As one noted to his wife, "there is no telling one day where we will be the next." Although many of the men were chilly in the cool autumn air, there was little sickness. Fortunately, ample supplies of potatoes, pumpkins, cornbread, beef, molasses, and raw sugar cane fortified the men. The sugar cane proved a special treat, and Walker's men ate whole fields of it. Indeed the soldiers had "as much plunder as we can haul."[20]

While the 28th Texas and other units in Walker's division enjoyed their plentiful food supplies, United States forces reached Opelousas on 21 October and three days later marched into Washington. While Northern forces crawled into Washington, a drama in the Confederate high command ended. Smith, the commander of the Trans-Mississippi Department, had cautioned Taylor, warning that a defeat would be demoralizing. Smith believed it was safest to retreat until the enemy became tired of pursuit. He warned that Taylor must attack the enemy only if virtually assured of success. Taylor, meanwhile, had believed a hard strike at the enemy before they ventured further into Louisiana was best. This same disagreement concerning strategy would be replayed in March and April 1864 during the Red River campaign. Accordingly, Taylor devised an ambush, or bluff, three miles north of Washington near the community of Moundville on 24 October. Taylor positioned Walker's division in line of battle across a field with some of the men standing in a ditch. Artillerymen situated the cannon of six batteries to sweep the road leading from Washington to Moundville. Brig. Gen. James P. Major's cavalry brigade was also present, primarily to act as skirmishers and to press the enemy in case of victory. Taylor also formed a new brigade for Walker's division composed of one regiment from each brigade. The regiments selected for the new brigade were the 18th Texas from Hawes's brigade, the 11th Texas from Randal's brigade, and the 15th Texas from Flournoy's brigade. Taylor assigned Col. Oran M. Roberts of the 11th Texas as commander of this temporary brigade, whose mission was to reinforce the cavalry and act as skirmishers. As preparations were completed, Walker's men "thought that we were going to get into it" as they observed Union Brig. Gen. Albert L. Lee's cavalry force ride into view. The encounter was brief. Skirmishers from each side almost immediately fired at each other. Roberts's brigade succeeded in killing and wounding several enemy soldiers. As the sound of skirmisher fire crackled across the field, a woman on horseback galloped across the field until she reached a point in front of the 11th Texas. She exhorted the men to advance and whip the Yankees. Astonished by this lady and encouraged by her words, Roberts's brigade drove forward and pressed back the enemy. The Federals, pursued by Confederate cavalry and Roberts's brigade, retired all the way to Opelousas. This, as matters turned out, marked the northernmost advance of Franklin's army. Walker's division, following the ambush, fell back two miles and two days later moved back twelve miles to Holmesville to guard communications for the army. The most important event for Walker's division when it retired was the arrival of Brig. Gen. William R. Scurry to command Flournoy's brigade. Scurry, a Mexican War veteran, had served prominently in the ill-fated New Mexico campaign in 1862 and had earned a promotion to brigadier general for his activities in that venture. More recently he had aided in the recapture of Galveston, Texas, in January 1863. The brigade enthusiastically greeted him, and bands serenaded him.[21]

Meanwhile, Franklin's campaign was in its final stages. General Franklin was considering abandoning the whole affair. His brigades were spread from New Iberia to Opelousas, a distance of thirty miles, so that forage could be obtained more easily. One division, consisting of two brigades of the 13th Corps commanded by Brig. Gen. Stephen G. Burbridge, occupied Opelousas. There were no reserves nearby to support Burbridge, and Taylor soon learned of the division's isolation and determined to attack it. Two brigades of Green's cavalry, accompanied by Roberts's newly organized brigade, attacked Burbridge's division on 2 November and drove the Federals seven miles south to Bayou Bourbeau. The next day Green's and Roberts's men attacked again, inflicting 716 casualties and suffering 180 casualties by comparison. The 11th Texas of Randal's brigade suffered four killed, fifteen wounded, and thirty-two missing. Colonel Roberts won much praise for the handling of his troops at Bayou Bourbeau. Franklin decided after the battle of Bayou Bourbeau to withdraw to New Iberia. By 17 November the campaign was over. The Union thrust had served to open tensions between Taylor and Smith and revealed the potential havoc that a well-organized Union thrust could have in Louisiana.[22]

While Green's and Roberts's men were attacking Burbridge, the rest of Walker's division drilled, and an execution of a deserter from the 28th Texas took place. Sometime in either September or October, Confederate troops caught Pvt. J. J. Boman of Company K trying to desert to the enemy. Boman had joined the 28th on 12 July 1863 when he transferred from the 3rd Louisiana Cavalry. At the same time, Pvt. Frederick H. Bird of Company K transferred to the 3rd Louisiana. Reasons for this trade in personnel between the two units is unknown. A court sentenced Boman to be shot to death, a decision read to Boman by Martin V. Smith on 1 November. At Private Boman's request, Smith stayed with the man from the time of sentencing until his death on the morning of 2 November. The two men talked often, and Smith prayed for the sentenced man. On Monday morning Smith baptized Boman and conducted him to the execution site. Smith escorted Boman before the division, gathered to witness the execution, and led Boman to the grave. After praying, Smith bandaged Boman's "eyes and tied him by his request to the post. He died without a struggle. Said he *was willing*. Twas a hard trial for me." To some in the ranks the death of Boman was "the deserved fate" of a traitor.[23]

Six days after this emotional event, the 28th Texas and the rest of the division marched to the Mississippi River to prey on enemy transports. Before the movement Roberts's temporary brigade was broken up, and the regiments returned to their respective brigades. Walker's division marched through Evergreen, then to Moreauville, fourteen miles west of Simmesport, and on to Simmesport. While waiting for engineers to construct a pontoon bridge out of dried logs and "'coolers from neighboring sugar houses" across the Atchafalaya River at Simmesport, the men fished in the river. Impatient with the engineers' progress, the division crossed the river on flat boats. On 15 November the pioneer corps, the 12th Texas, and five batteries traveled to the banks of the Mississippi. The men emplaced the guns "immediately upon the river" and waited for enemy transports. On 19 November the artillerymen fired their cannon at the transport *Black Hawk* and damaged it. The fire from Capt. William Edgar's Texas Artillery proved particularly effective by "setting fire to her upper works" and "shattering the [pilot] House." Supporting fire was provided by infantrymen from the 16th Texas. Five enemy gunboats retaliated that evening by shelling the Confederate batteries "very heavily" for three hours. In the meantime, the Confederate soldiers apparently hugged the ground behind a levee since officers ordered them not to waste ammunition on the heavily armored gunboats. The shelling killed two Confederates, and according to Dr. Cade, both men were from Mouton's division. One man, playing cards "near the top of the levee," was killed by a cannonball.[24]

For the rest of November there was occasional shelling and firing on transports and an abortive movement to capture Plaquemine. The men were uncomfortable because of the cold, rainy weather and a shortage of tents. Dr. Cade reported that there were only two tents per regiment although Captain Petty's company in the 17th Texas possessed five tents. In spite of the inclement weather, the religious meetings led by Martin Smith continued in the brigade. Some of the men in Scurry's brigade stole hogs. This act angered Scurry who ordered a hog skinned and the skin placed around one of the thieves. The culprit was then marched through the brigade accompanied by laughing, hog calls, and various remarks. On 1 December the division marched south toward Plaquemine, twelve miles south of Baton Rouge on the Mississippi. Walker was ordered to capture the garrison at Plaquemine, but he ordered the advance halted forty miles from Plaquemine on 3 December. Walker had received information that the enemy knew of his advance, and he believed it wisest simply to abandon the march. Also, the Atchafalaya River was rising rapidly and Walker feared the pontoon bridges would be swept away thus trapping the division on the east side. On 13 December the division arrived at Simmesport thus ending their service along the Mississippi for the year.[25]

From mid-December 1863 until the end of February 1864, the division was in winter encampment and worked on fortifications. On 15 December, Hawes's and Randal's brigades marched toward Marksville, situated roughly halfway between Alexandria and Simmesport on the Red River. Near Marksville these two brigades went into winter quarters while Scurry's brigade remained near the Atchafalaya River.[26]

For several months Walker's division remained comparatively inactive. In the 28th Texas officer examinations occurred in December and January. Officer examinations began in the Confederate military in October 1862 to ensure that an officer had the necessary knowledge for his rank, but these tests only "gradually acquired force." In the 28th Texas, perhaps as in other units, officers were given preparation time. On 8 December, Captain Perry spent much of the day studying tactics but did not take the examination until 7 January. A military board examined the officers. Perry was tested primarily by Maj. Henry G. Hall of the 28th Texas. In the 28th, Perry passed his examination but 1st Lt. James S. Wagnon and 2nd Lt. Rene

Fitzpatrick failed their tests. Interestingly, neither Wagnon nor Fitzpatrick lost his commission according to the compiled service records. Wagnon eventually became captain of Company F. Perhaps men were allowed to retake the examinations. Besides preparing for tests, officers in the regiment often acquired material or other items to improve their uniforms. Dr. Cade, with the help of Dr. O. A. Fitts, purchased a regulation color green silk sash for his uniform. Dr. Cade's wife, Allie, gathered other items for his uniform, including gold stars, a black coat, gray cloth and gold cord for the pants, and velvet for stripes down the sides of the pants. Captain Perry purchased nearly five yards of cloth for a gray overcoat.[27]

Both officers and men spent much time in camp gathering food. Captain Perry reported on the poor quality of beef and the general unavailability of pork. Enlisted men generally received bread, molasses, and poor beef as their rations. In Captain Petty's regiment, the 17th Texas, a number of men buried a quantity of poor beef to the sound of bells and much beating on pots and pans. As a result of the beef burial, fifty men were arrested because the unit's colonel viewed the ceremony as a personal affront. Luckily the colonel soon released the fifty men when he was assured the ceremony was not meant as an insult. Officers generally were in a better position to obtain good food. Captain Perry, for instance, purchased two pigs for ten dollars each and then proceeded to fatten them with camp leftovers.[28]

In early January the regiment began building "little board huts and shelters." Their campsite was in a forest, which provided ample supplies of wood for the men to use. The regiment constructed good shelters and probably used Spanish moss for bedding as the 14th Texas Infantry did. Captain Perry reported that his hut had a large chimney that filled one end of his hut. Other soldiers must have scrambled to build ample fireplaces, for it was a cold winter, apparently the coldest in the vicinity since 1822.[29]

During the winter of 1863–1864, the health of the men was good, other than frequent colds, and furloughs were granted more freely. One of the few men in the regiment seriously ill that winter was staff officer W. A. Tarlton, a lawyer by profession, who enlisted in the 28th Texas at age thirty-six in Company F. In late February, Tarlton was extremely ill. Captain Perry, a friend of Tarlton's, acquired a room in Marksville for Tarlton and even hired people to care for him constantly. On 23 February, Tarlton died as a result of typhoid fever, an illness that had literally driven him "altogether out of his mind. The Doctors call it Insanity." Generally good health and the introduction of a regular system of furloughs raised the morale of the men. From five to ten furloughs were allowed for each company in the 28th, generally in February. Apparently the men eligible for these leaves were those who had not had a leave in a long time. In the 19th Texas, in Private Farrow's company, a drawing was held for the coveted furloughs. Undoubtedly, the chance to go home after sometimes-lengthy absences raised morale.[30]

Those who remained in the regiment spent much of their time drilling and constructing fortifications. By late January the 28th Texas drilled regularly on a nearby prairie. All the other regiments did likewise in anticipation of a competition between the best drilled regiments in Hawes's and Randal's brigades. The prize was a "fine flag, and some say a few furloughs along with it." Probably each brigade held a competition to choose their participant in the match drill. The competitors were the 12th Texas of Hawes's brigade against the 11th Texas of Randal's brigade. General Walker personally presented the coveted flag to the 12th Texas, the winner of the contest. Such competitions provided the soldiers with a greater motivation for drilling. Besides gaining greater expertise on the drill field, the men worked on reinforcing and, to some extent, rebuilding Fort DeRussy on the Red River. This fort was approximately forty miles downstream from Alexandria and roughly fifty-five miles upstream from the mouth of the Red River. The fort had been partially destroyed by U.S. naval forces on 9 May 1863 during the Vicksburg campaign. Although General Taylor believed such fortifications were virtually useless since infantry could usually seize them, General Smith ordered Fort DeRussy rebuilt. Accordingly, the men from Hawes's brigade, Randal's brigade, and work parties of slaves reinforced the fort and constructed "an iron-casemated battery and other works." The men also labored on a "raft" designed to be placed as an obstruction across the river. On 29 February the men heard of the passage of five enemy gunboats into the Red River and up the Ouachita River to Fort Beauregard. Concurrently, a Federal column from Natchez occupied the fort abandoned earlier by Confederate forces.[31]

These events probably interested the men of the 28th, but great discontent within their unit created the most excitement. Many men in the 28th remained angry at the government's order for them to dismount in 1862 and were disgusted that cavalry units were formed after their own dismounting. Suspicions arose that the government had betrayed them, and many pointed to the payment of infantry wages rather than the higher cavalry pay as evidence of the government's deception. These long-standing complaints among the soldiers of the unit perhaps would have remained irritations only, but a third event added the final ingredient to a volatile mix. For several months at least, Confederate agents had traded cotton to the enemy in return for medicine, clothing, and other supplies. This cotton trade caused a great deal of discontent in Walker's division, particularly among dismounted units like the 28th that were already angry at the government. The soldiers did "not believe in fighting and trading with our enemies at the same time" and believed "they derive no benefit from it and think the trade is carried on for the benefit of the high officials." Private soldiers were keenly aware that such items like coffee went to division head-quarters rather than to the men in the ranks. An enlisted man in the division even composed and "published a scurrilous song expressing their contempt and dislike of the trade."[32]

Anger in regard to the cotton trade and other irritations culminated in mutinies in the 28th Texas, in Gould's Battalion, and excitement in the 14th Texas Infantry. On 4 and 5 March approximately half of the 28th (primarily Companies A, F, H, I, and K) refused to do duty. Officers brought these "unmanageable" companies under control by arresting the ringleaders. Captain Perry arrested four men in his company and believed all of them would be shot after a trial. Included in the number arrested in Company F was Pvt. Jacob Beahm, "a bad case." The incident might have ended quietly with the arrest of the inciters, but then Lt. Col. Eli H. Baxter, under orders from Randal, arrested the commanders of the companies primarily involved in the mutiny. Capt. J. W. Fuller (Company A), Lt. Thomas M. Lambright (Company K), Capt. John A. McLemore (Company I), Capt. J. C. Means (Company H), and Captain Perry (Company F) were con-fined to "Regimental Quarters" but released on 12 March because of the upcoming campaign. Baxter's actions seemed like cowardice to the enraged officers, who had not known of the mutiny in advance and had not partici-pated in the affair. Baxter eventually feared that during a court-martial the officers would blame him for the incident, and he turned "white when he thinks of what he has done."[33]

The unit was moved away from other troops to a point near Pearl Lake, about seven miles southwest of Marksville. For the most part the mutineers were "penitant" and mostly were "very much ashamed of their conduct." On the eve of their most important service, this mutiny had unsettled the regiment, causing remorse among the mutineers and opening a rift between Baxter and half of his company commanders. Baxter hoped "for a fight. Then all things will be dropped." He soon got his wish.[34]

By mid-March 1864 the 28th Texas was a seasoned unit although they had not yet engaged in a large pitched battle, unlike most Confederate units east of the Mississippi River. The 28th Texas survived, and perhaps emerged strengthened by the division's crisis of morale and the religious revivals that swept through the division in the autumn of 1863. Also, the unit's embarrassment over the mutiny perhaps increased the soldiers' determination to perform well in the upcoming campaign. The various activities of the previous months—marching, drilling, blocking Franklin's advance, bombarding enemy transports, and building fortifications—all served to prepare the unit for its most important duty of the war: the Red River campaign.

CHAPTER 6

The Red River Campaign

*I shall fight like I was standing at the threshold of my
door fighting against robbers. . . . This is a time for
brave hearts, and I feel like I can fight by the side of
the foremost men. Our Division is in fine spirits. They
will fight like heroes when the day comes. Depend on
this. They are in Earnest. . . .*
—CAPT. THEOPHILUS PERRY, 28TH TEXAS CAVALRY,
23 MARCH 1864

From March to the end of April 1864, the 28th Texas Cavalry (dismounted) saw its only heavy combat actions of the war. It and the other units of Walker's division would equal the famous feat of Maj. Gen. Thomas J. Jackson's men who marched 350 miles and fought four battles in one month, earning his men the nickname of "foot cavalry." Walker's division marched 628 miles in forty-nine days and fought three battles (although part of the regiment was engaged in an unsuccessful stand at Fort DeRussy near Alexandria on 14 March) that generally were larger than

Jackson's battles in the Shenandoah Valley. For the most part, the unit acquitted itself well and suffered one of the highest casualty rates in Walker's division.[1]

In the spring of 1864 Union forces finally attempted a coordinated invasion of northern Louisiana involving troops in both Louisiana and Arkansas. Maj. Gen. Nathaniel P. Banks commanded a Louisiana army that consisted of segments led by Maj. Gen. William B. Franklin and Brig. Gen. A. J. Smith. Parts of the 13th Corps and the 19th Corps, many of them veterans of Franklin's overland campaign in the fall, composed Franklin's force. This portion totaled about seventeen thousand men and, accompanied by Banks, intended to move from Berwick Bay, along Bayou Teche, to Alexandria on the Red River where they would meet A. J. Smith's men. Smith's troops were on loan from Maj. Gen. William T. Sherman and consisted of two divisions of the 16th Corps and one division from the 17th Corps. These were proud midwestern soldiers from the Army of the Tennessee, veterans of heavy service at such places as Fort Donelson, Shiloh, Iuka, Corinth, and Vicksburg. Sherman sent these men to Banks with two stipulations: they would advance no further than Shreveport and they would be returned by 15 April. Comprising about ten thousand men, Smith's force planned to move by water from Vicksburg to the mouth of the Red River. There, Adm. David D. Porter's fleet of transports and gunboats (totaling about two hundred guns) would meet Smith. This combined force intended to sweep up the Red River, capturing Simmesport and Fort DeRussy while advancing toward Alexandria and then Shreveport. Additionally twelve thousand men under Maj. Gen. Frederick Steele planned to march southward from Fort Smith and Little Rock, Arkansas, and aim toward Shreveport, Louisiana.[2]

The motivations for the Union invasion combined military objectives and politics. Union forces hoped to capture Shreveport, the headquarters of the Trans-Mississippi Department, and invade Texas. There were other, more complex reasons for Banks's campaign. The Union government feared an alliance between Mexico, then under a puppet government established by France, and the Confederacy. Accordingly, the Union was determined to invade Texas and stifle the threat of French involvement with the Confederacy. Cotton provided another motivation for the Red River campaign. Northern textile mills, by the end of 1863, faced a severe cotton shortage because of a diminished cotton supply from the American South and England's monopoly on cotton from India. The Red River campaign would enable the United States military and government-authorized traders to acquire cotton from Southerners. In turn, the North would presumably win the loyalty of Louisiana planters by opening up a lucrative market for their crops.[3]

The Federal advance up the Red River and the corresponding movement from Arkansas surprised neither Lt. Gen. Edmund Kirby Smith nor Maj. Gen. Richard Taylor. Both men had long believed the enemy intended to advance up Red River and move down from Arkansas. The Red River valley offered ample forage for an army and had been a target of Banks in 1863. Taylor had accurate knowledge of the Union plans because of his impressive network of informants. Wisely, Taylor concentrated on preparing for the inevitable Federal thrust. Subordinates established supply depots for his army through the valley northwest of Alexandria; officials encouraged civilians to leave; soldiers confiscated horses, mules, and wagons and burned some cotton. Reserves, primarily cavalry, gathered in east Texas and the Indian Territory. Taylor concentrated his own army between Alexandria and Simmesport, and cavalry patrolled the area between Simmesport and Opelousas. Soldiers strengthened Fort DeRussy on the Red River, constructed fortifications (nicknamed Fort Humbug) near Simmesport, and fortified Camden, Arkansas. In spite of these preparations, Taylor believed his smaller force of about ten thousand would have to retreat, and officers were given orders to retreat in the face of a general enemy advance.[4]

On 12 March a division from the 16th Corps seized Simmesport and Fort Humbug without a struggle. This thrust triggered the retreat of Maj. Gen. John G. Walker's division from the area. The 28th Texas left their Pearl Lake camp the next day but only marched two miles before they halted. During the long delay, the men leaned on their guns, while others, like Capt. Theophilus Perry, laid their oil cloths on the ground, rolled up in blankets, and napped. The next day the 28th moved to Mansura, situated on a prairie five miles south of Marksville and commanding "a view of the surrounding country for several miles." Near Mansura the entire division formed in line of battle on the prairie east of Bayou de Glaize for about half an hour. One observer, Felix Pierre Poché of Brig. Gen. Alfred A. Mouton's division, thought it a grand sight as the regiments wheeled into line, batteries moved here and there, and aides-de-camp galloped furiously around the prairie bearing orders. Walker, though, quickly ordered a retreat when he realized the enemy could cut him off behind his lines at Evergreen. The 28th Texas remained east of the bayou as pickets while their brigade marched toward Cheneyville, about fifteen miles southwest of Mansura. During their picket the men probably heard cannonading from Fort DeRussy near nightfall. At 1:00 A.M. the unit withdrew across the bridge, watched it burn, and moved toward Cheneyville.[5]

Thirty-four men of Company D, commanded by Capt. A. L. Adams, and at least one man from Company I were stationed in Fort DeRussy. Union troops of the 16th Corps marched from Marksville to the fort on 14 March and the 1st Division formed in line of battle across the Marksville–Fort DeRussy road. Situated inland from Red River on a nearly dry bayou, a double parapet connected the fort to a water battery seven hundred yards away overlooking the river. The men of the 28th served at the water battery, and late in the afternoon of the fourteenth, they and other men at the battery came under "heavy artillery fire into the rear of the water battery" from land-based artillery batteries. As Union gunboats also pounded them, they fired one shot from the battery (the only gun that could "be trailed upon the enemy") then climbed over the parapet to the land side for protection. Meanwhile, Union infantry charged the fort meeting only "scattered fire" and plunged over the breastworks "as fast as blackbirds" according to a Confederate soldier. The Union attackers easily conquered the garrison of only about three hundred and fifty men. The men by the water battery realized the inevitability of capture unless they escaped soon. The ranking officer at the battery, a Captain Hutton, disappeared, leaving Adams in charge, but Adams promptly led out most of Company D along with Hutton's men. After leaving the area, Hutton's men discarded their weapons and vanished into the forest. The enemy captured only twelve men of the 28th (eleven from Company D and one from Company I) at Fort DeRussy, thanks to the clear-headed actions of Captain Adams. The twenty-three soldiers who escaped arrived back in the regiment on 17 March. The loss of only twelve men at Fort DeRussy was among the lowest losses of Walker's division at this action. More common were the forty-five and thirty-five men captured respectively from the 11th Texas Infantry and the 19th Texas Infantry.[6]

The Federals also captured Pvt. Jacob Beahm of Company F, a ringleader in the recent mutiny, near Fort DeRussy. Although Beahm was trying to desert to the enemy, the Federals believed him to be part of the fort's

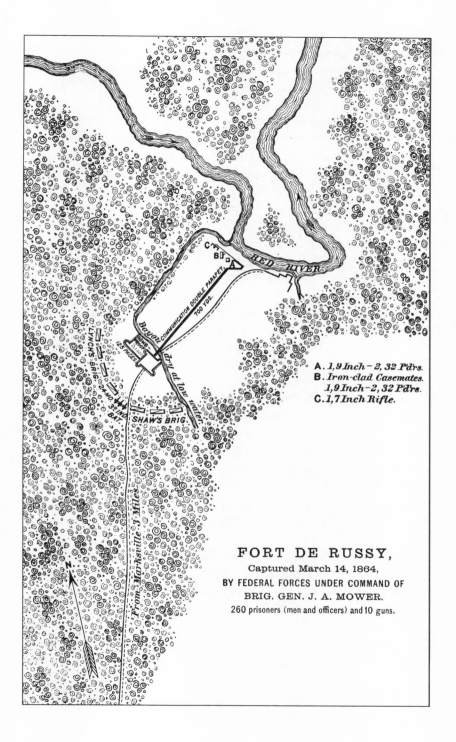

FORT DE RUSSY,
Captured March 14, 1864,
BY FEDERAL FORCES UNDER COMMAND OF
BRIG. GEN. J. A. MOWER.
260 prisoners (men and officers) and 10 guns.

A. 1, 9 Inch − 2, 32 Pdrs.
B. Iron-clad Casemates.
1, 9 Inch − 2, 32 Pdrs.
C. 1, 7 Inch Rifle.

garrison and imprisoned him in New Orleans for six months. At the end of that time, Beahm took the oath of allegiance. The other captives of the 28th were transported by gunboat, along with other prisoners, to Baton Rouge and temporary confinement in the penitentiary. Late in the evening of 17 March the men boarded boats and arrived in New Orleans the next day. The citizens of New Orleans welcomed the captives excitedly by sailing around the transports and "throwing us apples, oranges, and other such treats." The men were imprisoned in a two-acre-square enclosure in New Orleans where the men complained of short rations, gambled, made rings and other small objects and bided their time as best they could. Luckily their imprisonment was rather short, and they were exchanged in either June or July 1864. Five of the men of the 28th suffered from such illnesses as pneumonia, dysentery, and fevers while confined; however, none died while in the hands of their captors. As these men traveled to New Orleans, their unit quickly marched to the northwest.[7]

During the cool days from 15 to 17 March, the 28th marched about forty-five to fifty miles northwest to escape the enemy advance. After arriving in Cheneyville on the fifteenth, the regiment apparently joined the other brigade units, and the next day they marched twenty-six miles northwest. On the seventeenth the weary men arrived at Carroll Jones's, the home of a wealthy free black and the site of one of Taylor's supply depots, thirty-five miles northwest of Alexandria. Here, Mouton's division joined Walker's men, creating a force that numbered about seven thousand men. The tiring march to Carroll Jones's rated as one of the division's most excruciating moves of the war. Perry's feet developed blisters "as large as guinea eggs," and Dr. Cade's eyes ached from the dust, cold wind, and lack of sleep. Cade probably echoed the sentiments of many soldiers when he yearned for a cup of coffee. In spite of the retreat, Captain Perry reported proudly that his men "marched like heroes. . . . We have fought the battle 'with our legs' as Napolean often said."[8]

The division attempted to rest for four days in cold and occasionally rainy weather that made sleep difficult. Most men possessed only a blanket for protection, and some tried to construct simple shelters from the rain with them. The baggage train, consisting of only one wagon for each regiment, went to the rear on the nineteenth, leaving the men with one blanket each and necessary cooking utensils. A disastrous event on 21 March forced Taylor's army to retreat further into the piney woods of northwest

Louisiana. On that cold and rainy night a Union force captured most of the 2nd Louisiana Cavalry, plus Capt. William Edgar's fine battery of Walker's division, at Henderson Hill, approximately thirty miles south of Natchitoches. Since the 2nd Louisiana represented most of Taylor's cavalry force, the loss of this scouting arm meant that retreat was necessary.[9]

The day after the Henderson Hill debacle, the 28th trudged out of camp toward old Fort Jesup, twenty-one miles southwest of Natchitoches. Somewhere in the vast forest "at an old camp-meeting ground," Walker's division halted again, this time for eight days. The chilly and rainy weather again punished the men. All of the division burned pine knots that turned their skin and clothing black, much to their amusement and possible chagrin. Food supplies were scarce for the division with the men subsisting on "poor beef and cornbread." In this camp the division again reshuffled baggage, and this time each man was allowed to store a blanket and eight pounds of clothing in the train. Presumably space had been created for these items by the burning of tents, for only one tent was saved for each company. Perry prepared a valise that contained, among other things, his writing utensils.[10]

In the midst of this retreat, the men reflected definite divisions of thought regarding the withdrawal. A number of men remained determined to defeat the enemy. Perry was one of these men. He believed that a small but stubborn army could be successful against the larger Union forces in the piney woods. Prophetically and confidently, Perry predicted the campaign would end within six weeks. Determination to fight well filled Perry, a spirit that he believed infected all of the division. Still, in spite of Perry's optimism, low morale and pessimism influenced the thoughts of some soldiers. Pvt. S. W. Farrow of the 19th Texas Infantry, disgruntled over low food rations, believed the army would be forced to retreat to Shreveport and into Texas within two months. He also claimed many soldiers were talking of leaving for home. A cautious soldier of the 14th Texas Infantry (Randal's brigade) advised his wife "to bury your bacon which you can easily do in those 2 large hogsheads, and cover the top with boards" in case of an enemy advance into Texas.[11]

As Confederate troops retreated, the Union force stalled at Alexandria. Banks's force arrived in Alexandria on 25 March, several days late due to heavy rainfall on their route through southern Louisiana. When they arrived, the sight of naval men busily carting away valuable cotton as a prize of war

Richard J. Thompson, Jr.
& Donald S. Frazier

ARKANSAS

White River

Arkansas River

Fort
Smith

Little Rock ✪

Pine
Bluff

Jenkins'
Ferry

Arkadelphia

Ouachita River

Saline River

Tulip

Princeton

Marks'
Mills

Washington

Poison
Springs

Camden

Red River

Mississippi River

Marshall

Minden

Shreveport

LOUISIANA

Red River

Mansfield

Pleasant
Hill

Campti

Grand Ecore

Natchitoches

Fort
Jesup

Henderson Hill

TEXAS

Carroll
Jones's Home

Pineville

Alexandria

Ft. DeRussy

Cheneyville

Mansura

Marksville

Pearl Lake

Simmesport

**The Red River–
Jenkins' Ferry Campaign**

Opelousas

stunned Banks. Additionally, a message from Lt. Gen. Ulysses S. Grant, with its insistent reminder of the loan status of Smith's troops, troubled Banks. If Banks's force captured Shreveport by mid-April, then Grant suggested that Banks garrison the town and send the bulk of his troops to New Orleans. If unable to capture Shreveport by mid-April, Banks was to return Smith's troops soon. Finally, in a major disappointment, the Red River failed to rise substantially for the first time since 1855. Low water delayed the movement of Porter's fleet over the falls at Alexandria and into the upper Red until the end of March. Besides pondering military issues, Banks also dabbled in politics. Before Banks left New Orleans in March, a Unionist governor was inaugurated, and a new state administration, loyal to the Union, went to work. Now a convention needed to be called to rework the antebellum Louisiana constitution. Banks called an election in Alexandria for the purpose of choosing delegates to this constitutional convention. Roughly handled by prior Union armies, only three hundred Alexandria residents cast ballots, and Admiral Porter later deemed the election a "farce."[12]

While Union troops rested in Alexandria and subsequently began probes to the northwest, the Confederate army moved farther away to Mansfield. On 31 March Walker's division passed old Fort Jesup and continued northwest to Pleasant Hill, twenty miles northwest of Fort Jesup, where they arrived on 1 April. Along the way to Pleasant Hill, the soldiers observed a number of civilians "aroused to the highest pitch of excitement" and fleeing from their homes. At Pleasant Hill, the men formed in line of battle "and remained on arms all night." The men stayed only briefly at Pleasant Hill before marching twenty miles northwest to Mansfield in DeSoto Parish and camping seven miles on the other side of the town on 4 April. For several men of Company K, this march into DeSoto Parish was a homecoming, and they would fight only a few miles from their homes.[13]

The enemy, meantime, marched northwest along the Red River with the Navy conveying A. J. Smith's men. Banks's force reached Natchitoches on 1 April and soon after Grand Ecore. At Grand Ecore, Banks's decision to leave the protection of the navy and strike off into the piney woods to Pleasant Hill changed the course of the campaign. Banks, through lack of reconnaissance and overreliance on the word of a river pilot, failed to learn of a road that continued to follow the river all the way to Shreveport. The army left Grand Ecore on 6 April, and the navy steamed away toward Shreveport the following day. While moving toward Pleasant Hill, Union cavalry frequently clashed with Texas cavalry only recently arrived to complement Taylor's army.[14]

As the Union infantry marched toward Pleasant Hill, Walker's division rested in camp and again rearranged the baggage. Some of the men were unhealthy, some suffering from pneumonia and others from fevers. Col. Horace Randal's brigade presumably received spiritual succor by listening to a Dr. Wright, a Baptist missionary, speak on the evening of the fifth. As the soldiers engaged in various activities, they witnessed the concentration of Taylor's army near Mansfield. Mouton and Walker were joined by Brig. Gen. Thomas Green's cavalry on 6 April. Brig. Gen. Thomas J. Churchill's two divisions, consisting of Arkansas and Missouri men, reached Keatchie, twenty miles northwest of Mansfield, also on 6 April. Kirby Smith had ordered these men from Arkansas to join Taylor in spite of the expectation of a Union advance from Arkansas.[15]

The common soldiers remained unaware of tensions in the high command. An argument between Smith and Taylor simply reiterated their disagreements during Franklin's overland campaign in the fall of 1863. Smith willingly surrendered territory to draw the Federals deeper into Louisiana in hopes of creating the opportunity to defeat the enemy in parts. Although Taylor understood Smith's logic, Taylor was disturbed at surrendering huge chunks of his home state to the enemy, and he wanted to attack either Banks or Steele. Smith's agonizing indecision in selecting whether to attack Banks or Steele first fueled Taylor's impatience. Smith initially decided to fight Banks, but by 3 April he settled on attacking Steele because of Steele's smaller force. On 6 April, Smith and Taylor conferred at Mansfield where Smith discussed moving against Steele and mentioned the possibility of a siege at Shreveport and a retreat into Texas. Alarmed by the latter two possibilities, the combative Taylor determined the next day to make a stand southeast of Mansfield. In his opinion, the enemy had to be attacked while moving along the single road south of Mansfield, because once north of Mansfield the Union army would have the luxury of three roads leading to Shreveport. Accordingly on 7 April Taylor selected the ground that his army would occupy the next day in an effort to halt the enemy. Taylor issued orders to his division commanders, Walker and Mouton, to prepare for an advance the next morning. The soldiers received orders "to cook one day's rations, and to be ready to leave at four o'clock the following morning."[16]

On 8 April at daybreak the 28th Texas and the other units of the division marched through Mansfield enjoying a lovely spring day as the bands played "Dixie." Much to the delight of the men, the ladies threw flowers into the road and called for the men to halt the odious invader. Some men of the division remained in Mansfield to prepare houses for hospitals and to serve as guards. As the Greyhounds swung along down the road toward Pleasant Hill, they saw Green, Mouton, Taylor, and Walker along the road busy in consultation and continued for three miles until they reached the site Taylor had selected for a defense. Officers posted the troops on the edge of some woods "fronting an open field eight hundred yards in width by twelve hundred in length, through the center of which the road to Pleasant Hill passed." On the horizon a gentle forested incline called Honeycutt Hill met the mens' eyes. Across the opening, a fence separated the field from a forest that was "open on the higher ground and filled with underwood on the lower."[17]

Confederate troop dispositions were completed by about 2:00 P.M. On the right side of the road Taylor placed the brigades of Randal, Brig. Gen. Thomas N. Waul, and Brig. Gen. William R. Scurry. Two cavalry regiments under Brig. Gen. Hamilton P. Bee anchored the right of the line. In the road itself and to the rear of the main line, Taylor placed Col. Xavier B. Debray's 26th Texas Cavalry regiment. Randal's brigade moved into line "at a quick step, in their usual rollicking and bold style, overflowing with impatient and long-restrained ardor for the fight." Mouton's division of Louisianans and Texans formed on the left side of the road, and Brig. Gen. James P. Major's cavalry division formed on the extreme left. Artillery batteries were situated at intervals, but the wooded terrain generally rendered their service ineffective.[18]

As the men of Taylor's army anxiously waited, a Union column slowly drew near, headed by cavalry commanded by Brig. Gen. Albert L. Lee. Because of constant skirmishing with the stubborn Confederate cavalry since dawn, Lee's cavalry had traveled only six miles before they reached the clearing about noon. Union cavalrymen promptly drove Confederate skirmishers off Honeycutt Hill and discovered infantry and cavalry in the woods beyond. Throughout the afternoon, Federal troops continued to arrive and were situated on Honeycutt Hill. By four o'clock the Union battle line stretched along Honeycutt Hill with Albert Lee's cavalry brigade on the left, followed on the right by the 23rd Wisconsin Infantry of Col.

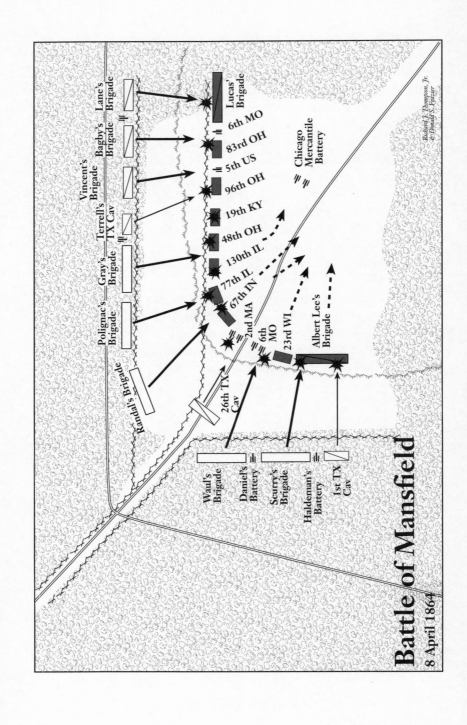

Battle of Mansfield

8 April 1864

Lane's Brigade
Bagby's Brigade
Vincent's Brigade
Terrell's TX Cav
Gray's Brigade
Polignac's Brigade
Randal's Brigade

Lucas' Brigade
6th MO
83rd OH
5th US
96th OH
19th KY
48th OH
130th IL
77th IL
67th IN
2nd MA
6th MO
23rd WI
Albert Lee's Brigade

Chicago Mercantile Battery

26th TX Cav

Waul's Brigade
Daniel's Battery
Scurry's Brigade
Haldeman's Battery
1st TX Cav

Richard J. Thompson, Jr.
& Donald S. Frazier

Frank Emerson's brigade, then two batteries posted across the road to Pleasant Hill. On the right of the road two more units of Emerson's brigade were posted (the 67th Indiana Infantry and the 77th Illinois Infantry). The Union battlefront then ran due east behind a rail fence bordering the field. Just to the right of the 77th Illinois, the 130th Illinois Infantry and the 48th Ohio Infantry of Col. Joseph W. Vance's brigade were situated. Curiously, the 19th Kentucky Infantry of Emerson's brigade was next in line and on the right the 96th Ohio Infantry, Battery G of the 5th United States Artillery, the 83rd Ohio Infantry, the 6th Missouri Artillery, and cavalrymen from Col. Thomas J. Lucas's brigade. All of the infantry units were veteran ones with Vicksburg being their most important campaign experience thus far. However, their force only reached a strength of about 4,800 men compared to 8,800 in Taylor's army. Probably 400 to 440 men stood in the ranks of the 28th Texas that day, and the 11th Texas Infantry, also of Randal's brigade, numbered 422.[19]

As the afternoon passed, Walker's division tore down the rail fence in front of them and "piled up the rails as breastworks." While engaged in this work, the men heard occasional skirmisher fire from the cavalry, but the enemy remained unseen. Taylor eventually believed the enemy was strengthening its right in preparation for an attack, so Taylor modified his troop dispositions to meet this presumed threat. Infantry skirmishers and the 26th Texas Cavalry filed into the field to mask the movement of Randal's brigade across the road and the subsequent repositioning of Scurry and Waul to fill the gap left by Randal. These alterations were completed by four o'clock when Taylor ordered an assault.[20]

Earlier in the day, Taylor had ridden down the line to Col. Henry Gray's brigade composed of Louisiana regiments of Mouton's division. Taylor recalled that he told the Louisianans: "As they were fighting in defense of their own soil I wished the Louisiana troops to draw the first blood." About 4:00 P.M. Taylor ordered an advance, and Mouton's division charged across the field under a severe and costly fire, paused at the fence on the far side, and moved into the woods. Walker's men, unable to see Mouton's gallant charge heard artillery and small arms fire, though Maj. Robert S. Gould of Randal's brigade said the sounds were fuzzy. Seeing Mouton's men cross into the woods, Taylor next ordered Randal's brigade into the fray. The regiments, including the 28th, crossed the rail fence, aligned themselves and stepped into the field en echelon and advanced for approximately one-quarter of a mile until they reached the woods. The sound of gunfire increased in volume as they approached the wood where Mouton's men had shattered the 19th Kentucky, the 48th Ohio, the 130th Illinois, and the 77th Illinois Infantry. Occasional bullets whizzed by as they entered the trees and saw many of the exhausted survivors of Mouton's division. Randal's men eagerly fired into the forest at the retreating enemy. Discovering the position of the remaining enemy line, Randal's regiments smashed into the right flank of the 67th Indiana and pushed the stubborn unit toward the Pleasant Hill road.[21]

The remainder of Walker's division and Bee's cavalry went forward after Randal's attack "was well developed." General Walker encouraged the troops by advising them to "'aim low boys, and trust in God.'" These Texans yelled "like Indians," pushed back the 23rd Wisconsin and the 67th Indiana and captured three cannon. Soon after, Union Brig. Gen. Thomas E. G. Ransom ordered a retreat into the forest bordering a clearing east of Honeycutt Hill. The enemy retreated to the edge of the clearing closely pursued by the double-quicking and yelling Confederates. Here, the 3rd Division of the 13th Corps had arrived as reinforcements with the 1st Brigade situated on the right of the road and the 2nd Brigade on the left of the road. These men of Iowa, Indiana, Ohio, and Wisconsin checked the Confederates for about one hour. Eventually the Confederates, among them Randal's brigade, broke through the enemy line, causing utter panic among the Federals. The Union wagon train served as a barrier in the narrow road, and Union soldiers went berserk as they tried to escape the Southerners. Franklin fell wounded here, and Banks unsuccessfully tried to reform his terrified men. Randal's brigade captured a large part of the beleaguered wagon train, and the division as a whole scooped up abandoned artillery pieces.[22]

Union troops ran along the road and through the forest for two miles until they reached a new position, established by Brig. William H. Emory and the 1st Division of the 19th Corps, along the east side of a ravine on a hill in rear of a peach orchard. The Confederates gamely followed but were greatly disordered because of the terrain and the earlier attacks. The 28th Texas and other units scrambled into the ravine anyway, passing several men clinging to the sides for protection from enemy bullets. After climbing out of the ravine, the Confederates faced a heavy fire at dusk in the peach orchard with Union volleys creating "a continuous stream of fire." Nevertheless, they charged toward the Union troops on the hill several times, all unsuccessfully. The engagement here lasted for only fifteen or twenty minutes, yet a Union veteran claimed the musketry fire surpassed that at either Shiloh or Champion's Hill. Confederate troops were unable to carry the Union position because of disorganization and exhaustion. They withdrew to a water source and bivouacked. During that cold night, some Confederates guarded the road while prisoners were marched to the rear and captured supplies were transported to the rear. Some of the 14th Texas Infantry of Randal's brigade were sent to bring in some ambulances that Union teamsters had driven into the forest away from the road. Soldiers managed to confiscate overcoats and other desired supplies.[23]

Taylor's army correctly claimed a victory at Mansfield. Union casualties out of a total of twelve thousand men engaged (including those in the second and third stand) totaled 113 killed, 581 wounded, and 1,541 missing. Additionally, Confederates captured a number of small arms, twenty cannon, a large number of wagons, and about one thousand horses and mules. Southern forces suffered about one thousand men killed or wounded, two-thirds from Mouton's division. Mouton himself was killed in the charge. Randal's brigade received few casualties, and most probably occurred at the peach orchard.

TABLE 4
Casualties in Randal's Brigade at Mansfield, Louisiana
8 APRIL 1864

	KILLED	WOUNDED	MISSING
28th Texas Cavalry	4	17	0
11th Texas Infantry	2	6	2
14th Texas Infantry	1	15	1
Gould's Battalion	2	14	3
Total	9	52	6

Source for Table 4: Johansson, "Two 'Lost' Battle Reports," 174.

The 28th Texas suffered more casualties than any other unit in the brigade and apparently acquitted themselves well in their first large-scale battle. In his report of the campaign, Taylor complimented Randal by stating, "In vigor, energy, and daring Randal surpassed my expectations, high as they were of him and his fine brigade."[24]

The battle was also significant because Banks ordered a retreat from the Mansfield area after a council of war. Their withdrawal began about midnight, and they reached Pleasant Hill, eleven miles to the south, about 8:30 A.M. Meanwhile, Churchill's men from Arkansas and Missouri marched from Keatchie to Mansfield (a distance of twenty miles) on the day of the battle. They had little rest before stopping to cook rations and again marching to join the rest of the army. Sometime after dawn, the Confederates moved toward Pleasant Hill, about eleven miles away. Green's cavalrymen took the lead, followed by Churchill's men, Walker's division, and Mouton's division, now commanded by Brig. Gen. Camille A. J. M. de Polignac. Men of the 28th and others stared at the gear littering the route of the Federal retreat. Knapsacks, cooking utensils, wounded and dead Federals, and burning wagons were strewn across the road. As they neared Pleasant Hill, the cavalry passed by, escorting to the rear a group of Union prisoners wearing Zouave uniforms. The exotic clothing amazed the shabbily attired Confederates who proclaimed that Lincoln must now be sending women to fight, and the Texans "had too much honor to fight women." Between one and two o'clock, the troops arrived at Pleasant Hill, and Taylor allowed them to rest for two hours. The divisions of Walker and Polignac were exhausted from the battle of the previous day, and Churchill's men had marched an incredible forty-five miles in thirty-six hours.[25]

The village of Pleasant Hill sat on a plateau "a mile wide from east to west." Two important roads formed a junction in the town (the road from Mansfield and one from the Sabine River) and continued on to Grand Ecore. Taylor hoped to drive Banks's force toward Grand Ecore, well away from the protection of the navy that was well above that point. About three o'clock Taylor began placing his troops in a position to attack. He sent Churchill and part of the cavalry to the right where they would advance through woods that sloped gradually downhill toward the enemy. Walker's division filled the center with Randal on the left, Waul in the center, and Scurry on the right. Taylor placed Randal and Waul near the edge of an open field, dotted with small pine trees, that inclined gently downhill toward the Federal position. The cavalry of Bee and Majors took the left side, and Polignac's division formed a reserve. Churchill's men would open the attack by aiming northeast toward the road and flank the enemy. Walker's men would advance at the sound of Churchill's attack and try to connect with Churchill's line. Finally, Debray's 26th Texas Cavalry and Col.

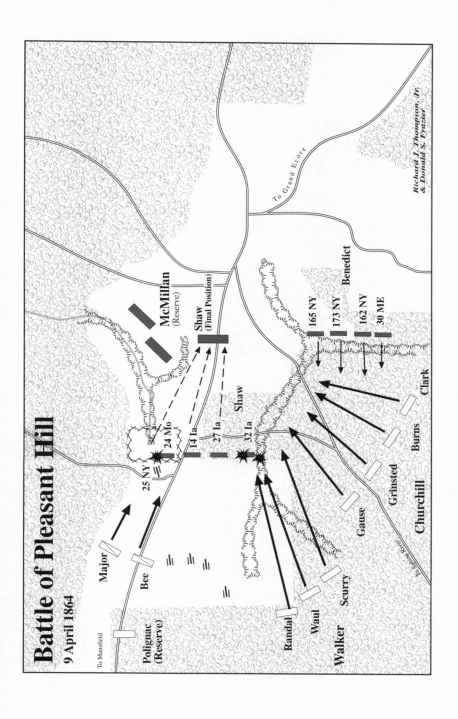

Battle of Pleasant Hill
9 April 1864

To Mansfield

Major

Bee

Polignac
(Reserve)

McMillan
(Reserve)

Shaw
(Final Position)

24 Mo

14 Ia

27 Ia

32 Ia

25 NY

Shaw

Randal

Waul

Scurry

Gause

WALKER

Churchill

Grinsted

Burns

Clark

Benedict

165 NY

173 NY

162 NY

30 ME

To Grand Ecore

Sabine River

Richard J. Thompson, Jr.
& Donald S. Frazier

Augustus Buchel's cavalry unit of Bee's division were to charge through the village when the enemy melted in confusion. On this day, the armies were nearly equal in number. Taylor's force numbered 12,500, and the enemy totaled 12,193. Randal estimated that his brigade totaled 800 men on the day of the battle.[26]

Confederate artillery bombarded the 25th New York Artillery, and Churchill's advance began about four-thirty. Randal's brigade waited in the wood, and some of the men flinched as occasional artillery shells exploded in the treetops. At five o'clock the men heard the distinct sounds of Churchill's attack, and Walker's division moved to the northeast "in beautiful order." Randal's men marched forward past a section of Capt. T. D. Nettles's Texas Battery, the Louisiana battery of Capt. J. A. A. West, and the Texans of Capt. William G. Moseley's battery as all of the brigades advanced as if on a parade ground. The enemy, crouched behind rails in the wood beyond, clearly heard the Confederate officers giving commands until the wounded began to fall with shrieks and cries. Occasionally men in the brigade returned this annoying fire, but most of the men reserved their fire until reaching a fence. Walker's division steadily moved into the forest where they methodically cut up Col. William T. Shaw's brigade. The 32nd Iowa on Randal's front suffered casualties of 35 killed, 115 wounded, and 60 missing. Lt. William Smith's section of Nettles's battery joined in the carnage by advancing behind Randal's men and firing into the enemy at "Canister Range." Unfortunately for the division, General Walker received "a severe contusion in the groin" at this stage, and Taylor ordered him off the field. In the confusion, Taylor found it difficult to locate the brigade commanders and any cohesion was lost due to Walker's wounding.[27]

Churchill's attack appeared successful as his men jubilantly entered the town itself, but they had not really flanked the enemy and were consequently attacked on their own right flank and driven back. Col. Lucien C. Gause's brigade fell back in confusion on Scurry's, causing disorder, and the enemy, sensing an opportunity, attacked Scurry and captured a number of men. Scurry's men started to withdraw in the face of the enemy assault, and Taylor ordered Randal and Waul to charge to lessen the pressure on Scurry. These two men led "on their fine brigades with skill and energy," pressed back the enemy, and rescued Scurry. Unfortunately, in the excitement and confusion Waul's brigade accidentally fired into Randal's brigade, forcing Randal to dispatch several couriers to warn Waul of his mistake.

Sometime during the battle, Captain Perry was shot in the leg "while gallantly heading his company." The two armies continued fighting over the ground west of the village until dusk, and at nightfall, the greatly disordered army fell back to a water source six miles away. Major Gould believed Randal's brigade was the last to withdraw.[28]

The Federals won a tactical victory by holding their position that day, but their subsequent retreat made it a strategic defeat. Northern casualties totaled 1,369 and Southern losses, 1,626. Randal's brigade suffered more severely than the day before.

TABLE 5
Casualties in Randal's Brigade at Pleasant Hill, Louisiana
9 APRIL 1864

	KILLED	WOUNDED	MISSING
28th Texas Cavalry	9	44	2
11th Texas Infantry	3	18	0
14th Texas Infantry	5	29	1
Gould's Battalion	5	9	3
Total	22	100	6

Source for Table 5: Johansson, "Two 'Lost' Battle Reports," 175.

Again, the 28th Texas suffered the heaviest losses in the brigade. Total regimental losses (counting the mortally wounded as killed) for the two days were 19 killed, 55 wounded, and 2 missing. The Pleasant Hill battlefield in particular horrified the men. Pvt. William F. Mills of Company A "went back on the [Pleasant Hill] battlefield the next day to bury the dead. The like of dead men I never saw before in my life. Some had their heads shot off; some had their arms and legs shot off. . . ." A surgeon, meanwhile, amputated Captain Perry's leg, and medical personnel transported him to Mansfield, probably to one of the houses transformed into a hospital. There he died on 17 April, leaving a grieving widow and an infant son. Perry had indeed fulfilled his promise to fight to his utmost. Seven officers, including Lt. Col. Baxter and four company commanders, were wounded; however, only two, Perry and 1st Lt. J. B. Allen (Company D), died. The majority of the wounds in the regiment were slight, but thirteen men received severe injuries. It is not known whether any of these soldiers subsequently died. Women and the medical personnel tended to the wounded as best they could. A soldier of Randal's brigade reported that women took the wounded "milk soup coffee and loaf bread." The injured were crowded together into houses and churches. Fortunately, all but one man was rescued after a nurse dropped a lighted candle on "cotton scattered over the floor" of the Baptist Church in Mansfield that was being used as a hospital.[29]

In his after-action report Randal cited nine men in the regiment for gallantry in the actions at Mansfield and Pleasant Hill. These were color bearer James M. Benton (Company K), Cpl. Horace B. Bishop (Company G), Lt. William G. Blain (Company H), Pvt. F. R. Compton (Company H), Capt. Patrick Henry (Company B), Adj. George T. Howard, Pvt. James Kolb (Company G), Capt. John A. McLemore (Company I), and Capt. Theophilus Perry (Company F). Additionally, two men of Randal's staff who had enlisted in the 28th were cited. These were 1st Lt. George B. Campbell and Leonard Randal Jr., who was "ever conspicuous in leading my men on to action."[30]

Taylor ordered Brig. Gen. Thomas Green's cavalry and Brig. Gen. Camille A. J. M. de Polignac's infantry division, only five thousand men, to pursue Maj. Gen. Nathaniel P. Banks's entire army along the Red River. At Blair's Landing, forty-five miles upriver from Grand Ecore, the cavalry impetuously attacked the powerful Union gunboats resulting in Green's death on 12 April. Banks considered moving again toward Shreveport, but Maj. Gen. William T. Sherman wanted Brig. Gen. A. J. Smith's troops returned and Adm. David D. Porter warned of the falling water level of the Red River. On 22 April, Banks's army left Grand Ecore and quickly moved southeast toward Natchitoches and Alexandria. As the Union troops hastily marched through the countryside, A. J. Smith's men wreaked havoc, looting and burning as they went. The Union army arrived in Alexandria on 26 April and was joined two days later by the navy, which had encountered much difficulty from harassing Confederates and the falling water level. The powerful ironclad *Eastport* had run aground under heavy gunfire from Polignac's men and artillery fire, and, unable to shift the *Eastport*, naval men destroyed her. Confederate troops damaged three other gunboats and destroyed two transports on the harrowing journey down the Red River.[31]

At Alexandria Maj. Gen. Richard Taylor's tiny army besieged the larger Union army of about thirty thousand. Banks's army halted at Alexandria to provide protection to the navy flotilla as it moved over the falls at Alexandria. The water level fell to just a few inches and the boats were saved only by the construction of large wing dams engineered by Lt. Col. Joseph Bailey. By 13 May all the gunboats had passed over the falls, Banks's force continued its retreat, and A. J. Smith's men burned the city of Alexandria to the ground. Much to Taylor's anger, Banks escaped down the river.[32]

The 28th Texas and the rest of Walker's division, however, did not participate in the pursuit of Banks. Instead, General Smith had ordered them to Arkansas, where he remained determined to destroy Steele's army. Taylor felt that once Steele learned of Banks's defeat, Steele's own retreat would be inevitable. On 13 April, Smith promised to return Churchill and Walker to Taylor if Steele retreated. As Taylor pursued Banks down the Red River with the troops of Bee, Green, and Polignac, he discovered on 15 April that Smith was pursuing the retreating Steele in spite of his promise.[33]

CHAPTER 7

Jenkins' Ferry

The men were heedless in their confusion.
—MAJ. HENRY G. HALL, 28TH TEXAS CAVALRY

The day after the battle of Pleasant Hill, Maj. Gen. John G. Walker's division withdrew toward Mansfield and on the eleventh camped north of the town. Here they heard the sad news of Brig. Gen. Thomas Green's death while impetuously encouraging his cavalry to fire on Union gunboats at Blair's Landing. For two days the soldiers rested near Mansfield and probably rejoiced at Col. Horace Randal's promotion to brigadier general by Lt. Gen. Edmund Kirby Smith, effective 8 April. On 14 April the division left camp and headed toward Shreveport, the first leg in the march toward Arkansas to block the movement of Maj. Gen. Frederick Steele's threatening army. On the fifteenth the 3rd Texas Infantry joined Brig. Gen. William R. Scurry's brigade as reinforcements, and the division crossed the Red River on a pontoon bridge at Shreveport. Three days later, the division marched through Minden, thirty miles northeast of Shreveport. The bands energetically played "Dixie," and the ladies heartily welcomed the men by waving handkerchiefs and cheering. The troops remained at Minden until the twentieth when Kirby Smith joined the columns of Brig. Gen. Thomas J. Churchill and Walker and personally took command of the expedition. A congratulatory message written by Kirby Smith and read to the men heartened the troops. As a reward for their victories, Kirby Smith allowed the men of Walker's division to inscribe "Mansfield" and "Pleasant Hill" on their banners as battle honors. On the twentieth, the soldiers made a short march of six miles and camped northeast of Minden along Walnut Creek. The men stayed at this camp until the morning of the twenty-fourth. Although the weather was "dark, gloomy, and very damp" during their time along Walnut Creek, the soldiers busily socialized with civilians. Women, some traveling from as far as twenty miles away, visited the encampment, listened to the division bands, and invited soldiers to dinner. Reluctantly, the men took up the march again on the twenty-fourth crossing the state line into Arkansas that day. The men now marched steadily and by the morning of the twenty-eighth, the two divisions arrived at Camden, Arkansas, eighty miles northeast of Shreveport. At Camden, orders reduced the transportation for the division to a single ambulance for each regiment, and the men were ordered to carry their own rations and ammunition. While in Camden, the men of the 28th Texas first saw Maj. Gen. Sterling Price, whose three cavalry divisions had harassed Steele's army for days. As the soldiers left Camden the civilians hailed the Confederates as their "deliverers," and the men crossed the Ouachita River on a makeshift bridge. On 29 April the division passed through Princeton, nearly forty miles southwest of Pine Bluff. The next day the Confederate infantry finally reached the enemy who was trying to cross the Saline River, about fifteen miles north of Princeton.[1]

Originally, Steele's Union army, with additional elements, was to march southwest from Little Rock and converge with Maj. Gen. Nathaniel P. Banks's army at Shreveport. Steele faced a daunting task. Required to travel across southwestern Arkansas with its sparse population and poor transportation network, Steele compounded the problem by being ill-prepared. Steele had neglected to "stockpile" food for the men and fodder for the animals. Steele planned to first feint toward Washington, Confederate Arkansas's capital, and then march to Camden, seventy-five miles southwest from Little Rock. From Camden, Steele hoped to institute a supply line to Little Rock. Opposing Steele's veterans was a force of about eighty-five hundred consisting mostly of Arkansas, Indian, Missouri, and Texas cavalrymen under the command of Sterling Price. Wisely and effectively, Price used his cavalry to annoy the enemy with hit-and-run attacks.[2]

Steele's army of about eighty-five hundred men left Little Rock on 23 March and were harassed increasingly by Confederate cavalry. Maneuvering slowly, Steele's army finally covered the fifty miles to Arkadelphia by 29 March. On 9 April, Brig. Gen. John M. Thayer's five-thousand-man force from Fort Smith reinforced Steele's army. By then, Union troops were on half rations, and Confederate cavalry had begun their successful tactics of harassment. On 15 April hungry Union soldiers entered Camden, the first goal of the expedition. From Camden, Thayer ordered an expedition to forage west of Camden; a Confederate force ambushed the expedition on 18 April at Poison Springs with the loss of many full wagons and over two hundred men killed (many from the 1st Kansas Colored Infantry). A wagon train from Little Rock finally resupplied Steele's army, but Confederate cavalry attacked the returning wagon train and escort at Marks' Mills five days later with heavy Union loss. By this time, Steele had learned of Banks's retreat and was feeling increasingly isolated, Steele decided to retreat to Little Rock. The only road back was northeastward through Princeton, across the Saline River, and on to Little Rock. Steele's army left Camden on 26 April and were exhausted, hungry, and desperate by the time they reached Jenkins' Ferry on the Saline on 29 April. The stage was set for the possible destruction of Steele's weary force.[3]

On 30 April the tired and hungry men of the 28th Texas awakened and left Princeton at 2:00 A.M. Walker's Division had approximately twenty-two miles to march before reaching the enemy at Jenkins' Ferry. According to Pvt. Horace Bishop of the 28th, the men were allowed to rest for five minutes after each three miles, and "what sleep we got was during those five minutes." At daybreak a heavy rainfall began and lasted for an hour followed by intermittent showers throughout the day. Sometime between 6:00 and 7:00 A.M the division passed through Tulip about eight miles past Princeton in the rain. At Tulip the soldiers heard a rumor that the enemy had passed through about two hours earlier. Although the story proved false, Pvt. Joseph P. Blessington stated that "although broken down with fatigue, [the troops] became fired with new life and energy, and redoubled their efforts to overhaul the flying foe." In addition, local residents, particularly women, greeted the division "and with wild enthusiasm cheered us on to the coming struggle." After leaving Tulip the men began to hear cannon fire from the northeast. For the last three miles, the men marched through mud and standing water. The rain and the earlier passage of Churchill's division and Brig. Gen. Mosby M. Parsons's division churned up the road so that it was in poor condition. In spite of the encouragement of civilians, lack of sleep and terrible marching conditions so fatigued the men that many in the division were "unable to get up to the fight." Private Blessington believed that half of Walker's effective force was absent from the battlefield.[4]

Walker's division heard the increasing sound of gunfire as they slogged nearer the battlefield about 10:30 A.M. Union troops had bridged the flooded Saline on the twenty-ninth and were working hard to push wagons and artillery through the slough to the bridge. The combatants fought the battle primarily on the south side of the road to Camden. Three cultivated fields, Kelly's, Cooper's, and Jiles's, bordered the south side of the road at intervals. Along the eastern edge of Cooper's field, Union troops had created a crude barricade of logs. All three fields were separated by timber, and forest also grew along the southern edge of all the fields. On the north side of the road and paralleling it was Cox Creek, more timber, and a "cane swamp." The space between the timber on the south side of the fields and the creek to the north was only about a quarter mile in width. The battlefield, then, was constricted and left little room for maneuvering. Additionally, much of the field was a virtual bog. In that cramped space approximately six thousand Confederates were engaged that day against four thousand of the enemy.[5]

While Walker's men marched to the battleground, the battle passed through three phases under the direction of Kirby Smith: the action of Confederate cavalry, the attack of Churchill's division, and the assault of Parsons's division. The cavalry action began near daybreak when Missouri cavalrymen of Col. Colton Greene's brigade of Maj. Gen. John S. Marmaduke's division began a reconnaissance of Union lines. The dismounted cavalrymen pushed back Union skirmishers through Jiles's field but were halted in Cooper's field when Greene noticed with alarm that the Union line overlapped his right. By this time, men of Churchill's Arkansas division had arrived on the battlefield and were resting after their hard march from Tulip. Price soon decided to send one of Churchill's brigades in to aid the cavalrymen, beginning the set of circumstances that led to Churchill's three brigades being committed piecemeal into the battle. The next Confederate troops to enter the fight were the soldiers of Parsons's Missouri division. Kirby Smith hoped to have Parsons's men attack with Walker's when the Texans arrived, but instead the Missourians were sent into the maelstrom to aid Churchill's Arkansans. Again, piecemeal attacks resulted in little except an added effusion of blood.[6]

By the time Walker's men entered the battlefield, Smith had learned of a branch of the main road. Kirby Smith believed that Walker's men could use this road to outflank the enemy. Accordingly, Brig. Gen. Thomas N. Waul's brigade continued down the road as Churchill's troops had done, but Randal's and Scurry's brigades marched down the branch road. The intent was for these two brigades to flank the enemy position. Before moving down the road, the men of Randal's brigade unslung their knapsacks and blankets, piled them on the saturated soil, and loaded their guns. Some guns were so wet that they could not be effectively loaded, and there was no time to completely dry the weapons. From here the problems only grew worse. The men marched for a mile through muddy goo that varied in depth from ankle deep to knee deep. At times a man cursed as he lost a shoe in the muck, and more weapons became wet as some soldiers tripped and fell into the water. Their route seemed impossible, so the troops turned and marched back one-half mile before orders arrived from Smith to turn around and press on.[7]

Maj. Henry G. Hall of the 28th and Randal were fortunate to be on horseback, and they rode together toward the firing. Hall observed that when the two men fully heard the gunfire, Randal's "countenance changed, a dark shade came over his face and particularly around his eyes. I cannot tell how I looked but I felt cheerful and resolute and the blood burned in my cheeks and my ears." The men wearily marched toward the sound of the firing from Waul's brigade whose skirmishers had engaged the enemy. Soon Waul's men charged into the enemy's "sheet of flame," and the gunfire rapidly increased in intensity. Randal's orders were to align his brigade on Waul's right and Scurry was to position himself to the right of Randal's brigade. The 28th Texas formed into line of battle in the forest about four hundred yards from the enemy in difficult circumstances. It is impossible to ascertain the brigade alignment with certainty, but judging from sources, the brigade alignment was, from left to right, the 11th Texas or the 14th Texas, Gould's Battalion, the 28th Texas, and either the 11th Texas or the

14th Texas. As the brigade aligned, the splashing of the water made it almost impossible to hear the orders of the officers, and most soldiers simply imitated the movements of those closest to the officers. One officer at least, Major Hall, was so tired he had difficulty speaking loudly and resorted for the most part to arm gestures. The regiment had to redo their line several times in the water as officers strove toward the proper alignment. At least the time spent in these maneuvers allowed some soldiers who had fallen back on the march to rejoin their comrades. In spite of all these efforts, the left of Randal's brigade ended up behind Waul's, and Randal's and Scurry's brigades shifted to the right to correct their position. By this time the men came under occasional enemy fire. The general idea now was to charge across Cooper's field, dotted with dead trees, toward an unseen enemy that crouched behind rude breastworks. Unfortunately for the men the two brigades had not outflanked the enemy and would be advancing into a deadly crossfire.[8]

The regiment began the charge with three disadvantages—they were exhausted, the condition of some of the weapons was poor, and the enemy was unseen. Nevertheless, they slogged through the woods toward the field as other units in Randal's and Scurry's brigades did also, and men began to fall. Two of the first to be shot were two Shelby County farmers: Pvt. Aruse Walling (Company A), who fell fifty or sixty yards from the field, and Pvt. Isaac Hays (Company A) who dropped dead at the edge of the opening. These early casualties caused some consternation, but Randal and other officers urged the troops onward. Randal's brigade advanced into the field toward the 50th Indiana Infantry and the 33rd Iowa Infantry, but as the men came under heavy fire from the front and to the right, order began to break down about one hundred yards from the sheltered enemy. Men of the 28th and Gould's Battalion crowded behind the "few dead trees in the field in such numbers that all except the ones nearest to each tree were more exposed to the enemy's cross-fire than they would have been in open lines." Major Hall galloped back to the fence lining the field and asked a brigade staff officer for advice, and the reply was to advance. Major Gould galloped to Randal who also urged a continued advance. Both Hall and Gould encouraged their respective soldiers to advance, but by that time it was too late to retrieve the situation and regimental discipline collapsed. Then confusion developed on the left of the brigade. There, Randal had fallen

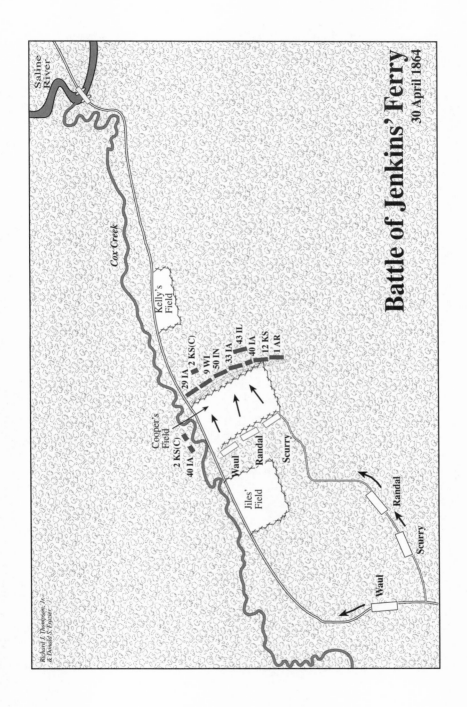

Battle of Jenkins' Ferry
30 April 1864

Saline River

Cox Creek

Kelly's Field

Cooper's Field

Jiles' Field

29 IA
2 KS(C)
9 WI
50 IN
33 IA
43 IL
40 IA
12 KS
1 AR

2 KS(C)
40 IA

Waul
Randal
Scurry

Randal
Scurry

Waul

Richard J. Thompson, Jr.
& Donald S. Frazier

"severely wounded in the abdomen" while exhorting the left of the brigade. Soon after this event a rumor spread among the already demoralized soldiers that a retreat had been ordered. One after another the men of the 28th retreated to the forest although they were "too tired to run fast."[9]

The officers of the brigade worked out a new chain of command in the wake of Randal's wounding. Lt. Col. Eli H. Baxter Jr. of the 28th took command of the brigade and Major Hall succeeded to command of the regiment. At about this time, Scurry also fell mortally wounded, and men of that brigade started to retreat. On the left, Waul was also struck, but he was able to stay on the battlefield until the fighting ended. Hall ordered the color bearer to plant the flag, and Hall attempted to rally the men. Even General Price, according to Hall, helped in the rallying effort. Eventually the troops established a small battle line, and two more men were wounded here when a Union regiment, probably the 43rd Illinois, advanced into the field and fired several volleys. The 28th returned fire even though Hall tried to prevent them from firing before being able to see. Soon after, Churchill's men arrived in the sector about twelve-thirty and covered Walker's withdrawal. Both sides stopped fighting, the Federals retired across their pontoon bridge, and the division withdrew to a point two miles from the battlefield. Later in the afternoon, some men returned to the battlefield to search for missing comrades after Union forces had retreated across the river. Capt. John T. Stark of the 13th Texas Cavalry (dismounted) expressed amazement at the sight of "hundreds of men engaged in pillaging the burning wagons[.] Trunks, boxes[,] and chests were soon broken open and their contents rifled. . . ."[10]

The battle was a great disappointment to Confederate hopes to destroy the enemy. Terrain, the weather, stubborn enemy resistance, and most crucial, the piecemeal attacks of the infantry, contributed to the defeat. Casualties probably reached one thousand among the Confederates and about seven hundred in the Union force. Randal's brigade suffered severely in the fighting.[11]

The 28th suffered one of the highest casualty rates among Confederate troops that day. Only the 12th Texas (Waul's brigade), with eight killed and sixty-eight wounded, and the 33rd Arkansas (Brig. Gen. James C. Tappan's brigade), with twenty-one killed and seventy-one wounded, had higher casualties. One officer, 2nd Lt. Rene Fitzpatrick of Company F, was killed and four more, all lieutenants, were wounded. One man, Pvt. John Amason of Company A, fell wounded and then was captured by Union forces. His captors took him to Little Rock where he died of measles in prison on 4 June. The regiment as a whole suffered an unusually high ratio of killed to wounded men that day. In addition, nineteen of the forty wounded suffered severe wounds, and interestingly the majority of the wounded men were wounded either in an arm, a hand, a shoulder, or the chest with very few leg wounds. The unusual ratio plus the high proportion of wounds above the waist may have been caused by the method of firing by the 33rd Iowa Infantry, one of the foes of Randal's men. The Iowans, bothered by the thick smoke "learned to stoop down, and look under the smoke sufficiently to discover the precise position of the rebel masses; and then a horizontal fire at the level of the breast, could not fail to hit its mark, unless a tree stood in the way." The 28th was also caught in a crossfire and the way men crowded behind trees also created inviting masses of men for the enemy to fire at. The position of the 28th, the breakdown of regimental discipline, and enemy marksmanship all contributed to the high casualties suffered at Jenkins' Ferry.[12]

TABLE 6
Casualties in Randal's Brigade at Jenkins' Ferry, Arkansas
30 APRIL 1864

	KILLED	WOUNDED	MISSING
28th Texas Cavalry	20	40	1
11th Texas Infantry	9	39	0
14th Texas Infantry	8	23	0
Gould's Battalion	7	9	0
Total	44	111	1

Source for Table 6: Alwyn Barr, "Texan Losses in the Red River Campaign, 1864," *Texas Military History* 3 (Summer 1963): 106; Dotson, *Who's Who of the Confederacy*, 86; *Houston Daily Telegraph*, 16 May 1864.

In the entire campaign the 28th Texas suffered casualties of 38 killed, 95 wounded, 13 captured, and 2 men missing for a total of 148. These losses were the third highest for any regiment in Walker's division during the Red River campaign and the battle of Jenkins' Ferry. Higher losses were suffered by the 16th Texas Infantry (9 killed, 72 wounded, and 98 captured or missing) and the 17th Texas Infantry (18 killed, 45 wounded, and 100 captured or missing), but a substantial proportion of their losses were men captured at Pleasant Hill. Walker's division as a whole had a severe casualty rate of at least 143 killed, 667 wounded, and 428 captured or missing for a total of 1,238 during the entire campaign. The strength of the division totaled 3,800 soldiers on 8 April at Mansfield. The overall proportion of losses in Walker's division, then, was probably 32 to 33 percent. Although this was certainly a severe casualty rate, it was not particularly unusual during the Civil War.[13]

During the campaign the 28th Texas fought at least as well as any other unit in Walker's division and marched in extraordinary fashion. In one of the most dramatic campaigns of the war, the smaller Confederate army capitalized on enemy errors to repel the North's most serious attempt to conquer the Trans-Mississippi Confederacy. As a consequence, Southern soldiers protected Texas from invasion and prolonged the war by at least two months and perhaps longer.[14]

At the conclusion of the battle of Jenkins' Ferry, the men were "completely exhausted" and emotionally spent. Details carrying shovels, spades, and pickaxes traveled to the battlefield to bury the dead of both sides, and as on any battleground, hideous sights of mangled and swollen corpses met the eyes of the soldiers. During this grisly task, the news of the death of Scurry on 1 May reached the men. Horace Randal died the next day, only an hour after Scurry's burial in Tulip, Arkansas, and, like Scurry, he was buried with military honors. Unfortunately, Randal died without the comfort and presence of his wife, who, greatly stricken, arrived six hours after his death. To the men of the 28th, the loss of Randal was undoubtedly an emotional one. When the 28th was organized in 1862, there were a number of soldiers who did not like Randal, but as a soldier said at the time, "now they would not give him up as Col[.] if they could help themselves." In honor of the fallen generals, Kirby Smith ordered the regiments of Randal's and Scurry's old brigades to drape their flags in mourning for thirty days.[15]

News of the regiment's casualties traveled slowly compared to today's speedy communications. A casualty list for Mansfield and Pleasant Hill finally appeared in the *Galveston Weekly News* on 10 May, followed six days later by the Jenkins' Ferry list in the *Houston Daily Telegraph*. Perhaps the news was spread earlier by letters home or by furloughed soldiers who conveyed the shocking news to family members. Pvt. Benjamin H. Schooler, a blacksmith from Shelby County, had enlisted in Company A on 2 April 1862 at age thirty-eight. Although on detached duty in late 1862 and throughout the summer of 1863, he stood in the ranks at the battle of Jenkins' Ferry where he was killed, leaving a widow and five children as survivors. Pvt. T. B. Selman of Cherokee County had enlisted at age twenty in Company E. He left a family headed by his mother, who owned eleven slaves, and composed of several siblings who operated the family farm. An exceptionally sturdy soldier, company officers recorded Private Selman as present at every roll call, except for a brief period of detached duty in 1862, and never listed him as sick. Still, his good fortune deserted him at either Mansfield or Pleasant Hill where he died.[16]

Field hospitals treated the numerous wounded soldiers near the actual fighting. Here, medical personnel treated and released those with minor wounds, while men with mortal wounds received "little treatment but support." Since physicians frequently performed amputations on severely wounded limbs, the sight of a field hospital frightened soldiers and often left a lasting impression. One hospital at Pleasant Hill resembled a "butcher's shamble, with maimed and bloody men lying on all sides; some with their arms off; some with their legs off; some awaiting their time, while the doctors, with upturned cuffs and bloody hands, are flourishing their knives and saws, and piles of bloody-looking limbs are strewn around them." Wagons transported soldiers with less-severe wounds to the Shreveport General Hospital, after treatment at a field hospital, for recuperation or perhaps further care. The Shreveport hospital admitted 160 men from 11 to 16 April with the diagnosis of "vulnus scolpetarium," or a gunshot wound, and later transferred some of these soldiers to branch hospitals.[17]

Men with severe wounds often spent long periods of time in the hospital. Others suffered disabling wounds and were as lost to the regiment as those soldiers who were killed. The Shreveport hospital admitted a Rusk County farmer, Pvt. R. B. Kelly (Company E), on 11 April as a result of a wound at either Mansfield or Pleasant Hill. Kelly spent the summer of 1864 in the Shreveport hospital and later at the Keatchi hospital, recuperating from his wound and suffering from diarrhea. Pvt. Albert J. Yarbro of Company H, wounded severely in the arm on 8 or 9 April, was admitted at Shreveport on 16 April. Authorities then furloughed this twenty-year-old for sixty days to allow his family or a local family to care for him. A year after being wounded severely in the arm at Jenkins' Ferry, 2nd Lt. M. M. Samples of Company K was still listed as wounded, and he awaited papers of retirement or discharge.[18]

While Maj. Gen. Richard Taylor tried to bag Banks, the units of Walker's division marched southward in a vain attempt to reinforce Taylor. On 4 May, only four days after the battle of Jenkins' Ferry, the division left camp and reached the Camden area, about thirty-five miles south and a little west of their previous camp. Dr. Edward W. Cade wryly commented, "Our officials appear to think that our division is made out of iron. . . . It would almost make your heart bleed could you see the haggard and worn looks of our men. Now 600 miles Since we started from Marksville La. I see from the Texas papers that our Brigade is Scarcely mentioned."[19]

CHAPTER 8

The Last Year

When the news of Lee's surrender reached us, the effect was sad, dreadful. Such depression I have never felt or seen. Hope seemed to have fled. We kept up the usual form of parades and drills, but it was without spirit.
— MAJ. ROBERT S. GOULD, GOULD'S BATTALION

On the route to Louisiana on 12 May, Brig. Gen. Robert P. Maclay, former chief of staff for Walker, became commander of Randal's former brigade while Brig. Gen. Richard Waterhouse, former colonel of the 19th Texas Infantry, became the new commander of Scurry's old brigade. Maclay, a native Pennsylvanian, was graduated with the 1840 United States Military Academy class. A veteran of the Seminole War and the Mexican War, Maclay resigned in 1860 to become a Louisiana planter. Although conceding that Maclay "is a very nice gentleman," Dr. Edward Cade commented that "no one can replace Randal with us." The appointment of Maclay increasingly rankled the men who believed that one of the brigade's unit commanders should have been promoted. As late as January

Robert P. Maclay

*Photo courtesy of the Special Collections Division
of the USMA Library, West Point, New York*

1865 there was "great dissatisfaction" and officers of the brigade worked on a petition asking for a different commander.[1]

Under the new commanders, the division passed through Homer, Louisiana, forty miles northeast of Shreveport, on 14 May. The citizens of Homer received the division enthusiastically, and young ladies gave bouquets of flowers to some of the soldiers. Dr. Cade, the pleased recipient of several bouquets, perhaps alarmed his wife by declaring, "I was almost tempted to remain a few days on account of the number of *beautiful* young ladies there. . . . Especially with a beautiful blue eyed fair haired blonde was I Smitten. I am getting to be quite a lady's man." Leaving Homer, the division tramped through Mount Lebanon, forty-five miles west of Monroe, where ladies gave gifts to the soldiers, marched southeast from that town and arrived at Pineville, across the Red River from Alexandria, on 22 May. They arrived nine days too late to aid Taylor in his efforts to halt Banks.[2]

For the rest of May and throughout June, the division enjoyed a relatively peaceful time. The camp near Pineville rested on wooded hills near "a cool, sparkling rivulet." Unfortunately, flies infested the camp, and the division left on 4 June and moved twenty-one miles downstream. At this site, details of men labored to cut down the riverbank to allow wagons to cross the river. Before the men completed this task, officials canceled the order and work halted. On 7 June, in a tremendous downpour, the camp flooded and water washed away cooking utensils and other items. Amidst much profanity and wisecracks, soldiers quacked like ducks in the rain-sodden camp. The division marched back toward Pineville on 13 June and moved southeast of Alexandria two days later in search of a good camp. During this movement, the soldiers learned of an important change in their high command. Taylor, increasingly annoyed by Smith's removal of Walker's division and Smith's subsequent claim of a great victory at Jenkins' Ferry, wrote a "vituperative" letter to Smith. Taylor hoped to be relieved of command, and Smith obliged him on 10 June and then sent part of the correspondence to President Jefferson Davis. On 17 June the men in the ranks learned of Taylor's dismissal and the appointment of Walker to his place. The loss of Walker upset the men. They nearly idolized him, and they regretted the departure of a gentleman known to salute even the dirtiest looking private soldier on the march. Brig. Gen. William H. King of the 18th Texas Infantry became temporary commander of the division.[3]

By the end of June the division had settled into an area about twenty miles southeast of Alexandria. The men nicknamed one of their camp sites "Camp Vermin" for its profusion of mosquitoes, ticks, and other insects. Diarrhea afflicted many of the soldiers, such as Pvt. S. W. Farrow of the 19th Texas Infantry and Dr. Cade. A monotonous diet of bread and beef, only occasionally enlivened by vegetables, perhaps weakened the general health of the men. Although Dr. Cade claimed he had eaten vegetables only twice that year, other physicians, such as Miles J. Birdsong of the 28th Texas, fared better because they received food, such as eggs and butter, from civilians in return for promising them medical care. In their lonesome camps, afflicted by insects and disease, a recurrence of religious revivals comforted the division. In Waterhouse's brigade, a Baptist minister named Mason baptized soldiers and preached regularly. As for Martin V. Smith, who had resigned in the fall of 1863 to become missionary for Randal's old brigade, he stayed with the division for three weeks in the summer of 1864 and then left for Texas. His brother-in-law, Dr. Cade, exclaimed, "This is what becomes of his promises made in getting his resignation accepted."[4]

The soldiers scarcely rested before embarking on a movement to the Mississippi River after breaking camp on 23 July. The following day, the men marched through the nearly dry lake bed of Catahoula Lake, twenty miles northeast of Alexandria. The troops reached Harrisonburg, approximately forty-five miles northeast of Alexandria, on 25 July and remained there until mid-August. Perhaps as early as 1 August the men discussed with increasing discontent the rumor that officers would order them to cross the Mississippi River to aid their comrades on the east side of the great river.[5]

While the common soldiers marched and gossiped, a series of dispatches from the east side of the Mississippi threw the Trans-Mississippi high command into confusion. In the midst of attempts to prepare Maj. Gen. Sterling Price's troops for a cavalry raid into Missouri, Smith received a dispatch from Lt. Gen. Stephen D. Lee, temporary commander of the Department of Alabama, Mississippi, and East Louisiana. Lee informed Smith of the movement of a Union force numbering twenty-thousand toward Mobile, Alabama, and asked Smith to transfer troops to help stop the Union offensive. Lee also stated that he had conferred with Gen. Braxton Bragg, President Davis's personal military advisor, giving the implication to Smith that Davis approved of the transfer of troops. On 28 July, Smith received another dispatch from Lee that included a message from

Bragg informing Smith that Davis ordered Taylor's (Confederate officials were unaware of his dismissal) infantry across the Mississippi where Taylor would supersede Lee. Smith accordingly reinstated Taylor and placed him in charge of the movement across the river. Walker's old division, Polignac's division, and Brig. Gen. Allen Thomas's Louisiana brigade, altogether totaling nine to ten thousand men, would march to the Mississippi under Taylor and be ferried across in pontoon boats.[6]

The scheme concerned both Smith and Taylor. Smith feared the resistance of Trans-Mississippi troops to the plan, and he asked Walker to consider taking temporary command of his former division until they crossed, but Walker eventually declined this idea. Smith also pointed out to Bragg that only eight thousand infantry would be left in the District of Texas and Arkansas to counter serious enemy offensives. Taylor expressed concerns about supplying the troops once they crossed, about enemy gunboats on the river, and about transportation on the east side of the river. None of these misgivings, though, prevented the actual march of the soldiers toward the waterway on 16 August. After crossing the Ouachita River at Harrisonburg, the soldiers of the 28th and other regiments marched east toward the Tensas River where they met the pontoon train. These soldiers eventually marched to within five miles of the river before increased Union naval patrols caused Taylor to halt the movement on 19 August.[7]

Desertions of Confederate troops reached a peak soon after Taylor rescinded the order to cross the Mississippi. In the spring of 1862, twenty-two thousand Confederate troops had crossed to the east side of the Mississippi with little incident and few desertions. Both groups of Southerners feared that communication would be weak or nonexistent over the Mississippi, but there were additional underlying reasons for the greater discontent among the later group. In addition to the usual complaints about food and furloughs, the men in Walker's division had not been paid in a year, and a number of field officers were absent, so there was less control over the enlisted men. For example, Maj. Robert S. Gould commanded Maclay's brigade during much of this crucial time, and besides Gould only one other field officer (a major) was present in that brigade.[8]

The desertions continued for a time after the movement stopped because the order to cancel the movement was slow in being communicated or because the men still feared a second attempt to cross. By 24 August about fifty men from Waterhouse's brigade and about two hundred each from

Maclay's and Waul's brigades had deserted. In Maclay's brigade an armed group of about one hundred deserters from the 11th Texas Infantry and the 28th Texas, considered to be "resolved and desperate," marched as a body through the picket lines one night. By this time Maclay had returned to the brigade, and he ordered Major Gould to take his battalion and the 14th Texas Infantry and bring back the deserters either dead or alive. At 1:00 A.M., Gould's force, accompanied by some cavalrymen, marched with loaded guns in pursuit of the deserters. One hundred yards from the deserters, who had camped for the night, Gould's force formed in line of battle and the cavalry placed themselves over the deserters' line of retreat. After the deserters refused to listen to Major Gould's adjutant, Gould himself, fearing he would be murdered, rode into the camp and asked for an audience. The men gathered around him as he made an impassioned speech pointing out reasons why they should return to duty. After his impromptu address a silence fell on the assembly until one soldier encouraged his comrades to return. By 8:00 A.M. Gould's force had successfully escorted the men back to camp where officers arrested the deserters, but none was ever seriously punished. As for Major Gould, he stated later, "I have always been prouder of that night, of the conduct of the battalion that night, and of its results, than of any other single act of the war."[9]

On the same day that Taylor canceled the movement, Smith received a dispatch from President Davis dated 8 August that said Davis had not given an order for the transfer of troops. Smith reiterated Taylor's order for the halt on 22 August and ordered Taylor to cross the river alone to become a department head in Mississippi. Smith also offered amnesties to deserters who returned at once to their units, but Maj. Gen. Simon B. Buckner, Smith's chief of staff, protested the amnesties and informed Smith that "the cases were more flagrant than I thought or than you have been led to suppose, amounting in at least one instance to an open mutinous outbreak under arms. . . ." In spite of the desertions during the month, the 11th Texas Infantry numbered 448, the 28th Texas fielded 380, the 14th Texas Infantry had 270 men, and Gould's Battalion, always small, numbered 155 for a total of 1,253 men in the ranks—more than at the battle of Pleasant Hill. Following the unsuccessful transfer, the troops fell back, much to the disappointment of Adjutant Volney Ellis who desired the transfer because, "I am almost willing to make . . . any sacrifice to end this war."[10]

At the end of August the units of the "Greyhound" division marched toward Monroe, fifty miles northwest of Harrisonburg, and arrived there on 6 September. Either on the march or soon after, Maj. Gen. John H. Forney, an 1848 graduate of the United States Military Academy, took command of the division. A veteran of frontier service, Forney had also taught tactics at the military academy but resigned his position in January 1861. Subsequently, Forney had raised and then commanded the 10th Alabama Infantry, fought early in Virginia, then commanded the District of the Gulf and later a division during the Vicksburg siege. A noted disciplinarian, Forney had been unpopular at times with his citizen soldiers. As early as August men in Walker's old division heard rumors of his impending appointment to their unit, and a number of men wrote to General Smith protesting Forney's appointment to the extent that Smith feared "that serious difficulty will arise" among the Texans. Still, the appointment was made because Forney was really the only available choice. The hot weather increased the soldiers' ill humor and forced them to rig up their blankets in camp as protection from the sun.[11]

From Monroe, Forney's men traveled to Monticello, Arkansas, forty-five miles southeast of Pine Bluff, between 14 and 20 September. A small party of forty men traveled ahead of the division to repair the road as necessary. This march particularly aggravated the main body of troops because Forney ordered roll call taken at each rest during the march. Pvt. Joseph P. Blessington of the 16th Texas Infantry bitterly recalled, "what his object was I am unable to say, unless it was to shorten the period of resting." Forney's division moved to Arkansas as part of a large shift of troops to Arkansas and secondarily to the Indian Territory. Smith situated the Trans-Mississippi infantry between Monticello and Camden as a diversion to keep Maj. Gen. Frederick Steele in Little Rock while Sterling Price led twelve thousand men on a raid into Missouri. The raiders started from Camden in late August as the Greyhounds recovered from their move toward the Mississippi. Price's raid all but ended on 23 October at Westport, Missouri, near Kansas City, where they suffered a devastating defeat.[12]

The soldiers of Forney's division concerned themselves little with the raid as Forney kept them busy with inspections and drills. They remained near Monticello from 20 September until 2 October, and the highlight of their stay was a grand inspection on 26 September. At 9:00 A.M. that morning, the men marched to the parade ground to await the arrival of Maj. Gen. John B. Magruder, the commander of the District of Arkansas.

John H. Forney
*Photo courtesy of the Special Collections Division
of the USMA Library, West Point, New York*

The Texans were amazed as "drawing our breath, and casting our eyes to the right, we perceived, at a distance, something resembling a *comet* with a long tail, advancing toward us. Further investigation plainly told us that what we took for a *comet* was nothing more nor less than the bunch of ostrich-feathers in General Magruder's hat." The band industriously played "Hail to the Chief" and then "Dixie" as Magruder rode along the lines. Then the regiments of the division passed in review of Magruder. One observer declared it "a grand sight" and noted that the many ladies (including Dr. Birdsong's wife) and children present enjoyed the occasion.[13]

Not long after this exciting incident, the men moved to Camden in early October and remained there until mid-November. The soldiers mostly worked on the fortifications at Camden. The execution of Capt. John Guynes, a fifty-year-old likable man of the 22nd Texas Infantry who had encouraged his men to desert while nearing the Mississippi, saddened many. In mid-November the division marched in the rain to Camp Sumter close to Shreveport. After a short stay at Camp Sumter, the troops went to Minden, thirty miles northeast of Shreveport, where they established a winter camp named Camp Magruder.[14]

Throughout December and until 26 January, the unit stayed at Camp Magruder where, upon arrival, they built sturdy log cabins. Private Farrow and his friends built a cabin "12 by 14 feet—we have comfortable fireplaces. We have Bed Scaffolds to sleep on, and stools to sit on—so we are well fixed up for Soldiers. We have chinked and daubed our houses. They are almost as tight as a jug." The troops completed most of the cabins before a heavy sleet storm pounded the area on 8 December. Four days after the storm the men were paid, some for the first time in two years. Gambling parties quickly formed throughout the encampment as some of the men gambled their meager earnings away. Christmas day was bleak as the men received no extra rations or "none of the O be joyful to kill trouble with," but the next day some units enjoyed a rousing time. In the 19th Texas Infantry, a captain brought a barrel of whiskey into camp and the men happily drank, many became drunk, and harmless fights resulted.[15]

By January ministers preached every day in camp, and the soldiers constructed a church. All of the preachers were Baptist, and Private Farrow claimed "there is not one fourth the wickedness in camp that there was 6 months ago." Pious men conducted Bible classes regularly in the division and formed an organization called the Christian Advocate primarily to aid the sick. General Forney, though, busied the soldiers with extensive military duties to attend to, including regular drill. A sham fight on 7 January before many spectators marked the biggest event at Camp Magruder. Although the audience enjoyed the performance, many of the soldiers were unamused at marching five miles to engage in a mock battle. One soldier mused that "I suppose Gen Forney has a pet Lady or two that he wishes amuse[d]. . . ."[16]

At the end of January, the division shifted their camp to a site near Shreveport and remained there until 21 February. Here, Forney further angered the men at a review conducted on 30 January. While marching to the parade ground several miles away, the sick and the tired who dropped out of the ranks were gathered up and "compelled to march a ring until the review was over. This treatment of the sick was loudly denounced by both officers and men." The big event, though, was a grand review and barbecue on 18 February. Thousands of civilians arrived for this event; one participant estimated a crowd of fifteen thousand. Generals Forney, Magruder, and Smith attended the event to watch the grand review and a sham fight. Special guests were the survivors of the 3rd Louisiana Infantry, veterans of Wilson's Creek, Pea Ridge, Corinth, Iuka, and service under Forney at Vicksburg. Speeches and large quantities of food further enlivened the gala affair.[17]

Forney's division bade farewell to Shreveport on 21 February when they marched ten miles outside the city and camped for about a week. Here, four recently dismounted Texas cavalry units augmented the division. Forney established the 4th Brigade under the command of Brigadier General King, consisting of one regiment from each of the old brigades and two of the new regiments. The 28th Texas left their old comrades to join the 16th Texas Infantry, the 18th Texas Infantry, the 34th Texas Cavalry (dismounted), and Col. J. M. Wells's dismounted cavalry (no numerical designation). Following this reorganization, the division marched through Mansfield on 8 March and then turned to march toward Texas. Six days later the men crossed the state line, entered their home state, and marched toward Hempstead, thirty miles northwest of Houston on the Houston and Texas Central Railroad. The soldiers now "went to sleep with lighter hearts than we did since we left our beloved State." The division crossed through the home territory of the 28th Texas, passing through Panola, Cherokee, and Houston counties. By 15 April, the division arrived at

Hempstead and settled into new duties such as drilling and the study of tactics by the officers.[18]

For the next month, many of the 304 men of the 28th Texas still on the roll in April 1865 were detached from camp. Company K had the largest number of men present (38), and Company I had the least with 23. However, on 10 April, Capt. John A. McLemore of Company I in a furlough request, noted he had three lieutenants and forty-three men present for duty in Company I. As a comparison, at the end of April, the 11th Texas Infantry listed a total of 520 men present for duty. Interestingly, only 67 men of the 28th Texas were present in camp at Hempstead. Most soldiers were either detached (143), absent with an illness (49), or on furlough (36). Another eighteen men were listed as deserters in April 1865. Many officers in the regiment apparently had little direct control over the enlisted men since many were detached to various duties in the commissary department, such as driving wagons or working at a local mill.[19]

In late April the rather fragmented group that composed the 28th Texas learned of the surrender of the Army of Northern Virginia on 9 April and that the Army of Tennessee was "surrounded." To encourage the soldiers, war speeches were made. One of these speeches occurred on 29 April "but there were not more than a third of the men that would listen to it. The others stood off some hundred yards and kept up a yell to break it up." In early May definite news of the capitulation of the Army of Tennessee reached the soldiers and still later the surrender of Lt. Gen. Richard Taylor's Department of Alabama, Mississippi, and East Louisiana. By mid-May the men in the Trans-Mississippi Department composed the last major Confederate army, and many soldiers wondered what action they should take. Forney, Magruder, and Smith all wrote addresses urging the men to stand fast, but on 8 May a Union army officer reached Smith and urged surrender. Smith called a Trans-Mississippi governors' conference at Marshall, Texas, where the attenders decided that continued fighting was impractical. Although the formal surrender did not occur until 26 May, it was quite clear to most that surrender was imminent.[20]

Forney's division was still intact in mid-May, but the end quickly neared. On 12 May a chaplain in the 16th Texas Infantry still solicited donations of food, clothing, and books for the division in the *Galveston Daily News*. Some soldiers heard rumors that their department had surrendered, however, and most by mid-May felt it useless to continue fighting. As one stated, "we are *beaten;* it is useless to disguise the fact that the majority of the soldiers are whipped and discouraged and think it useless to fight longer." Accordingly, desertions accelerated in most units. In Gould's Battalion many newer men in the unit deserted, but only two or three men from the original part of the battalion left. Perhaps the same trend occurred in other regiments as well. On 14 May some troops in Galveston mutinied, and Walker met with brigade and regimental leaders of Forney's division two days later and concluded that all "consider the contest a hopeless one, and will lay down their arms at the first appearance of the enemy." Three days later most of Forney's division disbanded, and the men seized food, wagons, and horses in Hempstead to expedite their return home. Some Trans-Mississippi troops looted and terrorized the region, but it is not known how the 28th Texas behaved in these final days. Gould's Battalion divided up supplies, traveled as an orderly group, and as the men reached their homes, they left the regiment. Major Gould "kept nothing save my tent, the equipment of a soldier and a spade. Others divided the wagons and mules. Lieut. Goodwyn took the ambulance." On 20 May, Brig. Gen. William H. Parsons's cavalry disbanded after heavy desertions. Obviously, the surrender on 26 May was only a formality in the Trans-Mississippi.[21]

Although the men disbanded several days before the surrender, their behavior was similar to that of Confederate soldiers in other armies. In Lee's proud Army of Northern Virginia many demoralized men simply refused to march further and allowed Union soldiers to capture them in early April. In the Army of Tennessee, mass desertions were common before their surrender on 26 April. The Confederacy had simply and suddenly collapsed in every theater of the war.[22]

Those Texans who returned home at the end of the war returned to a state that, unlike any other Southern state, had not been successfully invaded during the war. Many soldiers who returned to Texas were downcast, but many others felt relief that the war was over and confidence that they could be successful in civilian life. Fortunately for the 28th Texas, its losses during the war had been comparatively light (see Table 7). Only a small percentage of its men were battlefield casualties. As a comparison, the 3rd Texas Cavalry, also recruited in east Texas, had 7 percent of its members killed, 16 percent wounded, and 14 percent captured. The losses of both the 28th Texas and the 3rd Texas paled in comparison to the Texas regiments that served in the Army of Northern Virginia. For example, the 1st Texas

Infantry suffered 332 killed, and 620 wounded for a total of 952 in battle casualties alone. In regard to disease, the 28th Texas had nearly 10 percent of its soldiers die compared to 9 percent in the 3rd Texas Cavalry, and 12 percent in the 1st Texas. Only a small percentage (4.3) of the 28th Texas deserted as contrasted to other regiments like the 3rd Texas with a rate of nearly 7 percent. Of course these statistics obscure the unknown number of men who suffered from broken physical health, disabling wounds, or unstable mental health as a result of the war.[23]

TABLE 7
Summary of Losses in the 28th Texas Cavalry
1862–1865

Co.	Total Enrolled	KIA		WIA		Captured Missing		Died of Disease		Discharged		Deserted	
		No.	%	No.	%	No.	%	No.	%	No.	%	No.	%
A	125	3	2.4	11	8.8	1	0.8	13	10.4	7	5.6	3	2.4
B	113	2	1.8	8	7.1	0	0.0	9	8.0	3	2.7	1	0.9
C	96	6	6.3	7	7.3	1	1.1	4	4.2	8	8.3	9	9.4
D	92	3	3.3	10	10.9	11	12.0	5	5.4	16	17.4	2	2.2
E	104	5	4.8	6	5.8	0	0.0	7	6.7	4	3.8	9	8.7
F	92	3	3.3	9	9.8	6	6.5	7	7.6	4	4.3	5	5.4
G	88	1	1.1	7	8.0	0	0.0	13	14.8	4	4.5	1	1.1
H	104	7	6.7	10	9.6	0	0.0	14	13.5	4	3.8	7	6.7
I	105	4	3.8	5	4.8	1	1.0	18	17.1	14	13.3	6	5.7
K	114	4	3.5	23	20.2	0	0.0	11	9.6	10	8.8	1	0.9
	1033	38	3.7	96	9.3	20	1.9	101	9.8	74	7.2	44	4.3

With regard to marching, the regiment compiled an impressive record of rapid marches often in extreme weather conditions. These movements took place in Arkansas, Louisiana, and Texas but primarily in Louisiana. The geographical boundaries of the war for the 28th Texas extended from Little Rock, Arkansas, to approximately three hundred miles south to Opelousas, Louisiana, eastward to the Mississippi and westward, at least until 1865, to the Sabine River. This war zone was somewhat larger than the rather constricted area of operations of the Army of Northern Virginia but smaller than the region traversed by the wider ranging Army of Tennessee. In the arena of the 28th Texas, the regiment traveled approximately four thousand miles, primarily by foot, and concentrated mostly in the years

1863–1864. At least in one instance (during the Red River campaign and the Jenkins' Ferry campaign) Walker's division matched the feat of the more famous "foot cavalry" of Maj. Gen. Thomas J. Jackson's during the Shenandoah Valley campaign. The men of the 28th Texas could justifiably be proud of their marching prowess, shared by other units of Walker's Greyhounds.

Such marching skills contributed to their most important and dramatic success of the war—the Red River campaign. Walker's division participated heavily at the battles of Mansfield, Pleasant Hill, and Jenkins' Ferry and suffered severe losses as a result of their fighting. Their greatest success of the campaign, and perhaps of their wartime careers, was the victory at Mansfield, one of the most complete battlefield triumphs in any theater of the war. The veterans of Walker's division could also point with pride to their service in the fall of 1863 when Maj. Gen. William B. Franklin's over-land campaign was repulsed. The major failure of the war for the regiment and the Trans-Mississippi Department as a whole was the Vicksburg campaign. Through no fault of the common soldiers, Confederate troops at Vicksburg, Mississippi, were not aided materially by their Trans-Mississippi counterparts. Lack of cooperation between departments and bad timing rendered the services of Trans-Mississippi soldiers ineffective.

The 28th Texas was numerically only a small part of the overall Confederate war effort but was a relatively stable, effective regiment in perhaps the key division of the Trans-Mississippi army. In spite of grueling marches, extreme weather conditions, monotonous food, and sparse supplies of clothing, tents, and good weapons, the unit remained surprisingly loyal to their cause. It is true that the regiment was an independent and perhaps loosely controlled group as evidenced by their two mutinies, but other Confederate units also exhibited these same traits. The men were held together by a number of common bonds: many were married men, many were from east Texas, most engaged in agricultural occupations in civilian life, and many had a common religious background. Additionally, many may have shared a similar set of values concerning loyalty, honor, and courage. In common with most Civil War soldiers, the men of the 28th hoped to earn the respect of the homefolk by competent military service. Complaints and suffering of family members could disrupt a man's loyalty to the army, though, and lead to low morale or even desertion. The most noticeable instance of the power of home ties was the refusal of many of the unit's members to cross the Mississippi. Luckily Texas civilians suffered relatively little during the war as compared to other Southerners whose states were invaded, and this seemed to allow a delicate balance between loyalty to family and loyalty to the military to be maintained throughout much of the war. Only with the collapse of the eastern Confederate armies did the bonds that held the unit together break, leading to the regiment's disintegration. The 28th Texas answered its country's call and served steadfastly from 1862 to 1865 in an obscure but still important theater of the war.[24]

This photograph depicts Confederate veterans at a reunion near the turn of the twentieth century. Francis Marion Kolb, a veteran of Company G of the 28th Texas, is the eighth man from the left. *Photo courtesy of JoAnn M. Wood.*

APPENDIX A

ORGANIZATION OF WALKER'S TEXAS DIVISION DURING THE RED RIVER CAMPAIGN

Brig. Gen. Thomas N. Waul's brigade

12th Texas Infantry (sometimes referred to as the 8th Texas Infantry)
18th Texas Infantry
22nd Texas Infantry
13th Texas Cavalry (dismounted)
Capt. Horace Halderman's Texas battery

Col. Horace Randal's brigade

11th Texas Infantry
14th Texas Infantry
6th Texas Cavalry Battalion (dismounted) (Gould's battalion)
28th Texas Cavalry (dismounted)
Capt. J. M. Daniel's Texas battery

Brig. Gen. William R. Scurry's brigade

3rd Texas Infantry (joined the brigade in mid April 1864)
16th Texas Infantry
17th Texas Infantry
19th Texas Infantry
16th Texas Cavalry (dismounted)
Capt. William Edgar's Texas battery

CASUALTIES OF THE 28TH TEXAS CAVALRY

Newspaper casualty lists for the Red River campaign and the battle of Jenkins' Ferry list several men without compiled service records to indicate that they served in the 28th Texas Cavalry (these men are noted with an *). Inaccuracy of the newspapers lists is a possibility, but a regimental officer usually supplied the list and presumably knew the men serving in the unit. Many misspelled surnames were noted in all the casualty lists examined, so it is possible that the compiled service records do list the unknown man under a vastly different surname. The following list is compiled from the 10 May 1864 issue of the *Galveston Weekly News* (Mansfield and Pleasant Hill), the 16 May 1864 issue of the *Houston Daily Telegraph* (Jenkins' Ferry), the compiled service records of the 28th Texas Cavalry, and the 1860 U.S. Census. A complete record will show name and rank, age of the soldier in 1860, date of enlistment, county of residence, and casualty designation.

Brigade Staff

1st Lt. George B. Campbell, Company G, 24, April 20, 1862, Anderson, wounded slightly in the knee at Jenkins' Ferry

Brig. Gen. Horace Randal, 27, mortally wounded at Jenkins' Ferry; died on May 2, 1864

Headquarters Staff

Lt. Col. Eli H. Baxter, Company F, 26, May 10, 1862, Harrison, wounded slightly in the arm at either Mansfield or Pleasant Hill

Sgt. Maj. Henry J. Green, Company E, 23, April 28, 1862, Cherokee, wounded severely at either Mansfield or Pleasant Hill and arm amputated

Company A

OFFICERS

2nd Lt. Newel N. Yeary, 28, April 2, 1862, Shelby, wounded slightly in the leg at Mansfield or Pleasant Hill

ENLISTED MEN

Pvt. John Amason, 14, April 4, 1863, Shelby, wounded and captured at Jenkins' Ferry; died in prison at Little Rock, Arkansas

Pvt. Benjamin F. Beavers, April 2, 1862, wounded slightly in the hand at Jenkins' Ferry

Pvt. James Bralley, 35, April 13, 1863, Shelby, wounded slightly in the arm, leg, and hand at Jenkins' Ferry

Pvt. Isaac Hays, 25, April 2, 1862, Shelby, killed at Jenkins' Ferry

Cpl. Benjamin F. Lebo, 18, April 12, 1862, Shelby, wounded slightly at Mansfield or Pleasant Hill

Pvt. Stephen H. Oats, 15, May 15, 1863, Shelby, wounded severely in the jaw at Jenkins' Ferry

Pvt. Peter L. Rohus, wounded slightly in the side at Jenkins' Ferry

Pvt. H. H. Runnels, August 8, 1862, wounded severely in the breast at Mansfield or Pleasant Hill

Sgt. G. B. D. Rushing, 33, March 6, 1863, Shelby, wounded severely in the arms at Mansfield or Pleasant Hill

Pvt. Benjamin H. Schooler, 36, April 2, 1862, Shelby, killed at Jenkins' Ferry

Pvt. A. J. Shaw,* wounded severely in the hand at Jenkins' Ferry

Sgt. Henry C. Smith, April 2, 1862, wounded slightly in the face at Mansfield or Pleasant Hill

Pvt. Jefferson E. Thomas, April 2, 1862, wounded severely in the wrist at Jenkins' Ferry

Pvt. William A. Walling, 28, April 15, 1862, Shelby, killed at Jenkins' Ferry

Company B

ENLISTED MEN

Pvt. E. L. Gifford, 17, April 5, 1862, Cherokee, wounded slightly in the side at Mansfield or Pleasant Hill

Pvt. William M. Holloway, April 5, 1862, wounded slightly in the shoulder at Jenkins' Ferry

Pvt. R. L. Hudson, 25, August 8, 1862, Cherokee, killed at Mansfield or Pleasant Hill

Cpl. William Jones, 31, April 5, 1862, Cherokee, wounded slightly at Mansfield or Pleasant Hill

Pvt. William M. Lowe, 17, April 5, 1862, Cherokee, wounded slightly in the abdomen at Jenkins' Ferry

Pvt. R. W. McMinn, 17, October 22, 1863, Cherokee, wounded severely in the arm at Mansfield or Pleasant Hill

Pvt. J. F. Rice, October 12, 1863, wounded slightly in the thigh at Mansfield or Pleasant Hill

Pvt. C. L. Stafford, 23, April 5, 1862, Cherokee, killed at Jenkins' Ferry

Pvt. H. S. Walker, 29, May 3, 1862, Cherokee, wounded slightly in the head at Mansfield or Pleasant Hill

Sgt. William C. Woodall, 28, April 4, 1862, Cherokee, wounded slightly in the hand at Mansfield or Pleasant Hill

Company C

ENLISTED MEN

Sgt. James S. Anderson, 26, April 26, 1862, Panola, killed at Jenkins' Ferry

Pvt. John C. Anderson, 32, April 26, 1862, Panola, wounded slightly in the knee at Mansfield or Pleasant Hill

Pvt. J. A. Barber, April 26, 1862, wounded slightly in the arm at Jenkins' Ferry

Pvt. N. B. Campbell, April 26, 1862, killed at either Mansfield or Pleasant Hill

Pvt. Phillip Essry, April 26, 1862, wounded slightly in the fingers at Jenkins' Ferry

Pvt. D. Guttery,* wounded slightly in the thigh at Jenkins' Ferry

Pvt. E. C. Jones,* killed at either Mansfield or Pleasant Hill

Pvt. James Laham,* wounded slightly in the knee at Mansfield or Pleasant Hill

Pvt. J. T. McClendon, April 26, 1862, killed at either Mansfield or Pleasant Hill

Pvt. F. M. Pittman,* wounded slightly in the leg at either Mansfield or Pleasant Hill

Pvt. Hamelton Pollard, 37, April 26, 1863, Panola, wounded slightly in the side at either Mansfield or Pleasant Hill

Pvt. William A. Ritter, 27, April 26, 1862, Panola, killed at either Mansfield or Pleasant Hill

Pvt. W. P. Walker,* killed at either Mansfield or Pleasant Hill

Company D

OFFICERS

Capt. A. L. Adams, 33, May 3, 1862, Wood, wounded slightly in the hand at either Mansfield or Pleasant Hill

1st Lt. James B. Allen, April 24, 1862, killed at either Mansfield or Pleasant Hill

ENLISTED MEN

Pvt. James [——gs], wounded slightly at either Mansfield or Pleasant Hill

Pvt. Augustus H. Bonner, 15, June 28, 1862, Smith, captured at Fort DeRussy

Pvt. B. C. Chamness, 16, May 1, 1862, Rusk, captured at Fort DeRussy

Pvt. J. C. Chitwood, April 25, 1862, wounded slightly in the leg at either Mansfield or Pleasant Hill

Pvt. William Choate, 28, February 26, 1862, Smith, captured at Fort DeRussy

Pvt. J. C. Clingman, wounded severely in the leg at Jenkins' Ferry

Pvt. W. T. Gray, wounded slightly in the leg at either Mansfield or Pleasant Hill

Pvt. W. H. Gilliam, March 18, 1863, wounded severely in the shoulder at Jenkins' Ferry

Pvt. J. P. Hamilton, killed at Jenkins' Ferry

Pvt. James W. Ivy, 28, April 3, 1862, Rusk, captured at Fort DeRussy

Pvt. John W. King, May 2, 1862, wounded slightly in the hand at either Mansfield or Pleasant Hill

Pvt. W. H. Lowery, May 4, 1862, captured at Fort DeRussy

Pvt. Quitman A. McCright, 29, March 1, 1862, Wood, wounded slightly in the leg at either Mansfield or Pleasant Hill

Pvt. Samuel Meggs, 34, May 31, 1863, Cherokee, wounded severely in the arm at Jenkins' Ferry

Pvt. John R. Mooney, 35, May 5, 1862, Wood, captured at Fort DeRussy

Pvt. George D. Northcutt, 29, April 17, 1862, Rusk, killed at either Mansfield or Pleasant Hill

Pvt. Thomas W. Scott, 20, April 30, 1862, Rusk, captured at Fort DeRussy

Pvt. E. N. Stephenson, April 8, 1863, captured at Fort DeRussy

Pvt. Morris Ward, May 9, 1862, captured at Fort DeRussy

Sgt. C. N. White, 22, May 6, 1862, Smith, wounded slightly at Mansfield or Pleasant Hill

Pvt. J. J. Woodward, April 16, 1862, captured at Fort DeRussy

Pvt. J. S. Woodward, April 5, 1862, captured at Fort DeRussy

Company E

ENLISTED MEN

Pvt. J. T. Alexander,* wounded slightly in the hand at either Mansfield or Pleasant Hill

Pvt. John W. Carnes, 16, March 29, 1862, Cherokee, wounded slightly in the hand at either Mansfield or Pleasant Hill

Pvt. G. R. Clure, March 29, 1862, wounded slightly in the arm at Jenkins' Ferry

Pvt. W. C. Dawson, 15, May 9, 1862, Cherokee, wounded slightly in the arm at Jenkins' Ferry

Pvt. J. A. Dennis, February 6, 1863, killed at Jenkins' Ferry

Pvt. James Dowdy, June 2, 1862, killed at either Mansfield or Pleasant Hill

Pvt. James M. Loftis, February 26, 1862, wounded slightly in the hand at either Mansfield or Pleasant Hill

Pvt. J. M. Maddox, March 29, 1862, killed at Jenkins' Ferry

Pvt. William Oldham, December 12, 1862, wounded slightly in the leg at Jenkins' Ferry

Pvt. T. B. Selman, 18, March 29, 1862, Cherokee, killed at either Mansfield or Pleasant Hill

Cpl. T. H. Wynne, March 29, 1862, killed at Jenkins' Ferry

Company F

OFFICERS

1st Lt. A. J. Agnew, May 10, 1862, wounded slightly in the side at Jenkins' Ferry

2nd Lt. Rene Fitzpatrick Jr., 28, May 10, 1862, Harrison, killed at Jenkins' Ferry

Capt. Theophilus Perry, 27, May 10, 1862, Harrison, wounded dangerously at Pleasant Hill and leg amputated; died on April 17, 1864

ENLISTED MEN

Pvt. Joseph R. Bradfield, May 10, 1862, mortally wounded at either Mansfield or Pleasant Hill

1st Sgt. David G. Clark, May 10, 1862, wounded slightly in the leg at either Mansfield or Pleasant Hill

Pvt. James M. Curlin, May 10, 1862, missing at Pleasant Hill

Pvt. W. W. Gay, * missing at Pleasant Hill

Sgt. G. W. George, 30, May 10, 1862, Upshur, wounded slightly in the toe at Jenkins' Ferry

Pvt. J. D. Hartley, 15, May 10, 1862, Harrison, wounded in the arm at Jenkins' Ferry

Pvt. R. H. [Edward?] Hunter, 23, February 15, 1863, Harrison, wounded severely at either Mansfield or Pleasant Hill

Cpl. W. A. J. Lewis, May 10, 1862, wounded severely in the breast at Jenkins' Ferry

Pvt. D. Mahoen,* wounded severely in the arm at Jenkins' Ferry

Company G

OFFICERS

Capt. W. F. Roberts, April 20, 1862, wounded slightly in the shoulder at either Mansfield or Pleasant Hill

ENLISTED MEN

Pvt. Horace B. Bishop, June 20, 1862, wounded severely in the arm at Jenkins' Ferry

Pvt. R. M. Garrett, 37, April 20, 1862, Anderson, wounded severely in the thigh at Jenkins' Ferry

Pvt. William H. Kolb, 16, April 20, 1862, Anderson, killed at either Mansfield or Pleasant Hill

Sgt. James H. Lewis, April 20, 1862, wounded slightly in the chin at either Mansfield or Pleasant Hill

Pvt. William H. McDonald, April 20, 1862, wounded slightly at either Mansfield or Pleasant Hill

Cpl. Armstead Parker, 17, April 20, 1862, Anderson, wounded slightly at either Mansfield or Pleasant Hill

Pvt. W. T. Trim,* wounded severely in the foot and arm at Jenkins' Ferry

Company H

OFFICERS

2nd Lt. William G. Blain, 29, March 20, 1862, Freestone, wounded slightly in the thigh at Jenkins' Ferry

ENLISTED MEN

Pvt. J. C. Anderson, March 20, 1862, mortally wounded at either Mansfield or Pleasant Hill

Pvt. F. M. Bartlett, March 20, 1862, killed at Jenkins' Ferry

Pvt. F. M. Brown, March 20, 1862, killed at Jenkins' Ferry

Pvt. J. J. Burleson, 23, March 20, 1862, Freestone, killed at Jenkins' Ferry

Pvt. Henry G. Chancellor, 29, March 20, 1862, Freestone, wounded severely in the arm at either Mansfield or Pleasant Hill

Pvt. John W. Johnson, 21, March 20, 1862, Freestone, wounded slightly in the hip at either Mansfield or Pleasant Hill

Pvt. A. G. Lee, 30, March 20, 1862, Freestone, wounded slightly in the thigh at either Mansfield or Pleasant Hill

Pvt. J. F. McGraw, March 20, 1862, wounded severely in the neck at either Mansfield or Pleasant Hill

Sgt. E. A. Means, 29, April 25, 1862, Limestone, killed at Jenkins' Ferry

Pvt. John A. Netherland, 22, May 20, 1862, Freestone, wounded slightly in the shoulder at either Mansfield or Pleasant Hill

Cpl. W. E. Parsons, 21, May 20, 1862, Falls, mortally wounded at either Mansfield or Pleasant Hill

Pvt. E. D. Radford, 16, March 20, 1862, Freestone, wounded slightly in the leg at either Mansfield or Pleasant Hill

Pvt. L. M. Riley, 33, March 20, 1862, Freestone, killed at either Mansfield or Pleasant Hill

Pvt. James Strickland, 27, July 1, 1862, Freestone, wounded severely in the thigh at Jenkins' Ferry

Pvt. R. P. Varnell, 26, March 20, 1862, Freestone, wounded slightly in the arm at either Mansfield or Pleasant Hill

Pvt. Albert J. Yarbro, 16, March 20, 1862, Freestone, wounded severely in the arm at either Mansfield or Pleasant Hill

Company I

OFFICERS

2nd Lt. Morgan Rye, 32, June 11, 1862, Houston, wounded slightly in the arm and leg at Jenkins' Ferry

ENLISTED MEN

Pvt. John H. Albright, June 11, 1862, killed at Jenkins' Ferry

Pvt. Joseph M. Armstrong, 29, June 11, 1862, Houston, wounded severely in the back at Jenkins' Ferry

Pvt. William C. Aydelott, 27, December 10, 1862, Titus, captured at Fort DeRussy

Pvt. G. W. McKinney,* mortally wounded at either Mansfield or Pleasant Hill

Pvt. L. C. Mills, February 22, 1862, wounded slightly in the thigh at Jenkins' Ferry

Pvt. Chamer C. Scane, 33, June 11, 1862, Trinity, killed at Jenkins' Ferry

Pvt. Thomas J. Tipton, June 11, 1862, wounded severely in the hip at Jenkins' Ferry

Sgt. George W. Turner, 27, June 11, 1862, Houston, wounded slightly in the shoulder at Jenkins' Ferry

Pvt. John K. Wise, June 11, 1862, killed at Jenkins' Ferry

Company K

OFFICERS

2nd Lt. Thomas M. Lambright, 26, April 2, 1862, Shelby, wounded slightly in the body at either Mansfield or Pleasant Hill

Capt. William Neal Ramey, April 2, 1862, wounded slightly in the finger at either Mansfield or Pleasant Hill

2nd Lt. M. M. Samples, 23, May 3, 1862, Panola, wounded severely in the arm at Jenkins' Ferry

ENLISTED MEN

Color Sgt. James M. Benton, 16, March 1, 1863, Panola, wounded slightly in the arm at either Mansfield or Pleasant Hill

Pvt. Louis H. Bishop, 27, April 2, 1862, Panola, wounded slightly in the hand at either Mansfield or Pleasant Hill

Cpl. William P. Burns, April 2, 1862, wounded slightly in the head at either Mansfield or Pleasant Hill; killed at Jenkins' Ferry

Pvt. Henry Carroll, June 10, 1862, wounded slightly in the thigh at either Mansfield or Pleasant Hill; wounded severely in the arm at Jenkins' Ferry

Pvt. Thomas[?] N. Carroll, 43, June 10, 1862, Shelby, wounded slightly in the hand at either Mansfield or Pleasant Hill

Cpl. William F. Carter, 20, May 4, 1862, Panola, wounded dangerously in the neck and shoulder at either Mansfield or Pleasant Hill

Pvt. Gabriel R. W. Corley, June 8, 1862, wounded slightly in the shoulder at Jenkins' Ferry

Pvt. George Fleummons,* wounded severely in the hand at Jenkins' Ferry

Pvt. Archibald P. Gibbs, 20, May 2, 1862, Panola, wounded severely in the arm at either Mansfield or Pleasant Hill

Pvt. S. L. Harris, 14, Shelby, wounded severely in the arm at either Mansfield or Pleasant Hill

Pvt. Thomas Hill,* wounded dangerously in the thigh at Jenkins' Ferry

Sgt. William E. Midyett, May 2, 1862, killed at Jenkins' Ferry

Pvt. George T. Nail, April 15, 1862, wounded severely in the hip at Jenkins' Ferry

Pvt. Thomas M. Parrish, 21, April 2, 1862, wounded slightly in the leg at either Mansfield or Pleasant Hill; killed at Jenkins' Ferry

Pvt. G. F. Plemons,* wounded slightly in the hip at either Mansfield or Pleasant Hill

Cpl. William T. Pyle, September 20, 1862, mortally wounded at either Mansfield or Pleasant Hill

Pvt. O. F. Ramsey, 30, August 24, 1862, Panola, wounded slightly in the side at either Mansfield or Pleasant Hill; wounded slightly in the shoulder at Jenkins' Ferry

Pvt. Martin B. Stone, 27, May 10, 1862, Shelby, wounded slightly in the hand at either Mansfield or Pleasant Hill

Pvt. William C. Turpin, wounded slightly in the elbow at either Mansfield or Pleasant Hill

Pvt. J. M. White,* wounded severely in the thigh at Jenkins' Ferry

NOTES

INTRODUCTION

1. Joseph P. Blessington, *The Campaigns of Walker's Texas Division* (New York: Lange, Little & Co., 1875), 11. Useful introductions to the history of Walker's Texas Division are a preface written by Norman D. Brown in his edited edition of *Journey to Pleasant Hill: The Civil War Letters of Captain Elijah P. Petty, Walker's Texas Division, C.S.A.* (San Antonio: University of Texas Institute of Texan Cultures, 1982), xii-xiii; an introduction by Alwyn Barr in a reprint edition of Joseph P. Blessington, *The Campaigns of Walker's Texas Division* (1875; reprint, Austin, Tex.: Pemberton Press, 1968); and an introduction written by Norman D. Brown in the most recent reprint of Blessington's work published by State House Press of Austin, Tex., in 1994.

2. The neglect of the Trans-Mississippi has been partially rectified by Stephen B. Oates, *Confederate Cavalry West of the River* (Austin: University of Texas Press, 1961); Robert L. Kerby, *Kirby Smith's Confederacy: The Trans-Mississippi South, 1863–1865* (New York: Columbia University Press, 1972; reprint, Tuscaloosa: University of Alabama Press, 1991); Alvin Josephy, *The Civil War in the American West* (New York: A. A. Knopf, 1991); William L. Shea and Earl J. Hess, *Pea Ridge: Civil War Campaign in the West* (Chapel Hill: University of North Carolina Press, 1992); and Michael E. Banasik, *Embattled Arkansas: The Prairie Grove Campaign of 1862* (Wilmingon, N.C.: Broadfoot Publishing, 1996). See Richard Allen Sauers, comp., *The Gettysburg Campaign, June 3–August 1, 1863: A Comprehensive, Selectively Annotated Bibliography* (Westport, Conn.: Greenwood Press, 1982).

3. Histories about Confederate Trans-Mississippi units are mostly confined to this list: Joseph P. Blessington, *The Campaigns of Walker's Texas Division* (New York: Lange, Little & Co., 1875); Xavier Blanchard Debray, *A Sketch of the History of Debray's (26th) Regiment of Texas Cavalry* (1884; reprint, Waco, Tex.: Waco Village Press, 1961); W. E. Woodruff, *With the Light Guns in '61–'65: Reminiscences of Eleven Arkansas, Missouri, and Texas Light Batteries, in the Civil War* (1903; reprint, Little Rock, Ark.: Eagle Press, n.d.); Carl L. Duaine, *The Dead Men Wore Boots: An Account of the 32nd Texas Volunteer Cavalry, C.S.A., 1862–1865* (Austin, Tex.: San Felipe Press, 1966); Robert S. Weddle, *Plow-Horse Cavalry: The Caney Creek Boys of the Thirty-fourth Texas* (Austin, Tex.: Madrona Press,1974); Bradford K. Felmly and

John C. Grady, *Suffering to Silence: 29th Texas Cavalry, CSA, Regimental History* (Quanah, Tex.: Nortex Press, 1975); Anne Bailey, *Between the Enemy and Texas: Parsons's Texas Cavalry in the Civil War* (Fort Worth: Texas Christian University Press, 1989); and Anthony Rushing, *Ranks of Honor: A Regimental History of the Eleventh Arkansas Infantry and Poe's Battalion of Cavalry* (Little Rock, Ark.: n.p., 1990). Other important Confederate Trans-Mississippi sources are John Q. Anderson, ed., *A Texas Surgeon in the C.S.A.,* Confederate Centennial Studies, no. 6 (Tuscaloosa, Ala.: Confederate Publishing, 1957); Junius Newport Bragg, *Letters of a Confederate Surgeon* (Camden, Ark.: n.p., 1960); Brown, *Journey to Pleasant Hill;* and B. P. Gallaway, *The Ragged Rebel: A Common Soldier in W. H. Parson's Texas Cavalry, 1861–1865* (Austin: University of Texas Press, 1988).

    4. A brief overview of the historiography of unit histories and the "new" military history is contained in a foreword written by Emory M. Thomas in Warren Wilkinson, *Mother, May You Never See the Sights I Have Seen: The Fifty-Seventh Massachusetts Veteran Volunteers in the Army of the Potomac, 1864–1865* (New York: Harper and Row, 1990), xi–xii. Two of the early unit histories considered "classics" today are J. F. C. Caldwell, *The History of a Brigade of South Carolinians, Known First as 'Gregg's,' and Subsequently as 'McGowan's Brigade'* (1866; reprint, Dayton, Ohio: Morningside Bookshop, 1974) and Amos M. Judson, *History of the Eighty-Third Regiment Pennsylvania Volunteers* (1865; reprint, Dayton, Ohio: Morningside Bookshop, 1986). See also Bell Irvin Wiley, *The Life of Johnny Reb: The Common Soldier of the Confederacy* (Indianapolis, Ind.: Bobbs-Merrill, 1943; reprint, Baton Rouge, La.: Louisiana State University Press, 1986), and Bruce Catton, *Mr. Lincoln's Army* (New York: Doubleday, 1951). Among the best of the new generation of unit studies are John J. Pullen, *The Twentieth Maine* (Philadelphia: Lippincott, 1957); Alan T. Nolen, *The Iron Brigade* (New York: Macmillan, 1961); and James I. Robertson Jr, *The Stonewall Brigade* (Baton Rouge, Louisiana State University Press, 1963).

    5. Examples of this "new" military history are Joseph T. Glatthaar's *The March to the Sea and Beyond* (New York: New York University Press, 1985), Gerald F. Linderman's *Embattled Courage* (New York: The Free Press,1987), and Reid Mitchell's *Civil War Soldiers* (New York: Viking, 1988). Examples of the nontraditional approach in the study of Civil War regiments include Earl J. Hess, "The 12th Missouri Infantry: A Socio-Military Profile of a Union Regiment," (*Missouri Historical Review* 76 [October 1981]: 53–77) and David F. Riggs, "Sailors of the U. S. S. *Cairo:* Anatomy of a Gunboat Crew," (*Civil War History* 28 [September 1982]: 266–73). This method has also been employed to investigate more complex questions. Kevin Conley Ruffner explored the relationship between wealth and desertion patterns using this method in "Civil War Desertion from a Black Belt Regiment: An Examination of the 44th Virginia Infantry," in *The Edge of the South: Life in Nineteenth-Century Virginia,* eds. Edward L. Ayers and John C. Willis (Charlottesville: University Press of Virginia, 1991). Douglas Hale's provocative article "The Third Texas Cavalry: A Socioeconomic Profile of a Confederate Regiment," (*Military History of the Southwest* 19 [spring 1989]: 1–26) investigated the connection between wealth and rank and, finally, Martin Crawford, "Confederate Volunteering and Enlistment in Ashe County, North Carolina, 1861–1862," (*Civil War History* 37 [March 1991]: 29–50); William Marvel, "A Poor Man's Fight: Civil War Enlistment Patterns in Conway, New Hampshire," (*Historical New Hampshire* 43, no. 1 [1988]: 21–40); and W. J. Rorabaugh, "Who Fought for the North in the Civil War? Concord, Massachusetts, Enlistments," (*Journal of American History* 73 [December 1986]: 695–701) all discussed what kinds of men enlisted.

CHAPTER 1
THE ORGANIZATION OF THE REGIMENT

1. In the antebellum period, the word *peculiar* generally meant something particular or special. *The Compact Edition of the Oxford English Dictionary,* 3 vols. (Oxford: Oxford University Press, 1986), 2: 210. The term *military population* refers to all white males between the ages of fifteen and thirty-nine. Patricia L. Faust, ed., *Historical Times Illustrated Encyclopedia of the Civil War* (New York: Harper & Row, 1986), 750; Stephen B. Oates, *Confederate Cavalry West of the River* (Austin: University of Texas Press, 1961), 3–4, 75, 26–28.

2. Randolph B. Campbell, *A Southern Community in Crisis: Harrison County, Texas, 1850–1880* (Austin: Texas State Historical Association, 1983), 222–23.

3. R. M. Collins, *Chapters from the Unwritten History of the War Between the States* (1893; reprint, Dayton, Ohio: Morningside Bookshop, 1988), 9; Campbell, *Southern Community in Crisis,* 225–26.

4. Oates, *Confederate Cavalry,* 34–37.

5. James M. McPherson, *Ordeal by Fire: The Civil War and Reconstruction* (New York: McGraw-Hill, 1992), 184; James W. Geary, *We Need Men: The Union Draft in the Civil War* (DeKalb: Northern Illinois University Press, 1991), 167; Albert Burton Moore, *Conscription and Conflict in the Confederacy* (New York: Macmillan, 1924), 13–16, 67–68; Oates, *Confederate Cavalry,* 38, 44–47.

6. Leonard Randal to William L. Marcy, 20 January 1849, U.S. Military Academy Cadet Application Papers, 1805–1866, National Archives, Washington, D.C.; Max S. Lale, "A Letter from Leonard Randal to his Son," *East Texas Historical Association* 23, no. 2 (1985): 48; Horace Randal to David S. Kaufman, 12 April 1849, U.S. Military Academy Application Papers, 1805–1869; Official Register of the Officers and Cadets of the U.S. Military Academy, West Point, New York (1850), 16; Official Register (1851), 13; Official Register (1854), 8; Mark M. Boatner III, *The Civil War Dictionary* (New York: David McKay, 1959), 414, 474–77, 629, 812.

7. *(Marshall) Texas Republican,* 29 March 1862; Francis B. Heitman, *Historical Register and Dictionary of the United States Army, From its Organization, September 29, 1789, to March 2, 1903,* 2 vols. (Washington: Government Printing Office, 1903), 1: 814; Ron Tyler, ed., *New Handbook of Texas,* 6 vols. (Austin: Texas State Historical Association, 1996), 5: 436.

8. Gilbert E. Govan and James W. Livingood, eds., *The Haskell Memoirs* (New York: G. P. Putnam's Sons, 1960), 10; Tyler, *New Handbook of Texas,* 5: 436; Theophilus Perry to Thomas Person, 6 May 1862, Presley Carter Person Papers, Duke University Library; *(Marshall) Texas Republican,* 15, 29 March, 5 April 1862; U.S. War Department, *War of the Rebellion: A Compilation of the Official Records of the Union and Confederate Armies,* 128 vols. (Washington, D.C.: Government Printing Office, 1880–1901), ser. I, 5: 918; Lale, "Letter from Leonard Randal to his Son," 48.

9. The regions of the state are defined in Randolph B. Campbell and Richard G. Lowe, *Wealth and Power in Antebellum Texas* (College Station: Texas A&M University Press, 1977), 13–17.

10. Campbell and Lowe, *Wealth and Power,* 13, 15; Barnes F. Lathrop, *Migration Into East Texas, 1835–1860: A Study from the United States Census* (Austin: Texas State Historical

Association, 1940), 38, 51, 56; Joseph C. G. Kennedy, *Agriculture of the United States in 1860; Compiled from the Original Returns of the Eighth Census* (1864; reprint, New York: Norman Ross Publishing, 1990), 140–51.

11. *Statistics of the United States, (Including Mortality, Property, &c.,) in 1860; Compiled from the Original Returns and being the Final Exhibit of the Eighth Census, Under the Direction of the Secretary of the Interior* (1866; reprint, New York: Norman Ross Publishing, 1990), 471–72, 474.

12. The 1860 census does not list a population total for Marshall, Texas. Marshall's population is estimated in Campbell, *Southern Community in Crisis,* 22; Joseph C. G. Kennedy, *Population of the United States in 1860; Compiled from the Original Returns of the Eighth Census, Under the Direction of the Secretary of the Interior* (1864; reprint, New York: Norman Ross Publishing, 1990), 484–87.

13. *Statistics of the United States (Including Mortality, Property, &c.),* 329; Campbell, *Southern Community in Crisis,* 85–86; Douglas Hale, "The Third Texas Cavalry: A Socio-economic Profile of a Confederate Regiment," *Military History of the Southwest* 19 (spring 1989): 8.

14. *Manufacturers of the United States in 1860; Compiled from the Original Returns of the Eighth Census* (1865; reprint, New York: Norman Ross Publishing, 1990), 580, 583–85, 588–89.

15. Harold B. Simpson, *Texas in the War, 1861–1865* (Hillsboro, Tex.: Hill Junior College Press, 1965), xviii.

16. *(Marshall) Texas Republican,* 26 April, 10 May 1862; D. B. Martin to J. Y. Dashiell, 11 February, 3 April, 21 April 1862, Texas State Troops Records, Brigade Correspondence, 1861–1865, Box 401-825-15, Texas State Archives; National Archives and Records Administration, Compiled Service Records of Confederate Soldiers Who Served in Organizations from the State of Texas (microfilm M323), reel 93.

17. *(Marshall) Texas Republican,* 10 May 1862; Bureau of the Census, Eighth Census of the United States, 1860. Schedule I (Free Inhabitants), (microfilm M653), reel 1304, 428.

18. Campbell, *Southern Community in Crisis,* 206, 222–23; *(Marshall) Texas Republican,* 15, 22, 29 February, 1, 8, 15 March 1862; William M. Martin to J. Y. Dashiell, 8 April 1862, Brigade Correspondence, Box 401-825-16.

19. *(Marshall) Texas Republican,* 15 March, 24 May 1862; William DeRyee and R. E. Moore, *The Texas Album of the Eighth Legislature, 1860* (Austin, Tex.: Miner, Lambert & Perry, 1860), 24; correspondence with Dorothy Rapp, United States Military Academy Archives, 19 May 1992, in author's possession; Harold B. Simpson, *Hood's Texas Brigade: Lee's Grenadier Guard* (Waco: Texian Press, 1970), 28; Eighth Census, Schedule I, reel 1304, 396, Schedule II (Slave Inhabitants), reel 1312, 386; Mrs. Walter Gray Davis, "Henry Gerard Hall, 1833–1873," in *Who's Who of the Confederacy: A Symposium by the Members of the Albert Sidney Johnston Chapter No. 2060, United Daughters of the Confederacy,* comp., Susan Merle Dotson (San Antonio, Tex.: Naylor, 1966), 79.

20. Although many Southern states attempted to acquire weapons from the War Department before the outbreak of the war, these efforts were largely unsuccessful. As a result, the Confederacy only had 150,000 serviceable shoulder arms at the beginning of the war, and only 20,000 of these were rifles. As a result many units formed details to acquire

weapons. Edward W. Cade to Allie Cade, 8, 24, 29 June 1862, John Q. Anderson Collection, Texas State Archives, Austin, Tex.; *(Marshall) Texas Republican,* 28 June 1862; John Hope Franklin, *The Militant South, 1800–1861* (Cambridge, Mass.: Harvard University Press, 1956), 236; Bell Irvin Wiley, *The Life of Johnny Reb: The Common Soldier of the Confederacy* (Indianapolis, Ind.: Bobbs-Merrill, 1943; reprint, Baton Rouge: Louisiana State University Press, 1986), 286.

21. Edward W. Cade to Allie Cade, 8, 18, 24, 29 June, 3 July 1862, Anderson Collection.

22. *(Marshall) Texas Republican,* 5 July 1862; Compiled Service Records, reels 143–146.

23. *(Marshall) Texas Republican,* 5 July 1862; *Official Records* ser. I, 9: 718; Anne J. Bailey, *Between the Enemy and Texas: Parsons's Texas Cavalry in the Civil War* (Fort Worth: Texas Christian University Press, 1989), 29.

24. "Statement of facts about Col. Randall's [*sic*] Regt," 3 February 1863, Oran M. Roberts Papers, University of Texas at Austin, Center for American History; William M. Taylor to J. Y. Dashiell, 11 February, 8 April 1862, Brigade Correspondence, 1861–1865, Box 401-825-16.

25. Edward W. Cade to Allie Cade, 8 June 1862, Anderson Collection; *(Marshall) Texas Republican,* 5, 12 July, 9 August 1862; Marilyn McAdams Sibley, *Lone Stars and State Gazettes: Texas Newspapers before the Civil War* (College Station: Texas A&M Press, 1983), 351.

26. Muster Roll of the Freestone Freemen commanded by J. C. Means, 19th Brigade, #1532, Brigade Correspondence, 1861–1865, Box 401-826-8-9; "Statement of facts about Col. Randall's [*sic*] Regt," 3 February 1863, Oran M. Roberts Papers; Bailey, *Between the Enemy and Texas,* 231; Martin Hardwick Hall, *The Confederate Army of New Mexico* (Austin, Tex.: Presidial Press, 1978), 113.

27. Geary, *We Need Men,* 97; Moore, *Conscription and Conflict,* 13, 119; Ralph A. Wooster and Robert Wooster, "'Rarin' for a Fight': Texans in the Confederate Army," *Southwestern Historical Quarterly* 84 (April 1981): 395; Compiled Service Records, reels 143–146, see individual service records; Dotson, *Who's Who of the Confederacy,* 80; Lale, "Letter from Leonard Randal to his Son," 48.

28. Hale, "Third Texas Cavalry," 23; Wiley, *Life of Johnny Reb,* 347; Martin Crawford, "Confederate Volunteering and Enlistment in Ashe County, North Carolina, 1861–1862," *Civil War History* 37 (March 1991): 42–44.

29. Campbell and Lowe, *Wealth and Power,* 29. Campbell and Lowe defined the lower South as Alabama, Arkansas, Florida, Georgia, Louisiana, Mississippi, South Carolina, and Texas. Upper South states were Delaware, the District of Columbia, Kentucky, Maryland, Missouri, North Carolina, Tennessee, and Virginia; Hale, "Third Texas Cavalry," 23.

30. *Population of the United States in 1860,* 487.

31. Occupational percentages in Hale ("Third Texas Cavalry," 22–23) are agricultural (59 percent), students (10.4 percent), merchants and clerks (9 percent), artisans (8.2 percent). There were also "twenty-three school teachers, twenty-two lawyers, eleven physicians, and one loafer. . . ." In Hale ("Third Texas Cavalry," 14) the mean value for combined real and personal property was $14,814 for officers and $12,672 for enlisted men.

32. Eighth Census, Schedule I, reel 1290, 418, 424, 436; Record of the Comptroller of Public Accounts, Ad Valorem Tax Division, County Real and Personel Property Tax Rolls, Cherokee County, 1860.

33. *Manufacturers of the United States,* 588–89.

34. William M. Taylor to J. Y. Dashiell, 11 February, 8 April 1862, Brigade Correspondence, 1861–1865, Box 401-825-16; *Population of the United States,* 485 (percentage of slaves); Douglas Hale, "Third Texas Cavalry," 18, 26.

35. Eighth Census, Schedule I, reel 1304, 414–16, 433; Compiled Service Records, reels 144–146.

36. Charles D. Spurlin, comp., *Texas Veterans in the Mexican War: Muster Rolls of Texas Military Units* (Victoria, Tex.: Victoria College, 1984), 51, 91; Douglas Hale, "Life and Death Among the Lone Star Defenders: Cherokee County Boys in the Civil War," *East Texas Historical Journal* 29, no. 2 (1991): 31; Bailey, *Between the Enemy and Texas,* 231–32; Hall, *Confederate Army of New Mexico,* 113; Donald S. Frazier, *Blood & Treasure: Confederate Empire in the Southwest* (College Station: Texas A&M University Press, 1995), 162, 164–65.

37. Eighth Census, Schedule I, reel 1290, 437; *Biographical Encyclopedia of Texas* (New York: Southern Publishing, 1880), 188–89; Pauline Buck Hohes, *A Centennial History of Anderson County* (San Antonio: Naylor, 1936), 43.

38. Eighth Census, Schedule I, reel 1290, 415; reel 1296, 462; reel 1302, 389; reel 1303, 22; *A Memorial and Biographical History: McLennan, Falls, Bell and Coryell Counties, Texas* (Chicago: Lewis Publishing, 1893), 527–28.

39. Hale, "Third Texas Cavalry," 22; Simpson, *Hood's Texas Brigade,* 21; Crawford, "Confederate Volunteering," 39; Eighth Census, Schedule I, reel 1290, 415, reel 1297, 208; Hale, "Life and Death," 31; Hall, *Confederate Army of New Mexico,* 113.

CHAPTER 2
FROM TEXAS TO ARKANSAS

1. Theophilus Perry to Harriet Perry, 14, 18 July 1862, Presley Carter Person Papers, Duke University Library, Durham, N.C.

2. Theophilus Perry to Harriet Perry, 14, 17, 18 July 1862, Person Papers.

3. Theophilus Perry to Harriet Perry, 18 July 1862, Person Papers; *(Marshall) Texas Republican,* 26 July 1862; Edward W. Cade to Allie Cade, 13, 21, 29 July 1862, John Q. Anderson Collection, Texas State Archives, Austin, Tex.

4. Edward W. Cade to Allie Cade, 21 July 1862, Anderson Collection; *(Marshall) Texas Republican,* 26 July 1862; Stephen B. Oates, *Confederate Cavalry West of the River* (Austin: University of Texas Press, 1961), 47–48, 81–83.

5. Oates, *Confederate Cavalry,* 47–48; Biography and Diaries of R. S. Gould, 62, Robert Simenton Gould Papers, University of Texas at Austin, Center for American History; National Archives and Records Administration, Compiled Service Records of Confederate Soldiers Who Served in Organizations from the State of Texas (microfilm M323), reel 144.

6. Theophilus Perry to Harriet Perry, 23 July 1862, 5 August 1862, Person Papers; Edward W. Cade to Allie Cade, 29 July 1862, Anderson Collection.

7. Theophilus Perry to Harriet Perry, 5 August, 4 September 1862, Person Papers; Norman D. Brown, ed. *Journey to Pleasant Hill: The Civil War Letters of Captain Elijah P. Petty, Walker's Texas Division, C.S.A.* (San Antonio: The University of Texas Institute of Texan Cultures, 1982), 180; *(Marshall) Texas Republican,* 9 August 1862.

8.   Theophilus Perry to Harriet Perry, 4 September 1862, Person Papers; Robert S Gould, 62, Gould Papers; U.S. War Department, *War of the Rebellion: A Compilation of the Official Records of the Union and Confederate Armies,* 128 vols. (Washington, D.C.: Government Printing Office, 1880–1901), ser. I, 13: 881, 884; 22, pt. 1: 903–4, 22, pt. 2: 771, 805, 26, pt. 1, 393–95; *(Marshall) Texas Republican* 22 January 1863, 26 February 1863; "Statement of facts about Col. Randall's [*sic*] Regt," 3 February 1863, Oran M. Roberts Papers, University of Texas at Austin, Center for American History; Compiled Service Records, reel 143.

9.   Robert S. Gould, 62, Gould Papers; Theophilus Perry to Harriet Perry, 4, 5 September 1862, Person Papers; Edward W. Cade to Allie Cade, 16 September 1862, Anderson Collection.

10.   Ralph Masterson, ed., *Sketches from the Life of Dr. Horace Bishop* (San Angelo, Tex.[?]: n.p., ca. 1930), 8–9; Pat H. Martin to Mrs. S. E. Truit, 22 September 1862, James W. Truit Papers, University of Texas at Austin, Center for American History; Bell Irvin Wiley, *The Life of Johnny Reb: The Common Soldier of the Confederacy* (Indianapolis, Ind.: Bobbs-Merrill, 1943; reprint, Baton Rouge: Louisiana State University Press, 1986), 36–37.

11.   Edward W. Cade to Allie Cade, 16 September 1862, Anderson Collection; Theophilus Perry to Harriet Perry, 4, 5 September 1862, Person Papers; David M. Ray to his sister, 28 October 1862, David M. Ray Papers, University of Texas at Austin, Center for American History.

12.   James L. Nichols, *The Confederate Quartermaster in the Trans-Mississippi* (Austin: University of Texas Press, 1964), 27; Harriet Perry to Theophilus Perry, 15 September 1862, 23 September 1862, Person Papers; *Galveston (Tex.) Weekly News,* 3 December 1862; *Official Records,* ser. I, 13: 877; *(Marshall) Texas Republican,* 11, 18, 25 October 1862.

13.   Theophilus Perry to Harriet Perry, 21, 22 September, 4, 22 November 1862, Person Papers; Compiled Service Records, reels 143–146.

14.   Theophilus Perry to Harriet Perry, 4, 21 September 1862, Person Papers; Edward W. Cade to Allie Cade, 16 September 1862, Anderson Collection.

15.   Theophilus Perry to Harriet Perry, 21 September 1862, Person Papers; Mark M. Boatner III, *The Civil War Dictionary* (New York: David McKay, 1959), 406; "Statement of facts about Col. Randall's [*sic*] Regt," 3 February 1863, Oran M. Roberts Papers.

16.   In October 1862 a Unionist organization was uncovered in north Texas. In that same month, forty-six suspected Unionists were hanged in Cooke County, Texas. The most detailed study of the Great Hanging is Richard B. McCaslin, *Tainted Breeze: The Great Hanging at Gainesville, Texas, 1862* (Baton Rouge: Louisiana State University Press, 1993); Theophilus Perry to Harriet Perry, 4 September 1862, Person Papers; Edward W. Cade to Allie Cade, 16, 24, 28 September 1862, Anderson Collection; David M. Ray to his sister, 28 October 1862, Ray Papers; *(Marshall) Texas Republican,* 13 September 1862.

17.   The camp was named in honor of Brig. Gen. Allison Nelson, commander of the 10th Texas Infantry who died of disease on 7 October 1862. Jon Harrison, ed., "The Confederate Letters of John Simmons," 28, Hill College, Confederate Research Center, Hillsboro, Tex., 22nd Texas Infantry file; Edward W. Cade to Allie Cade, 8, 16, November 1862, Anderson Collection; Joseph P. Blessington, *The Campaigns of Walker's Texas Division, by a Private Soldier* (New York: Lange, Little & Co., 1875), 44; Patricia L. Faust, ed., *Historical Times Illustrated Encyclopedia of the Civil War* (New York: Harper & Row, 1986), 523; James

M. McPherson, *Ordeal By Fire: The Civil War and Reconstruction* (New York: McGraw-Hill, 1992), 385; Wiley, *The Life of Johnny Reb,* 244; David M. Ray to his sister, 28 October, 1862 (also mentions weather), Ray Papers.

18. Edward W. Cade to Allie Cade, 8, 16 November 1862, Anderson Collection; *(Marshall) Texas Republican,* 22 January 1863.

19. *(Marshall) Texas Republican,* 26 February 1863; Compiled Service Records, reels 143–146.

20. David M. Ray to his sister, 20 August 1862, Ray Papers; Theophilus Perry to Harriet Perry, 4 September 1862, Person Papers; Edward W. Cade to Allie Cade, 16 November 1862, Anderson Collection.

21. An excellent discussion of the transition from civilian to soldier is in Gerald F. Linderman, *Embattled Courage: The Experience of Combat in the American Civil War* (New York: Free Press, 1987), 113–24.

CHAPTER 3
THE VICKSBURG CAMPAIGN

1. Bayou Meto (the present-day spelling) is spelled various ways in contemporary letters, including "Meter" and "Metro." David M. Ray to his mother, 26 November 1862, David M. Ray Papers, University of Texas at Austin, Center for American History; Joseph P. Blessington, *The Campaigns of Walker's Texas Division, by a Private Soldier* (New York: Lange, Little & Co., 1875), 61–63; Theophilus Perry to Harriet Perry, 7 December 1862, Presley Carter Person Papers, Duke University Library, Durham, N.C.

2. Blessington, *Campaigns of Walker's Texas Division,* 63; Theophilus Perry to Harriet Perry, 10, 14 December 1862, Person Papers; Edwin C. Bearss, *The Campaign for Vicksburg,* 3 vols. (Dayton, Ohio: Morningside House, 1991), 1: 148, 349–50, 353; Patricia L. Faust, ed., *Historical Times Illustrated Encyclopedia of the Civil War* (New York: Harper & Row, 1986), 23; Mark M. Boatner III, *The Civil War Dictionary* (New York: David McKay, 1959), 24.

3. Blessington, *Campaigns of Walker's Texas Division,* 64–65; John C. Porter, "Early Days of Pittsburg, Texas, 1859–1874," 10–11, Hill College, Confederate Research Center, Hillsboro, Tex., 18th Texas Infantry file; Theophilus Perry to Harriet Perry, 14 December 1862, Person Papers.

4. Blessington, *Campaigns of Walker's Texas Division,* 72–73; Faust, *Historical Times Illustrated Encyclopedia,* 797; Ezra J. Warner, *Generals in Gray: Lives of the Confederate Commanders* (Baton Rouge: Louisiana State University Press, 1959), 320; Eldon Stephen Branda, ed., *The Handbook of Texas: A Supplement* (Austin: The Texas State Historical Association, 1976), 1076; Terrence J. Winschel, "To Rescue Gilbraltar: John G. Walker's Texas Division and the Relief of Fortress Vicksburg," *Civil War Regiments: A Journal of the American Civil War* 3, no. 3 (1993), 38–39.

5. Blessington, *Campaigns of Walker's Texas Division,* 66–75; John T. Stark to Martha Stark, 20 January 1863, Confederate Research Center, 13th Texas Cavalry file; Bearss, *Campaign for Vicksburg,* 1: 405, 418–19; David M. Ray to his mother, 28 January 1863, Ray Papers.

6. Blessington, *Campaigns of Walker's Texas Division,* 75; Norman D. Brown, ed., *Journey to Pleasant Hill: The Civil War Letters of Captain Elijah P. Petty, Walker's Texas Division,*

C.S.A. (San Antonio: University of Texas Institute of Texan Cultures, 1982), 136, 142–43; Edward W. Cade to Allie Cade, February 1863, John Q. Anderson Collection, Texas State Archives, Austin, Tex.

7. David M. Ray to his mother, 1 February 1863, Ray Papers; Theophilus Perry to Harriet Perry, 30 January 1863, Person Papers; Edward W. Cade to Allie Cade, 30 January, February 1863, Anderson Collection; Brown, *Journey to Pleasant Hill,* 134.

8. Edward W. Cade to Allie Cade, 30 January, 7, 22 February 1863, Anderson Collection; Theophilus Perry to Harriet Perry, 2 February 1863, Person Papers.

9. Brown, *Journey to Pleasant Hill,* 135; David M. Ray to his mother, 28 January 1863, Ray Papers; Edward W. Cade to Allie Cade, 22 February 1863, Anderson Collection; Faust, *Historical Times Illustrated Encyclopedia,* 366.

10. Boatner, *Civil War Dictionary,* 769–70; Faust, *Historical Times Illustrated Encyclopedia,* 695.

11. Brown, *Journey to Pleasant Hill,* 143; Blessington, *Campaigns of Walker's Texas Division,* 76–77; David M. Ray to his mother, 8 March 1863, Ray Papers.

12. Edward W. Cade to Allie Cade, 2 March 1863, Anderson Collection; David M. Ray to his mother, 8 March 1863, Ray Papers; Theophilus Perry to Harriet Perry, 11 March, 11 April 1863, Person Papers; Thomas W. Cutrer, ed., "'Bully for Flournoy's Regiment, We Are Some Punkins, You'll Bet': The Civil War Letters of Virgil Sullivan Rabb, Captain, Company 'I,' Sixteenth Texas Infantry, C.S.A.," *Military History of the Southwest* 19 (fall 1989): 175.

13. Theophilus Perry to Harriet Perry, February, 8 March 1863, Person Papers; Edward W. Cade to Allie Cade, 11 March 1863, Anderson Collection.

14. Edward W. Cade to Allie Cade, 13 March 1863, Anderson Collection; Brown, *Journey to Pleasant Hill,* 148; S. W. Farrow to Josephine Farrow, 13 March 1863, S. W. Farrow Papers, University of Texas at Austin, Center for American History.

15. Edward W. Cade to Allie Cade, 11, 22 March 1863, Anderson Collection; Lelia Bailey, "The Life and Public Career of O. M. Roberts, 1815–1883" (Ph.D. diss., University of Texas at Austin, 1932), 133–36; "Statement of facts about Col. Randall's [*sic*] Regt," 3 February 1863, Oran M. Roberts Papers, University of Texas at Austin, Center for American History; Brown, *Journey to Pleasant Hill,* 153.

16. The secretary of war provided Cade with a commission dating from 22 September 1862. Dr. Jones's commission dated from 14 October 1862, so Cade was named as ranking surgeon in Randal's brigade. Edward W. Cade to Allie Cade, 20 April, 9 July 1863, Anderson Collection.

17. Bearss, *Campaign for Vicksburg,* 3: 1154–55; Robert L. Kerby, *Kirby Smith's Confederacy: The Trans-Mississippi South, 1863–1865* (New York: Columbia University Press, 1972; reprint, Tuscaloosa: University of Alabama Press, 1991), 98–99, 105; Blessington, *Campaigns of Walker's Texas Division,* 78; Faust, *Historical Times Illustrated Encyclopedia,* 569.

18. Theophilus Perry to Harriet Perry, 23, 25 April 1863, Person Papers; Bearss, *Campaign for Vicksburg,* 3: 1203; S. W. Farrow to Josephine Farrow, 30 April 1863, Farrow Papers.

19. Blessington, *Campaigns of Walker's Texas Division,* 79; Brown, *Journey to Pleasant Hill,* 204–7; John G. Walker, "The War of Secession West of the Mississippi River during the Years 1863–4–& 5," 26, Myron G. Gwinner Collection, United States Military History Institute, Carlisle Barracks, Pennsylvania; S. W. Farrow to Josephine Farrow, 30 April 1863, Farrow Papers; Theophilus Perry to Harriet Perry, 18 May 1863, Person Papers.

20. S. W. Farrow to Josephine Farrow, 7 May 1863, Farrow Papers; Blessington, *Campaigns of Walker's Texas Division*, 80; Lawrence E. Estaville Jr., *Confederate Neckties: Louisiana Railroads in the Civil War* (Ruston: Louisiana Tech University, 1989), 61, 65; Theophilus Perry to Harriet Perry, 7 May 1863, Person Papers.

21. Porter, "Early Days of Pittsburg, Texas, 1859–1874,"14, Confederate Research Center, 18th Texas Infantry file; Brown, *Journey to Pleasant Hill*, 215; Bearss, *Campaign for Vicksburg*, 3: 700, 1158–60.

22. Bearss, *Campaign for Vicksburg*, 3: 1160, 1162, 1165–66; Kerby, *Kirby Smith's Confederacy*, 112.

23. Edward W. Cade to Allie Cade, 20 May 1863, Anderson Collection; Brown, *Journey to Pleasant Hill*, 217; Paul E. Steiner, *Disease in the Civil War: Natural Biological Warfare in 1861–1865* (Springfield, Ill.: Charles C. Thomas, 1968), 14–15; John Q. Anderson, ed., *Brokenburn: The Journal of Kate Stone, 1861–1868* (Baton Rouge: Louisiana State University Press, 1955), 212; Calvin D. Cowles, comp., *Atlas to Accompany the Official Records of the Union and Confederate Armies* (1891–1895; reprint, New York: Arno Press, 1978), plate 155; Theophilus Perry to Harriet Perry, 18 May 1863, Person Papers.

24. Theophilus Perry to Harriet Perry, 25 April, 18, 23 May 1863, Person Papers.

25. Faust, *Historical Times Illustrated Encyclopedia*, 743–44; See also T. Michael Parrish, *Richard Taylor: Soldier Prince of Dixie* (Chapel Hill: University of North Carolina Press, 1992) and Richard Taylor, *Destruction and Reconstruction: Personal Experiences of the Late War* (New York: D. Appleton and Company, 1879) for further information about Richard Taylor.

26. Blessington, *Campaigns of Walker's Texas Division*, 83; Theophilus Perry to Harriet Perry, 23, 27 May 1863, Person Papers; Cowles, *Atlas to Accompany the Official Records*, plate 155; Bearss, *Campaign for Vicksburg*, 2: 461, 480–81, 562, 3: 1166–67, 1174.

27. Brown, *Journey to Pleasant Hill*, 221, 228; Theophilus Perry to Harriet Perry, 27, 29 May 1863, Person Papers; Bearss, *Campaign for Vicksburg*, 3: 1168–69.

28. Blessington, *Campaigns of Walker's Texas Division*, 85; Brown, *Journey to Pleasant Hill*, 228–30.

29. Theophilus Perry to Harriet Perry, 1 June 1863, Person Papers; Cowles, *Atlas to Accompany the Official Records*, plate 155; Bearss, *Campaign for Vicksburg*, 3: 1170–72.

30. Bearss, *Campaign for Vicksburg*, 3: 1172–73, 1177; Cowles, *Atlas to Accompany the Official Records*, plate 155; Edward W. Cade to Allie Cade, early June 1863, Anderson Collection; Theophilus Perry to Harriet Perry, 1 June 1863, Person Papers.

31. Blessington, *Campaigns of Walker's Texas Division*, 94; Bearss, *Campaign for Vicksburg*, 3: 1174, 1177, 1186; Cowles, *Atlas to Accompany the Official Records*, plate 155; Theophilus Perry to Harriet Perry, 11 June 1863, Person Papers; Cowles.

32. The black regiments had been in service for less than two weeks. Theophilus Perry to Harriet Perry, 11 June 1863, Person Papers; Bearss, *Campaign for Vicksburg*, 3: 1175, 1179–88; Parrish, *Richard Taylor*, 289; U.S. War Department, *War of the Rebellion: A Compilation of the Official Records of the Union and Confederate Armies*, 128 vols, (Washington, D.C.: Government Printing Office, 1880–1901), ser. I, 24, pt. 2, 446–48; John D. Winters, *The Civil War in Louisiana* (Baton Rouge: Louisiana State University Press, 1963), 199–202.

33. Dudley Taylor Cornish, *The Sable Arm: Negro Troops in the Union Army, 1861–1865* (New York: Longmans, Green and Co., 1956), 145, 163; Joseph T. Glatthaar, *Forged in Battle: The Civil War Alliance of Black Soldiers and White Officers* (New York: The Free Press, 1990), 134; Bearss, *Campaign for Vicksburg*, 3: 1206; Bell Irvin Wiley, *The Life of Johnny Reb: The Common Soldier of the Confederacy* (Indianapolis, Ind.: Bobbs-Merrill, 1943; reprint, Baton Rouge: Louisiana State University Press, 1986), 314; *Official Records*, ser. I, 24, pt. 2: 459, 467.

34. The battle of Milliken's Bend occurred weeks before the famous action of the 54th Massachusetts Colored Regiment at Fort Wagner, South Carolina, on 18 July 1863. Faust, *Historical Illustrated Encyclopedia*, 480; Theophilus Perry to Harriet Perry, 11 June 1863, Person Papers; Anderson, *Brokenburn*, 219.

35. Bearss, *Campaign for Vicksburg*, 3: 1189–95; Edward W. Cade to Allie Cade, 14 June 1863, Anderson Collection; Theophilus Perry to Harriet Perry, 20 June, 9 July 1863, Person Papers.

36. Bearss, *Campaign for Vicksburg*, 3: 1198–201; Junius Newport Bragg, *Letters of a Confederate Surgeon* (Camden, Ark.: n.p., 1960), 142–43; Anne J. Bailey, "A Texas Cavalry Raid: Reaction to Black Soldiers and Contrabands," *Civil War History* 35 (June 1989): 146; S. W. Farrow to Josephine Farrow, 4 July 1863, Farrow Papers; Edward W. Cade to Allie Cade, 9 July 1863, Anderson Collection.

37. Bearss, *Campaign for Vicksburg*, 3: 1198–201; Bragg, *Letters of a Confederate Surgeon*, 142–43; Blessington, *Campaigns of Walker's Texas Division*, 114; *Official Records*, ser. I, 24, pt. 2: 466; Bailey, "Texas Cavalry Raid," 143–45; Jon Harrison, ed., "The Confederate Letters of John Simmons," 34, Confederate Research Center, 22nd Texas Infantry file.

38. Theophilus Perry to Harriet Perry, 4, 9 July 1863, Person Papers; National Archives and Records Administration, Compiled Service Records of Confederate Soldiers Who Served in Organizations from the State of Texas (microfilm M323), reel 143; Bearss, *Campaign for Vicksburg*, 3: 1202.

39. Ledger Book 4, 11th Texas Infantry Description Books, Texas State Archives, Austin, Tex.

CHAPTER 4
SOLDIER LIFE IN THE TRANS-MISSISSIPPI

1. Robert L. Kerby, *Kirby Smith's Confederacy: The Trans-Mississippi South, 1863–1865* (New York: Columbia University Press, 1972; reprint, Tuscaloosa: University of Alabama Press, 1991), 1; S. W. Farrow to Josephine Farrow, 11 July 1863, S. W. Farrow Papers, University of Texas at Austin, Center for American History; Theophilus Perry to Harriet Perry, 9 July 1863, Presley Carter Person Papers, Duke University Library, Durham, N.C.; Joseph P. Blessington, *The Campaigns of Walker's Division, by a Private Soldier* (New York: Lange, Little & Co., 1875), 116–17; Edward W. Cade to Allie Cade, 9 July 1863, John Q. Anderson Collection, Texas State Archives, Austin, Tex.; Thomas W. Cutrer, ed., "'An Experience in Soldier's Life': The Civil War Letters of Volney Ellis, Adjutant, Twelfth Texas Infantry, Walker's Texas Division, C.S.A.," *Military History of the Southwest* 22 (fall 1992): 133.

2. Edward W. Cade to Allie Cade, 16, 30 July 1863, Anderson Collection. The number of men present for duty in the 28th Texas Cavalry can be ascertained from the compiled

service records. In the reporting period of May–June 1863, 386 men were aggregate present. In July–August 1863, this increased to 429 men aggregate present. National Archives and Records Administration, Compiled Service Records of Confederate Soldiers Who Served in Organizations from the State of Texas (microfilm M323), reels 143–146; John G. Walker, "The War of Secession West of the Mississippi River during the Years 1863–4–& 5," 31, Myron G. Gwinner Collection, United States Military History Institute, Carlisle Barracks, Pennsylvania.

3. Theophilus Perry to Harriet Perry, 17 July 1863, Person Papers.

4. Edward W. Cade to Allie Cade, 9 July 1863, Anderson Collection; Paul E. Steiner, *Disease in the Civil War: Natural Biological Warfare in 1861–1865* (Springfield, Ill.: Charles C. Thomas, 1968), 16–17, 21, 23; H. H. Cunningham, *Doctors in Gray: The Confederate Medical Service* (Baton Rouge: Louisiana State University Press, 1958), 173–74.

5. J. Woodfin Wilson Jr., "Some Aspects of Medical Services in the Trans-Mississippi Department of the Confederate States of America, 1862–1865," *North Louisiana Historical Association Journal* 12, no. 4 (1981), 125, 128, 131, 133.

6. Walker, "The War of Secession," 31–32, Gwinner Collection; Compiled Service Records, reels 143–146; David M. Ray to his mother, 28 July 1863, David M. Ray Papers, University of Texas at Austin, Center for American History.

7. Compiled Service Records, reels 143–146.

8. Compiled Service Records, reels 143–146; Max S. Lale, "A Letter from Leonard Randal to his Son," *East Texas Historical Association* 23, no. 2 (1985): 48 (a copy of this letter is also in Leonard Randal's compiled service record).

9. Compiled Service Records, reel 143.

10. Compiled Service Records, reel 146.

11. Compiled Service Records, reels 143–146.

12. Douglas Hale, "The Third Texas Cavalry: A Socioeconomic Profile of a Confederate Regiment," *Military History of the Southwest* 19 (spring 1989): 14, 24–25.

13. Kerby, *Kirby Smith's Confederacy*, 1–2, 4–6, 12.

14. Kerby, *Kirby Smith's Confederacy*, 136, 143, 149.

15. Kerby, *Kirby Smith's Confederacy*, 143; James L. Nichols, *The Confederate Quartermaster in the Trans-Mississippi* (Austin: University of Texas Press, 1964), 14; Compiled Service Records, reels 143–146.

16. Compiled Service Records, reels 143–146; "Return of Captain J. M. Daniel's Company of the Lamar Artillery," May 1863, Louisiana Historical Association Collection, Tulane University Library, New Orleans, La.; Kerby, *Kirby Smith's Confederacy*, 68–69.

17. Edward W. Cade to Allie Cade, 9 July 1863, Anderson Collection; Compiled Service Records, reels 143–146; Theophilus Perry to Harriet Perry, 18 January 1864, Person Papers.

18. Albert Burton Moore, *Conscription and Conflict in the Confederacy* (New York: Macmillan, 1924), 115; Kerby, *Kirby Smith's Confederacy*, 89–91, 276.

19. Kerby, *Kirby Smith's Confederacy*, 73–75; Patricia L. Faust, ed., *Historical Times Illustrated Encyclopedia of the Civil War* (New York: Harper & Row, 1986), 282.

20. Kerby, *Kirby Smith's Confederacy*, 76–77; "Ordnance Report of Walker's Division in Camp near Alexandria, Louisiana," 8 August 1863, Louisiana Historical Association Collection.

21. U.S. War Department, *War of the Rebellion: A Compilation of the Official Records of the Union and Confederate Armies,* 128 vols. (Washington, D.C.: Government Printing Office, 1880–1901), ser. I, 26, pt. 1: 359, 394; James M. McPherson, *Ordeal by Fire: The Civil War and Reconstruction* (New York: McGraw-Hill, 1992), 198; "Report of Ordnance and Ordnance Stores for Walker's Division," 18 June 1864, Louisiana Historical Association Collection.

22. Bell Irvin Wiley, *The Life of Johnny Reb: The Common Soldier of the Confederacy* (Indianapolis, Ind.: Bobbs-Merrill, 1943; reprint, Baton Rouge: Louisiana State University Press, 1986), 290–91; Theophilus Perry to Harriet Perry, 5 September 1862, Person Papers; Francis A. Lord, *Civil War Collector's Encyclopedia: Arms, Uniforms, and Equipment of the Union and Confederacy* (Harrisburg, Pa.: Stackpole, 1963; reprint, Secaucus, N.J.: Castle Books, 1982), 247; Faust, *Historical Times Illustrated Encyclopedia,* 153; Janet B. Hewett et al, eds., *Supplement to the Official Records of the Union and Confederate Armies* (Wilmington, N.C.: Broadfoot Publishing, 1994–), part 1, 4: 831.

23. Ledger Book 4, 11th Texas Infantry Description Books, Texas State Archives, Austin, Tex.; Kerby, *Kirby Smith's Confederacy,* 64–65.

24. Blessington, *Campaigns of Walker's Texas Division,* 115; Kerby, *Kirby Smith's Confederacy,* 65–67.

25. S. W. Farrow to Josephine Farrow, 19 July, 6 August 1863, Farrow Papers; Edward W. Cade to Allie Cade, 10 September 1863, Anderson Collection; Theophilus Perry to Harriet Perry, 14 February 1864, Person Papers; Nichols, *Confederate Quartermaster,* 27–28; Compiled Service Records, reel 144.

26. Harriet Perry to Theophilus Perry, 24 September, 4 October 1862, Person Papers; Kerby, *Kirby Smith's Confederacy,* 67; Nichols, *Confederate Quartermaster,* 20–22, 25.

27. Allie Cade to Edward W. Cade, 6 September 1863, Anderson Collection; Harriet Perry to Theophilus Perry, 3 August, 4, 26 October 1862, Person Papers.

CHAPTER 5
WALKER'S GREYHOUNDS

1. Norman D. Brown, ed., *Journey to Pleasant Hill: The Civil War Letters of Captain Elijah P. Petty, Walker's Texas Division, C.S.A.* (San Antonio: University of Texas Institute of Texan Cultures, 1982), 302; Edwin C. Bearss, *The Campaign for Vicksburg,* 3 vols. (Dayton, Ohio: Morningside House, 1991), 3: 1166–67; T. Michael Parrish, *Richard Taylor: Soldier Prince of Dixie* (Chapel Hill: University of North Carolina Press, 1992), 300–303; Robert L. Kerby, *Kirby Smith's Confederacy: The Trans-Mississippi South, 1863–1865* (New York: Columbia University Press, 1972; reprint, Tuscaloosa: University of Alabama Press, 1991), 238.

2. Lelia Bailey, "The Life and Public Career of O. M. Roberts, 1815–1883" (Ph.D. diss., University of Texas at Austin, 1932), 139; Theophilus Perry to Harriet Perry, 17 July 1863, Presley Carter Person Papers, Duke University Library, Durham, N.C.; Joseph P. Blessington, *The Campaigns of Walker's Texas Division, by a Private Soldier* (New York: Lange, Little & Co., 1875), 127–28, 130–31; Calvin D. Cowles, comp., *Atlas to Accompany the Official Records of the Union and Confederate Armies* (1891–1895; reprint, New York: Arno Press, 1978), plate 155; Edward W. Cade to Allie Cade, 30 July 1863, John Q. Anderson Collection, Texas

State Archives, Austin, Tex.; S. W. Farrow to Josephine Farrow, 21 July, 6 August 1863, S. W. Farrow Papers, University of Texas at Austin, Center for American History; David M. Ray to his mother, 28 July 1863, David M. Ray Papers, University of Texas at Austin, Center for American History; John C. Porter, "Early Days of Pittsburg, Texas, 1859–1874," 18, Hill College, Confederate Research Center, Hillsboro, Tex., 18th Texas Infantry file.

3. S. W. Farrow to Josephine Farrow, 17 July 1863, Farrow Papers; Edward W. Cade to Allie Cade, 12, 16 July 1863, Anderson Collection; David M. Ray to his mother, 28 July 1863, Ray Papers; Parrish, *Richard Taylor,* 305–6.

4. Edward W. Cade to Allie Cade, 9 July 1863, Anderson Collection; S. W. Farrow to Josephine Farrow, 19, 30 July, 6 August 1863, Farrow Papers; Theophilus Perry to Harriet Perry, 12 July 1863, Person Papers.

5. Theophilus Perry to Harriet Perry, 12, 17 July 1863, Person Papers; S. W. Farrow to Josephine Farrow, 19, 30 July, 16 August 1863, Farrow Papers; Edward W. Cade to Allie Cade, 9 July 1863, Anderson Collection.

6. Theophilus Perry to Harriet Perry, 12, 17, 29 July 1863, Person Papers; National Archives and Records Administration, Compiled Service Records of Confederate Soldiers Who Served in Organizations from the State of Texas (microfilm M323), reels 143–146.

7. Edward W. Cade to Allie Cade, 22 September 1863, Anderson Collection; David M. Ray to Martha, 12 September 1863, David M. Ray to his mother, 11 September 1863, Ray Papers; Compiled Service Records, reels 143–146.

8. Bell Irvin Wiley, *The Life of Johnny Reb: The Common Soldier of the Confederacy* (Indianapolis, Ind.: Bobbs-Merrill, 1943; reprint, Baton Rouge: Louisiana State University Press, 1986), 174–75; Edward W. Cade to Allie Cade, 16 July, 24 November 1863, Anderson Collection; Theophilus Perry to Harriet Perry, 14 July 1862, Person Papers.

9. Wiley, *Life of Johnny Reb,* 180, 183–84; David M. Ray to Martha, 12 September 1863, Ray Papers; Compiled Service Records, reel 146.

10. Compiled Service Records, reel 146; *Memorial and Biographical History: McLennan, Falls, Bell and Coryell Counties, Texas* (Chicago: Lewis Publishing, 1893), 527–28; John Q. Anderson, ed., *A Texas Surgeon in the C.S.A.,* Confederate Centennial Studies (Tuscaloosa, Ala.: Confederate Publishing, 1957), 26, 83; Martin V. Smith to his sister Ella, 3 November 1863, Anderson Collection.

11. Theophilus Perry to Harriet Perry, 8 December 1863, Person Papers; Edward W. Cade to Allie Cade, 6 October, 20, 24 November, 11 December 1863, Anderson Collection; David M. Ray to Martha, 12 September 1863, David M. Ray to his mother, 11 October 1863, Ray Papers; Martin V. Smith to his sister Ella, 3 November 1863, Anderson Collection.

12. U.S. War Department, *War of the Rebellion: A Compilation of the Official Records of the Union and Confederate Armies,* 128 vols. (Washington, D.C.: Government Printing Office, 1880–1901), ser. I, 26, pt. 1: 273, 280–81, ser. I, 31, pt. 1: 817, 824; Cowles, *Atlas to Accompany the Official Records,* plate 155; John D. Winters, *The Civil War in Louisiana* (Baton Rouge: Louisiana State University Press, 1963), 302–3; Walter Lord, ed., *The Fremantle Diary: Being the Journal of Lieutenant Colonel Arthur James Lyon Fremantle, Coldstream Guards, on his Three Months in the Southern States* (Boston: Little, Brown, and Co., 1954), 74–75.

13. *Official Records of the Union and Confederate Armies,* ser. I, 26, pt. 1: 280–81; Cowles, *Atlas to Accompany the Official Records,* plate 155; Blessington, *Campaigns of Walker's Texas Division,* 53.

14. *Official Records of the Union and Confederate Armies,* ser. I, 26, pt. I: 274; Winters, *Civil War in Louisiana,* 303; Compiled Service Records, reel 145; Edward W. Cade to Allie Cade, 10, 13 September 1863, Anderson Collection.

15. Parrish, *Richard Taylor,* 307; Kerby, *Kirby Smith's Confederacy,* 224, 240, 242.

16. Patricia L. Faust, ed., *Historical Times Illustrated Encyclopedia of the Civil War* (New York: Harper & Row, 1986), 650; Mark M. Boatner III, *The Civil War Dictionary* (New York: David McKay, 1959), 716; Parrish, *Richard Taylor,* 308–9; *Official Records of the Union and Confederate Armies,* ser. I, 26, pt. 2: 280; David C. Edmonds, *Yankee Autumn in Acadiana: A Narrative of the Great Texas Overland Expedition through Southwestern Louisiana, October– December 1863* (Lafayette, La.: Acadiana Press, 1979), 10; Cowles, *Atlas to Accompany the Official Records,* plate 156.

17. Kerby, *Kirby Smith's Confederacy,* 243; Cowles, *Atlas to Accompany the Official Records,* plate 156.

18. Edmonds, *Yankee Autumn in Acadiana,* 213, 237; Brown, *Journey to Pleasant Hill,* 260–61; Thomas W. Cutrer, ed., "'Bully for Flournoy's Regiment, We Are Some Punkins, You'll Bet': The Civil War Letters of Virgil Sullivan Rabb, Captain, Company 'I,' Sixteenth Texas Infantry, C.S.A.," *Military History of the Southwest* 19 (fall 1989): 183; David M. Ray to Martha, 7 October 1863, Ray Papers; Cowles, *Atlas to Accompany the Official Records,* plate 156; Blessington, *Campaigns of Walker's Texas Division,* 132–33.

19. Brown, *Journey to Pleasant Hill,* 264–65, 267–69; Blessington, *Campaigns of Walker's Texas Division,* 133; Cowles, *Atlas to Accompany the Official Records,* plate 156; U.S. Naval War Records Office, *Official Records of the Union and Confederate Navies in the War of the Rebellion,* 30 vols. (Washington, D.C.: Government Printing Office, 1894–1922), ser. I, 25: 450–51, 456–57; S. W. Farrow to Josephine Farrow, 8 October 1863, Farrow Papers.

20. S. W. Farrow to Josephine Farrow, 8 October 1863, Farrow Papers; David M. Ray to Martha, 7 October 1863, David M. Ray to his mother, 11 October 1863, Ray Papers.

21. S. W. Farrow to Josephine Farrow, 28 October 1863, Farrow Papers; Parrish, *Richard Taylor,* 310–11; Kerby, *Kirby Smith's Confederacy,* 244–45; Edmonds, *Yankee Autumn in Acadiana,* 239–41; Blessington, *Campaigns of Walker's Texas Division,* 135–37; Faust, *Historical Times Illustrated Encyclopedia,* 663.

22. Kerby, *Kirby Smith's Confederacy,* 245–46; Edmonds, *Yankee Autumn in Acadiana,* 296, 353; *Official Records of the Union and Confederate Armies,* ser. I, 26, pt. I: 395; Bailey, "Life and Public Career of O. M. Roberts," 141–42.

23. Martin V. Smith to his sister Ella, 3 November 1863, Anderson Collection; Blessington, *Campaigns of Walker's Texas Division,* 137; Brown, *Journey to Pleasant Hill,* 276; Compiled Service Records, reel 143.

24. John G. Walker, "The War of Secession West of the Mississippi River during the Years 1863–4–& 5," 40, Myron G. Gwinner Collection, United States Military History Institute, Carlisle Barracks, Pennsylvania; Edward W. Cade to Allie Cade, 19, 20 November 1863, Anderson Collection; Janet B. Hewett et al, eds., *Supplement to the Official Records of the Union and Confederate Armies* (Wilmington, N.C.: Broadfoot Publishing,1994–), part 1, 4: 841–42; Blessington, *Campaigns of Walker's Texas Division,* 150–52; Brown, *Journey to Pleasant Hill,* 280–82.

25. Edward W. Cade to Allie Cade, 22, 24, 27, 28 November 1863, Anderson Collection; Brown, *Journey to Pleasant Hill,* 279, 286; Blessington, *Campaigns of Walker's Texas Division,* 153, 155, 157; Walker, "The War of Secession," 40, Gwinner Collection.

26. Blessington, *Campaigns of Walker's Texas Division,* 157; Cowles, *Atlas to Accompany the Official Records,* plate 155.

27. Gerald F. Linderman, *Embattled Courage: The Experience of Combat in the American Civil War* (New York: Free Press, 1987), 169; James M. McPherson, *Ordeal by Fire: The Civil War and Reconstruction* (New York: McGraw-Hill, 1992), 175; Theophilus Perry to Harriet Perry, 8 December 1863, 8, 12 January 1864, Person Papers; Compiled Service Records, reels 144, 146; Edward W. Cade to Allie Cade, 20 December 1863, Allie Cade to Edward W. Cade, 29 December 1863, Anderson Collection.

28. Theophilus Perry to Harriet Perry, 8, 12 January 1864, Person Papers; S. W. Farrow to Josephine Farrow, 14 February 1864, Farrow Papers; Brown, *Journey to Pleasant Hill,* 324–25.

29. Theophilus Perry to Harriet Perry, 8, 29 January 1864, Person Papers; J. H. Armstrong to Martha Armstrong, 19 December 1863, Hill College, Confederate Research Center, Hillsboro, Tex., 14th Texas Infantry file.

30. Theophilus Perry to Harriet Perry, 8 January, 21 February 1864, Person Papers; S. W. Farrow to Josephine Farrow, 7 February 1864, Farrow Papers; Compiled Service Records, reel 146; Brown, *Journey to Pleasant Hill,* 294.

31. Theophilus Perry to Harriet Perry, 29 January, 21 February, 1, 3 March 1864, Person Papers; Richard Taylor, *Destruction and Reconstruction: Personal Experiences in the Late War* (New York: D. Appleton and Company, 1879), 153; Blessington, *Campaigns of Walker's Texas Division,* 164; Parrish, *Richard Taylor,* 320; Bearss, *Campaign for Vicksburg,* 3: 699; Kerby, *Kirby Smith's Confederacy,* 287, 294; J. H. Armstrong to Martha Armstrong, 5 January 1864, Confederate Research Center, 14th Texas Infantry file.

32. David M. Ray to his mother, 6 March 1864, Ray Papers; Theophilus Perry to Harriet Perry, 9 March 1864, Person Papers.

33. Unfortunately, no other information can be provided about this mutiny. Questions pertaining to what sparked the mutiny or the final disposition of the inciters are unanswerable at this time. Theophilus Perry to Harriet Perry, 9, 13, 17 March 1864, Person Papers; J. H. Armstrong to Martha Armstrong, 9 March 1864, Confederate Research Center, 14th Texas Infantry file; Jon Harrison, ed., "The Confederate Letters of John Simmons," 39, Confederate Research Center, 22nd Texas Infantry file.

34. Theophilus Perry to Harriet Perry, 9, 13 March 1864, Person Papers; Ludwell H. Johnson, *Red River Campaign: Politics and Cotton in the Civil War* (Baltimore: Johns Hopkins Press, 1958), 90.

CHAPTER 6
THE RED RIVER CAMPAIGN

1. Patricia L. Faust, ed., *Historical Times Illustrated Encyclopedia* (New York: Harper & Row, 1986), 677; William Allan, *History of the Campaign of Gen. T. J. (Stonewall) Jackson in the Shenandoah Valley of Virginia from November 4, 1861, to June 17, 1862* (1912; reprint, Dayton, Ohio: Morningside Bookshop, 1974), 156, 162; John G. Walker, "The War of Secession West of the Mississippi River during the Years 1863–4–& 5," 68, Myron G. Gwinner Collection, United States Military History Institute, Carlisle Barracks, Pennsylvania.

2. Robert L. Kerby, *Kirby Smith's Confederacy: The Trans-Mississippi South, 1863–1865* (New York: Columbia University Press, 1972; reprint, Tuscaloosa: University of Alabama Press, 1991), 290–91; Richard Leslie Kiper Jr., "Dead-end at the Crossroads: The Battles of Mansfield (Sabine Crossroads) and Pleasant Hill, Louisiana, 8 and 9 April 1864" (master's thesis, Rice University, 1976), 182–86; Frederick H. Dyer, *A Compendium of the War of the Rebellion*, 2 vols. (1908; reprint, Dayton, Ohio: Morningside Bookshop, 1978), 1072, 1165, 1298; Ludwell H. Johnson, *Red River Campaign: Politics and Cotton in the Civil War* (Baltimore: Johns Hopkins Press, 1958), 84; T. Michael Parrish, *Richard Taylor: Soldier Prince of Dixie* (Chapel Hill: University of North Carolina Press, 1992), 322.

3. Ludwell H. Johnson, "The Red River Campaign," in *The Civil War Battlefield Guide*, ed. Frances H. Kennedy (Boston: Houghton Mifflin, 1990), 163; Johnson, *Red River Campaign*, 5–7, 13, 34–35, 45, 47; Parrish, *Richard Taylor*, 318.

4. Kerby, *Kirby Smith's Confederacy*, 283–86, 288; Parrish, *Richard Taylor*, 317–18.

5. Theophilus Perry to Harriet Perry, 13, 17 March 1864, Presley Carter Person Papers, Duke University Library, Durham, N.C.; Kerby, *Kirby Smith's Confederacy*, 295; Max S. Lale, "For Lack of a Nail," *East Texas Historical Journal* 30, no. 1 (1992): 36 (diary of Capt. N. S. Allen, 14th Texas Infantry); Edwin C. Bearss, ed., *A Louisiana Confederate: Diary of Felix Pierre Poché* (Natchitoches: Louisiana Studies Institute, Northwestern State University, 1972), 94; Johnson, *Red River Campaign*, 90.

6. U.S. War Department, *War of the Rebellion: A Compilation of the Official Records of the Union and Confederate Armies,* 128 vols. (Washington, D.C.: Government Printing Office, 1880–1901), ser. I, 34, pt. 1: 224, 305, 314, 600–601; John C. Porter, "Early Days of Pittsburg, Texas, 1859–1874," 27, Hill College, Confederate Research Center, Hillsboro, Tex., 18th Texas Infantry file; Edward W. Cade to Allie Cade, 18 March 1864, John Q. Anderson Collection, Texas State Archives, Austin, Tex.; Kerby, *Kirby Smith's Confederacy*, 295; Johnson, *Red River Campaign*, 93; National Archives and Records Administration, Compiled Service Records of Confederate Soldiers Who Served in Organizations from the State of Texas (microfilm M323), reels, 143–146.

7. Compiled Service Records, reels 143–146; Porter, "Early Days," Confederate Research Center, 18th Texas Infantry file.

8. Theophilus Perry to Harriet Perry, 17 March 1864, Person Papers; Harrison, Jon, ed., "The Confederate Letters of John Simmons," 40, Confederate Research Center, 22nd Texas Infantry file; Lale, "For Lack of a Nail," 37; Edward W. Cade to Allie Cade, 18 March 1864, Anderson Collection; Johnson, *Red River Campaign*, 96; Parrish, *Richard Taylor*, 327; Thomas W. Cutrer, ed., "'An Experience in Soldier's Life': The Civil War Letters of Volney Ellis, Adjutant, Twelfth Texas Infantry, Walker's Texas Division, C.S.A.," *Military History of the Southwest* 22 (fall 1992): 151.

9. Lale, "For Lack of a Nail," 37; Theophilus Perry to Harriet Perry, 19 March 1864, Person Papers; *Official Records,* ser. I, 34, pt. 1, 326, 562; Johnson, *Red River Campaign*, 97; Parrish, *Richard Taylor*, 321, 330.

10. Joseph P. Blessington, *The Campaigns of Walker's Texas Division by a Private Soldier* (New York; Lange, Little & Co., 1875), 178; Jon Harrison, ed., "The Confederate Letters of John Simmons," 41, Confederate Research Center, 22nd Texas Infantry file; Lale, "For Lack of a Nail," 37–38; Norman D. Brown, ed., *Journey to Pleasant Hill: The Civil War Letters of Captain Elijah P. Petty, Walker's Texas Division, C.S.A.* (San Antonio: University of Texas

Institute of Texan Cultures, 1982), 382; Edward W. Cade to Allie Cade, 22 March 1864, Anderson Collection; S. W. Farrow to Josephine Farrow, 23, 29 March 1864, S. W. Farrow Papers, University of Texas at Austin, Center for American History; Theophilus Perry to Harriet Perry, 23, 24 March 1864, Person Papers.

11. J. H. Armstrong to Martha Armstrong, 1 April 1864, Confederate Research Center, 14th Texas Infantry file; Theophilus Perry to Harriet Perry, 23 March 1864, Person Papers; S. W. Farrow to Josephine Farrow, 23, 29 March 1864, Farrow Papers.

12. Johnson, *Red River Campaign,* 83, 98–99, 101, 106–7, 109–10.

13. Blessington, *Campaigns of Walker's Texas Division,* 179; Lale, "For Lack of a Nail," 38–39; J. H. Armstrong to Martha Armstrong, 1 April 1864, Confederate Research Center, 14th Texas Infantry file; Calvin D. Cowles, comp., *Atlas to Accompany the Official Records of the Union and Confederate Armies* (1891–1895; reprint, New York: Arno Press, 1978), plate 158; Compiled Service Records, reels 143–146.

14. Johnson, *Red River Campaign,* 110–13, 115–17.

15. Lale, "For Lack of a Nail," 39; Edward W. Cade to Allie Cade, 5 April 1864, Anderson Collection; Kiper, "Dead-end at the Crossroads," 180; Taylor, *Destruction and Reconstruction,* 161; Johnson, *Red River Campaign,* 114, 119–20.

16. Blessington, *Campaigns of Walker's Texas Division,* 181; Parrish, *Richard Taylor,* 333–35; Johnson, *Red River Campaign,* 121–23, 129, 131; Taylor, *Destruction and Reconstruction,* 161–62.

17. Taylor, *Destruction and Reconstruction,* 160–61; Diary of Capt. John Thomas Stark, 8 April 1864, Confederate Research Center, 13th Texas Cavalry file; Lale, "For Lack of a Nail," 39; Blessington, *Campaigns of Walker's Texas Division,* 183; Johnson, *Red River Campaign,* 131; Parrish, *Richard Taylor,* 341.

18. Blessington, *Campaigns of Walker's Texas Division,* 185; *Galveston (Tex.) Weekly News,* 20 April 1864; *Official Records,* ser. I, 34, pt. 1, 563–64; Mark M. Boatner III, *The Civil War Dictionary* (New York: David McKay, 1959), 229; X. B. Debray, "A Sketch of Debray's Twenty-Sixth Regiment of Texas Cavalry," *Southern Historical Society Papers* 13 (1885): 158; Parrish, *Richard Taylor,* 341.

19. Johnson, *Red River Campaign,* 127–28, 133; Theodore P. Savas, "A Death at Mansfield: Col. James Hamilton Beard and the Consolidated Crescent Regiment," *Civil War Regiments: A Journal of the American Civil War* 4, no. 2 (1994): 95; Dyer, *A Compendium of the War of the Rebellion,* 2: 1079, 1100, 1144, 1205–6, 1519, 1535, 1539, 1683; Taylor, *Destruction and Reconstruction,* 162; Compiled Service Records, reels 143–146; Ledger Book 4, 11th Texas Infantry Description Books, Texas State Archives, Austin, Tex. Richard Taylor, in *Destruction and Reconstruction: Personal Experiences in the Late War* (New York: D. Appleton and Co., 1879), 162, stated the infantry of Mouton's division and Walker's division totaled about 5,300 on 8 April. In his memoirs written after the war, John G. Walker stated that his division numbered 3,800 on 8 April. If this number is accurate then Mouton's division numbered 1,500 on that day. Walker, "The War of Secession," 52, Gwinner Collection. In November 1863 Mouton's division had numbered 3,275 and Walker's, 4,843. *Official Records,* ser. I, 26, pt. 2, 465.

20. Biography and Diaries of R. S. Gould, 64, Robert Simenton Gould Papers, University of Texas at Austin, Center for American History; Blessington, *Campaigns of Walker's Texas Division,* 185–86; Lale, "For Lack of a Nail," 39; Taylor, *Destruction and Reconstruction,* 163; *Official Records,* ser. I, 34, pt. 1, 564.

21. Taylor, *Destruction and Reconstruction*, 162–63; Blessington, *Campaigns of Walker's Texas Division*, 187; Robert S. Gould, 64, Gould Papers; *Official Records*, ser. I, 34, pt. 1, 297, 564; Jane Harris Johansson and David H. Johansson, "Two 'Lost' Battle Reports: Horace Randal's and Joseph L. Brent's Reports of the Battles of Mansfield and Pleasant Hill, 8 and 9 April 1864," *Military History of the West* 23 (fall 1993): 173; Arthur W. Bergeron Jr., "A Colonel Gains His Wreath: Henry Gray's Louisiana Brigade at the Battle of Mansfield, April 8, 1864," *Civil War Regiments: A Journal of the American Civil War* 4, no. 2 (1994): 20; Savas, "A Death at Mansfield," 95.

22. *Official Records*, ser. I, 34, pt. 1, 169, 228, 564; Diary of Capt. John Thomas Stark, 8 April 1864, Confederate Research Center, 13th Texas Cavalry file; G. B. Layton to Nancy Blewett, 18 April 1864, Confederate Research Center, 13th Texas Cavalry file; Johnson, *Red River Campaign*, 135–37; Johansson, "Two 'Lost' Battle Reports," 173–74.

23. Diary of Capt. John Thomas Stark, 8 April 1864, Confederate Research Center, 13th Texas Cavalry file; Johnson, *Red River Campaign*, 138–39; Robert S Gould, 65, Gould Papers; William F. Mills to his father and mother, 12 April 1864, Mansfield, Louisiana, State Commemorative Area; Parrish, *Richard Taylor*, 351–52; J. H. Armstrong to Martha Armstrong, 13 April 1864, Confederate Research Center, 14th Texas Infantry file.

24. *Official Records*, ser. I, 34, pt. 1, 564; Johnson, *Red River Campaign*, 134–35, 140–41.

25. Blessington, *Campaigns of Walker's Texas Division*, 193; Johnson, *Red River Campaign*, 114, 146–47, 153; Parrish, *Richard Taylor*, 356; *Official Records*, ser. I, 34, pt. 1, 565–66.

26. Taylor, *Destruction and Reconstruction*, 165, 167; *Official Records*, ser. I, 34, pt. 1, 566–68; Tom J. Waxham, Terry G. Waxham, and H. G. Waxham, "Battle of Pleasant Hill, La., 9 April 1864, Opening Phase of Battle," map, Mansfield, Louisiana, State Commemorative Area; Parrish, *Richard Taylor*, 360; Johnson, *Red River Campaign*, 149, 154–55, 168; Eldon Stephen Branda, ed., *The Handbook of Texas: A Supplement* (Austin: Texas State Historical Association, 1976), 3: 118; Debray, "Sketch of Debray's Twenty-Sixth Regiment of Texas Cavalry," 158; Johansson, "Two 'Lost' Battle Reports," 174.

27. Robert S. Gould, 66–67, Gould Papers; Johansson, "Two 'Lost' Battle Reports," 178, 180; *Official Records*, ser. I, 34, pt. 1, 313, 567–68; Johnson, *Red River Campaign*, 155–58.

28. Taylor, *Destruction and Reconstruction*, 168–70; Johnson, *Red River Campaign*, 157–58, 160; *Official Records*, ser. I, 34, pt. 1, 568–69; Kiper, "Dead-end at the Crossroads," 180; Johansson, "Two 'Lost' Battle Reports," 174; Harriet Perry, undated eulogy, Person Papers; *Galveston (Tex.) Weekly News*, 10 May 1864; Debray, "Sketch of Debray's Twenty-Sixth Regiment of Texas Cavalry," 158–59; Robert S. Gould, 69, Gould Papers.

29. William F. Mills to his father and mother, 12 April 1864, Mansfield, Louisiana, State Commemorative Area; J. H. Armstrong to Martha Armstrong, 13 April 1864, Confederate Research Center, 14th Texas Infantry file; *Galveston (Tex.) Weekly News*, 20 April, 10 May 1864; Johansson, "Two 'Lost' Battle Reports," 175–76; Harriet Perry, undated eulogy, Person Papers.

30. Johansson, "Two 'Lost' Battle Reports," 175–76.

31. Parrish, *Richard Taylor*, 373, 375–76, 383; Johnson, *Red River Campaign*, 235, 238–41.

32. Parrish, *Richard Taylor*, 382, 385, 388–90; Johnson, *Red River Campaign*, 266.

33. Parrish, *Richard Taylor*, 370–72.

CHAPTER 7
JENKINS' FERRY

1. Susan Merle Dotson, comp., *Who's Who of the Confederacy: A Symposium by the Members of the Albert Sidney Johnston Chapter No. 2060, United Daughters of the Confederacy* (San Antonio, Tex.: Naylor, 1966), 83, 85 (a transcription of a letter written by Major Henry G. Hall to his mother, 8 May 1864); Joseph P. Blessington, *The Campaigns of Walker's Texas Division by a Private Soldier* (New York: Lange, Little & Co., 1875), 241–48; U.S. War Department, *War of the Rebellion: A Compilation of the Official Records of the Union and Confederate Armies,* 128 vols. (Washington, D.C.: Government Printing Office, 1880–1901), ser. I, 34, pt. 1, 549; 34, pt. 3, 764; David M. Ray to his mother, 7 May 1864, David M. Ray Papers, University of Texas at Austin, Center for American History; Diary of Capt. John Thomas Stark, 28 April 1864, Hill College, Confederate Research Center, Hillsboro, Tex., 13th Texas Cavalry file.

2. Patricia L. Faust, ed., *Historical Times Encyclopedia of the Civil War* (New York: Harper & Row, 1986), 106; Richard N. Current, ed., *Encyclopedia of the Confederacy,* 4 vols. (New York: Simon & Schuster, 1993), 1: 55–57; Ludwell H. Johnson, *Red River Campaign: Politics and Cotton in the Civil War* (Baltimore: Johns Hopkins Press, 1958), 174.

3. *Official Records,* ser. I, 34, pt. 1, 657; Current, *Encyclopedia,* 1: 55–57; Johnson, *Red River Campaign,* 174.

4. Masterson, Ralph, ed., *Sketches of the Life of Dr. Horace Bishop* (San Angelo, Tex.[?]: n.p., ca. 1930), 9; Blessington, *Campaigns of Walker's Texas Division,* 248; David M. Ray to his mother, 7 May 1864, Ray Papers; *Official Records,* ser. I, 34, pt. 1, 816; Dotson, *Who's Who of the Confederacy,* 83.

5. Johnson, *Red River Campaign,* 196–99, 202; Biography and Diaries of R. S. Gould, 70, Robert Simenton Gould Papers, University of Texas at Austin, Center for American History; Dotson, *Who's Who of the Confederacy,* 83–84; *Official Records,* ser. I, 34, pt. 1, 816; Edwin C. Bearss, *Steele's Retreat from Camden and the Battle of Jenkin's [sic] Ferry* (Little Rock: Arkansas Civil War Centennial Commission, 1967), 119, 121, 146.

6. Bearss, *Steele's Retreat from Camden,* 117–22, 135, 147–48.

7. Bearss, *Steele's Retreat from Camden,* 148–49; Dotson, *Who's Who of the Confederacy,* 84; Robert S. Gould, 70–71, Gould Papers.

8. Dotson, *Who's Who of the Confederacy,* 84–85; Bearss, *Steele's Retreat from Camden,* 152–53; *Official Records,* ser. I, 34, pt. 1, 816–17; Robert S. Gould, 71, Gould Papers.

9. Dotson, *Who's Who of the Confederacy,* 85; Robert S. Gould, 71–72, Gould Papers; Bearss, *Steele's Retreat from Camden,* 146.

10. Diary of Capt. John Thomas Stark, 30 April 1864, Confederate Research Center, 13th Texas Cavalry file; Dotson, *Who's Who of the Confederacy,* 85–86; Robert S. Gould, 71–72, Gould Papers; *Official Records,* ser. I, 34 pt. 1, 818; Bearss, *Steele's Retreat from Camden,* 155–59.

11. Johnson, *Red River Campaign,* 202–3.

12. A. F. Sperry, *History of the 33rd Iowa Infantry: Volunteer Regiment, 1863–1866* (1866; reprint, Pine Bluff, Ark.: Rare Book Pub., 1982 [?]): 91; *Official Records,* ser. I, 34, pt. 1, 787; Alwyn Barr, "Texan Losses in the Red River Campaign, 1864," *Texas Military History* 3 (summer 1963): 106; *Houston (Tex.) Daily Telegraph,* 16 May 1864; National Archives and Records Administration, Compiled Service Records of Confederate Soldiers Who Served

in Organizations from the State of Texas (microfilm M323), reel 143; Blessington, *Campaigns of Walker's Texas Division,* 256.

13. Barr, "Texan Losses in the Red River Campaign," 108–9; Richard Taylor, *Destruction and Reconstruction: Personal Experiences in the Late War* (New York: D. Appleton and Co., 1879), 162; Walker, "The War of Secession West of the Mississippi River during the Years 1863–4–& 5," 52, Myron G. Gwinner Collection, United States Military History Institute, Carlisle Barracks, Pennsylvania.

14. Johnson, *Red River Campaign,* 279.

15. Edward W. Cade to Allie Cade, 6 May 1864, John Q. Anderson Collection, Texas State Archives, Austin, Tex.; Pat H. Martin to Mrs. S. E. Truit, 22 September 1862, James W. Truit Papers, University of Texas at Austin, Center for American History; Blessington, *Campaigns of Walker's Texas Division,* 254, 256, 260.

16. *Galveston (Tex.) Weekly News,* 10 May 1864; *Houston (Tex.) Daily Telegraph,* 16 May 1864; Compiled Service Records, reel 146; National Archives, Eighth Census of the United States, 1860 (microfilm M653), Schedule I (Free Inhabitants), reel 1290, 419, reel 1304, 400, Schedule II (Slave Inhabitants), reel 1309, 200.

17. J. Woodfin Wilson Jr., "Civil War Medicine in North Louisiana," *North Louisiana Historical Association Journal* 17, no. 2–3 (1986): 59–60; Blessington, *Campaigns of Walker's Texas Division,* 201.

18. Compiled Service Records, reel 144, 146; Eighth Census, Schedule I, reel 1294, 396, reel 1304, 246; *Galveston (Tex.) Weekly News,* 10 May 1864; *Houston (Tex.) Daily Telegraph,* 16 May 1864.

19. Edward W. Cade to Allie Cade, 14 May 1864, Anderson Collection; Blessington, *Campaigns of Walker's Texas Division,* 260; Calvin D. Cowles, *Atlas to Accompany the Official Records of the Union and Confederate Armies* (1891–1895; reprint, New York: Arno Press, 1978), plate 154.

CHAPTER 8
THE LAST YEAR

1. Biography and Diaries of R. S. Gould, 80, Robert Simenton Gould Papers, University of Texas at Austin, Center for American History; Edward W. Cade to Allie Cade, 12, 14 May 1864, John Q. Anderson Collection, Texas State Archives, Austin, Tex.; Joseph P. Blessington, *The Campaigns of Walker's Texas Division by a Private Soldier* (New York: Lange, Little & Co., 1875), 261; Mark Mayo Boatner III, *The Civil War Dictionary* (New York: David McKay, 1959), 500, 894; W. D. Thompson to Oran M. Roberts, 5 January 1865, Oran M. Roberts Papers, University of Texas at Austin, Center for American History.

2. Edward W. Cade to Allie Cade, 14, 24 May 1864, Anderson Collection; Calvin D. Cowles, comp., *Atlas to Accompany the Official Records of the Union and Confederate Armies* (1891–1895; reprint, New York: Arno Press, 1978), plate 155, 158; Blessington, *Campaigns of Walker's Texas Division,* 261–63.

3. Thomas W. Cutrer, ed., "'An Experience in Soldier's Life': The Civil War Letters of Volney Ellis, Adjutant, Twelfth Texas Infantry, Walker's Texas Division, C.S.A.," *Military History of the Southwest* 22 (fall 1992): 163; Edward W. Cade to Allie Cade, 24 May 1864,

Anderson Collection; Blessington, *Campaigns of Walker's Texas Division*, 269–71; T. Michael Parrish, *Richard Taylor: Soldier Prince of Dixie* (Chapel Hill: University of North Carolina Press, 1992), 395–96; Robert L. Kerby, *Kirby Smith's Confederacy: The Trans-Mississippi South, 1863–1865* (New York: Columbia University Press, 1972; reprint, Tuscaloosa: University of Alabama Press, 1991), 321; Boatner, *Civil War Dictionary*, 463.

4. Blessington, *Campaigns of Walker's Texas Division*, 271; Edward W. Cade to Allie Cade, 8, 28 June, 3 July 1864, Anderson Collection; S. W. Farrow to Josephine Farrow, 8 June 1864, S. W. Farrow Papers, University of Texas at Austin, Center for American History; David M. Ray to his mother, 3 July 1864, David M. Ray Papers, University of Texas at Austin, Center for American History.

5. Blessington, *Campaigns of Walker's Texas Division*, 272; David M. Ray to his mother, 30 July 1864; Ray Papers; Cowles, *Atlas to Accompany the Official Records*, plate 155; Kerby, *Kirby Smith's Confederacy*, 328–29; U.S. War Department, *War of the Rebellion: A Compilation of the Official Records of the Union and Confederate Armies*, 128 vols. (Washington, D.C.: Government Printing Office, 1880–1901), ser. I, 41, pt. 1, 111–12.

6. Kerby, *Kirby Smith's Confederacy*, 323–25; *Official Records*, ser. I, 41, pt. 1, 89–90, 96, 103.

7. *Official Records*, ser. I, 41, pt. 1, 95–96, 101, 112; Kerby, *Kirby Smith's Confederacy*, 327; Blessington, *Campaigns of Walker's Texas Division*, 273.

8. Douglas Hale, *The Third Texas Cavalry in the Civil War* (Norman: University of Oklahoma, 1993), 103–5; *Official Records*, 41, pt. 1, 112; Robert S. Gould, 74, Gould Papers; Kerby, *Kirby Smith's Confederacy*, 328.

9. Robert S. Gould, 75–79, Gould Papers; David M. Ray to his mother, 24 August 1864, Ray Papers.

10. *Official Records*, ser. I, 41, pt. 1, 102, 117–18, 120; Cutrer, "An Experience in Soldier's Life,'" 166; Kerby, *Kirby Smith's Confederacy*, 330; Civil War Papers of Captain Thomas J. Foster, "Abstract of Provisions from the 1st day of August 1864 to the 31st day of August 1864," Hill College, Confederate Research Center, Hillsboro, Tex., 11th Texas Infantry file.

11. *Official Records*, ser. I, 41, pt. 1, 105; Blessington, *Campaigns of Walker's Texas Division*, 275–76; Cowles, *Atlas to Accompany the Official Records*, plate 155; C. S. During, 42–44, Diary of Cpl. M. W. Barber and Pvt. C. S. During, University of Texas at Austin, Center for American History; Patricia L. Faust, ed., *Historical Times Illustrated Encyclopedia of the Civil War* (New York: Harper & Row, 1986), 268; Kerby, *Kirby Smith's Confederacy*, 327.

12. Blessington, *Campaigns of Walker's Texas Division*, 277; Cowles, *Atlas to Accompany the Official Records*, plate 154; During, 45, Diary of Corporal M. W. Barber and Private C. S. During; Kerby, *Kirby Smith's Confederacy*, 332–33; Stephen B. Oates, *Confederate Cavalry West of the River* (Austin: University of Texas Press, 1961), 144, 150–51.

13. Blessington, *Campaigns of Walker's Texas Division*, 277–78; During, 47, Diary of Corporal M. W. Barber and Private C. S. During; Kerby, *Kirby Smith's Confederacy*, 334; David M. Ray to his mother, 8 October 1864, Ray Papers.

14. Blessington, *Campaigns of Walker's Texas Division*, 279–81; During, 50–53, Diary of M. W. Barber and Private C. S. During; Cowles, *Atlas to Accompany the Official Records*, plate 158.

15. S. W. Farrow to Josephine Farrow, 16, 25, 27 December 1864, Farrow Papers; Blessington, *Campaigns of Walker's Texas Division,* 281–82.

16. S. W. Farrow to Josephine Farrow, 7, 13 January 1865, Farrow Papers; *Galveston (Tex.) Weekly News,* 8 March 1865; Ledger Book I, 11th Texas Infantry Description Books, Texas State Archives, Austin, Tex.

17. Blessington, *Campaigns of Walker's Texas Division,* 285–87, 289–90; W. H. Tunnard, *A Southern Record: The History of the Third Regiment Louisiana Infantry* (1866; reprint, Dayton, Ohio: Morningside Bookshop, 1988), 332–35.

18. Blessington, *Campaigns of Walker's Texas Division,* 291–92, 299, 301–2; Cowles, *Atlas to Accompany the Official Records,* plate 157; John C. Porter, "Early Days of Pittsburg, Texas, 1859–1874," 37, Confederate Research Center, 18th Texas Infantry file.

19. National Archives and Records Administration, Compiled Service Records of Confederate Soldiers Who Served in Organizations from the State of Texas (microfilm M323), reels 143–146; Ledger I, 11th Texas Infantry Description Books.

20. Jon Harrison, ed., "The Confederate Letters of John Simmons," 52, Confederate Research Center, 22nd Texas Infantry file; Blessington, *Campaigns of Walker's Texas Division,* 303; David M. Ray to his mother, 15 May 1865, Ray Papers; Faust, *Historical Illustrated Encyclopedia of the Civil War,* 736; Robert S. Gould, 80, Gould Papers; Kerby, *Kirby Smith's Confederacy,* 417, 422–24; Joseph Howard Parks, *General Edmund Kirby Smith, C.S.A.* (Baton Rouge: Louisiana State University Press, 1954), 462, 465.

21. David M. Ray to his mother, 15 May 1865, Ray Papers; *Official Records,* ser. I, 48, pt. 2, 1308–9; Robert S. Gould, 80, 82, Gould Papers; *Galveston (Tex.) Daily News,* 14 May 1865; W. W. Heartsill, *Fourteen Hundred and 91 Days in the Confederate Army,* ed. Bell Irvin Wiley (Jackson, Tenn.: McCowat-Mercer Press, 1953; reprint, Wilmington, N.C.: Broadfoot Publishing, 1992), 244, 246; Parks, *General Edmund Kirby Smith,* 472–73; Blessington, *Campaigns of Walker's Texas Division,* 307.

22. Douglas Southall Freeman, *Lee's Lieutenants: A Study in Command,* 3 vols. (New York: Charles Scribner's Sons, 1944), 3: 713; Larry J. Daniel, *Soldiering in the Army of Tennessee: A Portrait of Life in a Confederate Army* (Chapel Hill: University of North Carolina Press, 1991), 167.

23. Robert S. Gould, 82, Gould Papers; Hale, *Third Texas Cavalry,* 277–78, 282–83; Harold B. Simpson, *Hood's Texas Brigade: Lee's Grenadier Guard* (Waco, Tex.: Texian Press, 1970), 468.

24. Reid Mitchell, "The Northern Soldier and His Community," in *Toward a Social History of the American Civil War: Exploratory Essays,* ed. Maris A. Vinovskis (New York: Cambridge University Press, 1990), 85–88.

BIBLIOGRAPHY

Manuscripts

DUKE UNIVERSITY LIBRARY, DURHAM, NORTH CAROLINA
Presley Carter Person Papers (Theophilus and Harriet Perry correspondence)

HILL COLLEGE, CONFEDERATE RESEARCH CENTER, HILLSBORO, TEXAS
11th Texas Infantry file (Thomas J. Foster)
13th Texas Cavalry (dismounted) file (G. B. Layton, John Thomas Stark)
14th Texas Infantry file (J. H. Armstrong)
18th Texas Infantry file (John C. Porter)
22nd Texas Infantry file (John Simmons)

MANSFIELD, LOUISIANA, STATE COMMEMORATIVE AREA
Letter of Private William F. Mills
Waxham, Tom J., Terry G, and H. G. "Battle of Pleasant Hill, La., 9 April 1864,
Opening Phase of Battle," map

TEXAS STATE ARCHIVES, AUSTIN
11th Texas Infantry Description Books
Confederate Pension Applications
Horace Randal Papers, 1854–1855
John Q. Anderson Collection (Edward W. Cade correspondence)
Muster Rolls, companies B, C, D, E, G, H, I, and K of the 28th Texas Cavalry
Texas State Troops Records, Brigade Correspondence, 1861–1865

TULANE UNIVERSITY LIBRARY, NEW ORLEANS, LOUISIANA,
MANUSCRIPTS SECTION
Louisiana Historical Association Collection, Trans-Mississippi Department Papers.

UNITED STATES MILITARY ACADEMY ARCHIVES, WEST POINT, NEW YORK

Official Register of the Officers and Cadets of the U.S. Military Academy, 1850–1854.

National Archives and Service Administration. U.S. Military Academy Cadet Application Papers, 1805–1866 (microfilm, M688).

UNIVERSITY OF NORTH CAROLINA, CHAPEL HILL

Southern Historical Collection (John G. Walker Papers)

UNIVERSITY OF NORTH TEXAS LIBRARY, DENTON

Bureau of the Census. Eighth Census of the United States, 1860. Schedule I (Free Inhabitants), and II (Slave Inhabitants), (microfilm, M653), reels 1287–1312.

Bureau of the Census. Non-Population Schedules, 1850–1880. Schedule IV (Productions of Agriculture), (microfilm, RG29), reels 3–7.

National Archives and Service Administration. Compiled Service Records of Confederate Soldiers Who Served in Organizations From the State of Texas (microfilm, M323), reels 93, 143–146.

Texas State Library. Records of the Comptroller of Public Accounts, Ad Valorem Tax Division. County Real and Personal Property Tax Rolls (microfilm).

UNIVERSITY OF TEXAS AT AUSTIN, CENTER FOR AMERICAN HISTORY

David M. Ray Papers

Diary of Cpl. M. W. Barber and Pvt. C. S. During

James W. Truit Papers

Oran M. Roberts Papers

Robert Simenton Gould Papers

Rufus R. Jones Papers

S. W. Farrow Papers

U.S. ARMY MILITARY HISTORY INSTITUTE, CARLISLE BARRACKS, PENNSYLVANIA

Civil War Times Illustrated Collection, Camille A. J. M. de Polignac Diary

Myron G. Gwinner Collection, John G. Walker Papers

Newspapers

Crockett (Tex.) Weekly Quid Nune
Galveston (Tex.) Daily News
Galveston (Tex.) Tri-Weekly News
Galveston (Tex.) Weekly News
Henderson East Texas Times
Henderson (Tex.) Times
Houston (Tex.) Daily Telegraph
(Marshall) Texas Republican
Tyler (Tex.) Reporter

Public Documents

Cowles, Calvin D., comp. *Atlas to Accompany the Official Records of the Union and Confederate Armies.* 1891–1895. Reprint, New York: Arno Press, 1978.

Heitman, Francis B. *Historical Register and Dictionary of the United States Army, From its Organization, September 29, 1789, to March 2, 1903.* 2 vols. Washington, D.C.: Government Printing Office, 1903.

Hewett, Janet B., Noah Andre Trudeau, and Bryce A. Suderow, eds. *Supplement to the Official Records of the Union and Confederate Armies.* Wilmington, N.C.: Broadfoot Publishing, 1994–

Kennedy, Joseph C. G. *Agriculture of the United States in 1860: Compiled from the Original Returns of the Eighth Census.* 1864. Reprint, New York: Norman Ross Publishing, 1990.

———. *Population of the United States in 1860: Compiled Under the Direction of the Secretary of the Interior.* 1864. Reprint, New York: Norman Ross Publishing, 1990.

Manufacturers of the United States in 1860: Compiled from the Original Returns of the Eighth Census. 1865. Reprint, New York: Norman Ross Publishing, 1990.

Statistics of the United States, (Including Mortality, Property, &c.,) in 1860: Compiled from the Original Returns and being the Final Exhibit of the Eighth Census, Under the Direction of the Secretary of the Interior. 1866. Reprint, New York: Norman Ross Publishing, 1990.

United States Naval War Records Office. *Official Records of the Union and Confederate Navies in the War of the Rebellion.* 30 vols. Washington, D.C.: Government Printing Office, 1894–1922.

United States War Department. *War of the Rebellion: A Compilation of the Official Records of the Union and Confederate Armies.* 128 vols. Washington, D.C.: Government Printing Office, 1880–1901.

Primary Sources

BOOKS

Anderson, John Q., ed. *Brokenburn: The Journal of Kate Stone, 1861–1868.* Baton Rouge: Louisiana State University Press, 1955.

————, ed. *A Texas Surgeon in the C.S.A.* Confederate Centennial Studies, Number Six. Tuscaloosa, Ala.: Confederate Publishing, 1957.

Bearss, Edwin C., ed. *A Louisiana Confederate: Diary of Felix Pierre Poché.* Natchitoches: Louisiana Studies Institute, Northwestern State University, 1972.

Blessington, Joseph P. *The Campaigns of Walker's Texas Division.* New York: Lange, Little & Co., 1875.

Bragg, Junius Newport. *Letters of a Confederate Surgeon.* Camden, Ark.: n.p., 1960.

Brown, Norman D., ed. *Journey to Pleasant Hill: The Civil War Letters of Captain Elijah P. Petty, Walker's Texas Division, C.S.A.* San Antonio: University of Texas Institute of Texan Cultures, 1982.

Caldwell, J. F. C. *The History of a Brigade of South Carolinians, Known First as 'Gregg's,' and Subsequently as 'McGowan's Brigade.'* 1866. Reprint, Dayton, Ohio: Morningside Bookshop, 1974.

Collins, R. M. *Chapters from the Unwritten History of the War Between the States.* 1893. Reprint, Dayton, Ohio: Morningside Bookshop, 1988.

Debray, Xavier Blanchard. *A Sketch of the History of Debray's (26th) Regiment of Texas Cavalry.* 1884. Reprint, Waco Tex. Waco Village Press, 1961.

DeRyee, William, and R. E. Moore. *The Texas Album of the Eighth Legislature, 1860.* Austin, Tex.: Miner, Lambert & Perry, 1860.

Dotson, Susan Merle, comp. *Who's Who of the Confederacy: A Symposium by the Members of the Albert Sidney Johnston Chapter No. 2060, United Daughters of the Confederacy.* San Antonio, Tex.: Naylor, 1966.

Govan, Gilbert E. and James W. Livingood, eds. *The Haskell Memoirs.* New York: G. P. Putnam's Sons, 1960.

Heartsill, W. W. *Fourteen Hundred and 91 Days in the Confederate Army.* Edited by Bell Irvin Wiley. Jackson, Tenn.: McCowat-Mercer Press, 1953. Reprint, Wilmington, N.C.: Broadfoot Publishing, 1992.

Holder, Anne Thiele. *Tennessee to Texas: Francis Richardson Tannehill, 1825–1864.* Austin, Tex.: Pemberton Press, 1966.

Judson, Amos M. *History of the Eighty-Third Regiment Pennsylvania Volunteers.* 1865. Reprint, Dayton, Ohio: Morningside Bookshop, 1986.

Lord, Walter, ed. *The Fremantle Diary: Being the Journal of Lieutenant Colonel Arthur James Lyon Fremantle, Coldstream Guards, on his Three Months in the Southern States.* Boston: Little, Brown, and Co., 1954.

Masterson, Ralph , ed. *Sketches from the Life of Dr. Horace Bishop.* San Angelo, Tex.[?]: n.p., ca. 1930.

Olmsted, Frederic Law. *Journey Through Texas: A Saddle-trip on the Southwestern Frontier.* Edited by James Howard. 1857. Reprint, Austin, Tex.: Von Boeckmann-Jones Press, 1962.

Sperry, A. F. *History of the 33rd Iowa Infantry: Volunteer Regiment, 1863–1866.* 1866. Reprint, Pine Bluff, Ark.: Rare Book Pub., 1982[?].

Taylor, Richard. *Destruction and Reconstruction: Personal Experiences of the Late War.* New York: D. Appleton and Company, 1879.

Tunnard, W. H. *A Southern Record: The History of the Third Regiment Louisiana Infantry.* 1866. Reprint, Dayton, Ohio: Morningside Bookshop, 1988.

Yeary, Mamie, comp. *Reminiscences of the Boys in Gray, 1861–1865.* 1912. Reprint, Dayton, Ohio: Morningside Press, 1986.

ARTICLES

Cutrer, Thomas W., ed. "'Bully for Flournoy's Regiment, We are some Punkins, You'll Bet': The Civil War Letters of Virgil Sullivan Rabb, Captain, Company 'I,' Sixteenth Texas Infantry, C.S.A." *Military History of the Southwest* 19 (fall 1989): 161–90; 20 (spring 1990): 61–96.

———, ed. "'An Experience in Soldier's Life': The Civil War Letters of Volney Ellis, Adjutant, Twelfth Texas Infantry, Walker's Texas Division, C.S.A." *Military History of the Southwest* 22 (fall 1992): 109–72.

Debray, X. B. "A Sketch of Debray's Twenty-Sixth Regiment of Texas Cavalry." *Southern Historical Society Papers* 13 (1885): 153–65.

Johansson, Jane Harris and David H. Johansson. "Two 'Lost' Battle Reports: Horace Randal's and Joseph L. Brent's Reports of the Battles of Mansfield and Pleasant Hill, 8 and 9 April 1864." *Military History of the West* 23 (fall 1993): 169–80.

Lale, Max S. "For Lack of a Nail." *East Texas Historical Journal* 30, no. 1 (1992): 34–43.

———. "A Letter from Leonard Randal to his Son." *East Texas Historical Association* 23, no. 2 (1985): 47–48.

———. "New Light on the Battle of Mansfield." *East Texas Historical Journal* 25 no. 2 (1987): 34–41.

Secondary Sources

BOOKS

Allan, William. *History of the Campaign of Gen. T. J. (Stonewall) Jackson in the Shenandoah Valley of Virginia from November 4, 1861, to June 17, 1862.* 1912. Reprint, Dayton, Ohio: Morningside Bookshop, 1974.

Anders, Leslie. *The Twenty-First Missouri: From Home Guard to Union Regiment.* Contributions in Military History, Number 11. Westport, Conn.: Greenwood Press, 1975.

Arceneaux, William. *Acadian General: Alfred Mouton and the Civil War.* 2nd ed. Lafayette: Center for Louisiana Studies, University of Southwestern Louisiana Press, 1981.

Bailey, Anne J. *Between the Enemy and Texas: Parsons's Texas Cavalry in the Civil War.* Fort Worth: Texas Christian University Press, 1989.

Bailey, Fred Arthur. *Class and Tennessee's Confederate Generation.* Chapel Hill: The University of North Carolina Press, 1987.

Banasik, Michael E. *Embattled Arkansas: The Prairie Grove Campaign of 1862.* Wilmingon, N.C.: Broadfoot Publishing, 1996.

Bearss, Edwin C. *The Campaign for Vicksburg.* 3 vols. Dayton, Ohio: Morningside House, 1991.

———. *Steele's Retreat from Camden and the Battle of Jenkin's [sic] Ferry.* Little Rock: Arkansas Civil War Centennial Commission, 1967.

Beers, Henry Putney. *The Confederacy: A Guide to the Archives of the Government of the Confederate States of America.* Washington, D.C.: National Archives and Records Administration, 1986.

Beringer, Richard E., Herman Hattaway, Archer Jones, and William N. Still Jr. *Why the South Lost the Civil War.* Athens: University of Georgia Press, 1986.

Betts, Vicki. *Smith County, Texas in the Civil War.* Tyler, Tex.: Jack T. Greer Memorial Fund of the Smith County Historical Society, 1978.

Biographical Encyclopedia of Texas. New York: Southern Publishing, 1880.

Boatner, Mark M., III. *The Civil War Dictionary.* New York: David McKay, 1959.

Branda, Eldon Stephen, ed. *The Handbook of Texas: A Supplement.* Austin: Texas State Historical Association, 1976.

Campbell, Randolph B. *A Southern Community in Crisis: Harrison County, Texas, 1850–1880.* Austin: Texas State Historical Association, 1983.

Campbell, Randolph B., and Richard G. Lowe. *Wealth and Power in Antebellum Texas.* College Station: Texas A&M University Press, 1977.

Castel, Albert. *General Sterling Price and the Civil War in the West.* Baton Rouge: Louisiana State University Press, 1968.

Catton, Bruce. *Mr. Lincoln's Army.* New York: Doubleday, 1951.

Cole, Garold L. *Civil War Eyewitnesses.* Columbia: University of South Carolina Press, 1988.

The Compact Edition of the Oxford English Dictionary. 3 vols. Oxford: Oxford University Press, 1986.

Cornish, Dudley Taylor. *The Sable Arm: Negro Troops in the Union Army, 1861–1865.* New York: Longmans, Green and Co., 1956.

Cunningham, H. H. *Doctors in Gray: The Confederate Medical Service.* Baton Rouge: Louisiana State University Press, 1958.

Current, Richard N., ed. *Encyclopedia of the Confederacy.* 4 vols. New York: Simon & Schuster, 1993.

Daniel, Larry J. *Soldiering in the Army of Tennessee: A Portrait of Life in a Confederate Army.* Chapel Hill: University of North Carolina Press, 1991.

Dougan, Michael B. *Confederate Arkansas: The People and Policies of a Frontier State in Wartime.* University, Ala.: University of Alabama Press, 1976.

Duaine, Carl L. *The Dead Men Wore Boots: An Account of the 32nd Texas Volunteer Cavalry, C.S.A., 1862–1865.* Austin, Tex.: San Felipe Press, 1966.

Dyer, Frederick H. *A Compendium of the War of the Rebellion.* 2 vols. 1908. Reprint, Dayton, Ohio: Morningside Bookshop, 1978.

Edmonds, David C. *Yankee Autumn in Acadiana: A Narrative of the Great Texas Overland Expedition through Southwestern Louisiana, October–December 1863.* Lafayette, La.: Acadiana Press, 1979.

Estaville, Lawrence E., Jr. *Confederate Neckties: Louisiana Railroads in the Civil War.* Ruston: Louisiana Tech University, 1989.

Evans, Clement, ed. *Confederate Military History: Extended Edition.* Vol. 15, *Texas.* 1899. Reprint, Wilmington, N.C.: Broadfoot Publishing Company, 1989.

Faust, Patricia L., ed. *Historical Times Illustrated Encyclopedia of the Civil War.* New York: Harper & Row, 1986.

Felmly, Bradford K., and John C. Grady. *Suffering to Silence: 29th Texas Cavalry, CSA, Regimental History.* Quanah, Tex.: Nortex Press, 1975.

Fox, William F. *Regimental Losses in the American Civil War, 1861–1865.* 1898. Reprint, Dayton, Ohio: Morningside Bookshop, 1974.

Franklin, John Hope. *The Militant South, 1800–1861.* Cambridge, Mass.: Harvard University Press, 1956.

Frazier, Donald S. *Blood & Treasure: Confederate Empire in the Southwest.* College Station: Texas A&M University Press, 1995.

Freeman, Douglas Southall. *Lee's Lieutenants: A Study in Command.* 3 vols. New York: Charles Scribner's Sons, 1942–1944.

Gallaway, B. P. *The Ragged Rebel: A Common Soldier in W. H. Parsons' Texas Cavalry, 1861–1865.* Austin: University of Texas Press, 1988.

Geary, James W. *We Need Men: The Union Draft in the Civil War.* DeKalb: Northern Illinois University Press, 1991.

Glatthaar, Joseph T. *Forged in Battle: The Civil War Alliance of Black Soldiers and White Officers.* New York: The Free Press, 1990.

Glatthaar, Joseph T. *The March to the Sea and Beyond: Sherman's Troops in the Savannah and Carolinas Campaigns.* New York: New York University Press, 1983.

Griffith, Paddy. *Battle Tactics of the Civil War.* New Haven: Yale University Press, 1989.

Hagerman, Edward. *The American Civil War and the Origins of Modern Warfare: Ideas, Organization, and Field Command.* Bloomington: Indiana University Press, 1988.

Hale, Douglas. *The Third Texas Cavalry in the Civil War.* Norman: University of Oklahoma Press, 1993.

Hall, Martin Hardwick. *The Confederate Army of New Mexico.* Austin, Tex.: Presidial Press, 1978.

Henderson, Harry McCorry. *Texas in the Confederacy.* San Antonio, Tex.: Naylor, 1955.

History of Houston County, 1687–1979. Tulsa, Okla.: Heritage Publishing, 1979.

Hohes, Pauline Buck. *A Centennial History of Anderson County.* San Antonio, Tex.: Naylor, 1936.

Jackson, Ronald Vern. *Texas 1860 Census Index.* North Salt Lake, Utah: Accelerated Indexing Systems International, 1982.

Johnson, Ludwell H. *Red River Campaign: Politics and Cotton in the Civil War.* Baltimore: Johns Hopkins University Press, 1958.

Josephy, Alvin. *The Civil War in the American West.* New York: A. A. Knopf, 1991.

Kerby, Robert L. *Kirby Smith's Confederacy: The Trans-Mississippi South, 1863–1865.* New York: Columbia University Press, 1972; reprint, Tuscaloosa: University of Alabama Press, 1991.

Lathrop, Barnes F. *Migration Into East Texas, 1835–1860: A Study from the United States Census.* Austin: Texas State Historical Association, 1949.

Linderman, Gerald F. *Embattled Courage: The Experience of Combat in the American Civil War.* New York: The Free Press, 1987.

Lonn, Ella. *Desertion during the Civil War.* 1928. Reprint, Gloucester, Mass.: Peter Smith, 1966.

Lord, Francis A. *Civil War Collector's Encyclopedia: Arms, Uniforms, and Equipment of the Union and Confederacy.* Harrisburg, Pa.: Stackpole, 1963. Reprint, Secaucus, N.J.: Castle Books, 1982.

Lowe, Richard G., and Randolph B. Campbell. *Planters & Plain Folk: Agriculture in Antebellum Texas.* Dallas, Tex.: Southern Methodist University, 1987.

McCaslin, Richard B. *Tainted Breeze: The Great Hanging at Gainesville, Texas, 1862.* Baton Rouge: Louisiana State University Press, 1993.

McPherson, James M. *Ordeal by Fire: The Civil War and Reconstruction.* New York: McGraw-Hill, 1992.

Memorial and Biographical History of Navarro, Henderson, Anderson, Limestone, Freestone and Leon Counties, Texas. Chicago: Lewis Publishing, 1893.

Memorial and Biographical History of McLennan, Falls, Bell and Coryell Counties, Texas. Chicago: Lewis Publishing, 1893.

Mitchell, Reid. *Civil War Soldiers.* New York: Viking, 1988.

Moore, Albert Burton. *Conscription and Conflict in the Confederacy.* New York: Macmillan, 1924.

Nolen, Alan T. *The Iron Brigade.* New York: Macmillan, 1961.

Nichols, James L. *The Confederate Quartermaster in the Trans-Mississippi.* Austin: University of Texas Press, 1964.

Nunn, W. C., ed. *Ten More Texans in Gray.* Hillsboro, Tex.: Hill Junior College Press, 1980.

———, ed. *Ten Texans in Gray.* Hillsboro, Tex.: Hill Junior College Press, 1968.

Oates, Stephen B. *Confederate Cavalry West of the River.* Austin: University of Texas Press, 1961.

Parks, Joseph Howard. *General Edmund Kirby Smith, C.S.A.* Baton Rouge: Louisiana State University Press, 1954.

Parrish, T. Michael. *Richard Taylor: Soldier Prince of Dixie*. Chapel Hill: University of North Carolina Press, 1992.

Pullen, John J. *The Twentieth Maine*. Philadelphia: Lippincott, 1957.

Robertson, James I., Jr. *Soldiers Blue and Gray*. Columbia: University of South Carolina Press, 1988.

————. *The Stonewall Brigade*. Baton Rouge: Louisiana State University Press, 1963.

Rushing, Anthony. *Ranks of Honor: A Regimental History of the Eleventh Arkansas Infantry and Poe's Battalion of Cavalry*. Little Rock, Ark.: n.p., 1990.

Shea, William L. and Earl J. Hess. *Pea Ridge: Civil War Campaign in the West*. Chapel Hill: University of North Carolina Press, 1992.

Sibley, Marilyn McAdams. *Lone Stars and State Gazettes: Texas Newspapers before the Civil War*. College Station: Texas A & M Press, 1983.

Simpson, Harold B. *Hood's Texas Brigade: Lee's Grenadier Guard*. Waco: Texian Press, 1970.

Spurlin, Charles D., comp. *Texas Veterans in the Mexican War: Muster Rolls of Texas Military Units*. Victoria, Tex.: Victoria College, 1984.

Steiner, Paul E. *Disease in the Civil War: Natural Biological Warfare in 1861–1865*. Springfield, Ill.: Charles C. Thomas, Publisher, 1968.

Tyler, Ron, ed. *New Handbook of Texas*. 6 vols. Austin: Texas State Historical Association, 1996.

Vinkovskis, Maris A., ed. *Toward a Social History of the Civil War: Exploratory Essays*. New York: Cambridge University Press, 1990.

Warren, Ezra J. *Generals in Gray: Lives of the Confederate Commanders*. Baton Rouge: Louisiana State University Press, 1959.

Weddle, Robert S. *Plow-Horse Cavalry: The Caney Creek Boys of the Thirty-fourth Texas*. Austin, Tex.: Madrona Press, 1974.

Wiley, Bell Irvin. *The Life of Johnny Reb: The Common Soldier of the Confederacy*. Indianapolis, Ind.: Bobbs-Merrill Company, 1943. Reprint, Baton Rouge: Louisiana State University Press, 1986.

Wilkinson, Warren. *Mother, May You Never See the Sights I Have Seen: The Fifty-Seventh Massachusetts Veteran Volunteers in the Army of the Potomac, 1864–1865*. New York: Harper and Row, 1990.

Winters, John D. *The Civil War in Louisiana*. Baton Rouge: Louisiana State University Press, 1963.

Woodworth, Stephen. *Jefferson Davis and His Generals: The Failure of Confederate Command in the West*. Lawrence: University Press of Kansas, 1990.

Wright, Marcus J., comp., and Harold B. Simpson, ed. *Texas in the War, 1861–1865*. Hillsboro, Tex.: Hill Junior College, 1965.

ARTICLES

Bailey, Anne J. "A Texas Cavalry Raid: Reaction to Black Soldiers and Contrabands." *Civil War History* 35 (June 1989): 138–52.

Barr, Alwyn. "Texan Losses in the Red River Campaign, 1864." *Texas Military History* 3 (summer 1963): 103–10.

Bergeron, Arthur W., Jr. "A Colonel Gains his Wreath: Henry Gray's Louisiana Brigade at the Battle of Mansfield, April 8, 1864." *Civil War Regiments: A Journal of the American Civil War* 4, no. 2 (1994): 1–25.

Cain, Marvin R. "A 'Face of Battle' Needed: An Assessment of Motives and Men in Civil War Historiography." *Civil War History* 28 (March 1982): 5–27.

Connelly, Thomas L. "Vicksburg: Strategic Point or Propaganda Device?" *Military Affairs* 34 (April 1970): 49–53.

Crawford, Martin. "Confederate Volunteering and Enlistments in Ashe County, North Carolina, 1861–1862." *Civil War History* 37 (March 1991): 29–50.

Crump, Tanya. "The Battle of Pleasant Hill." *North Louisiana Historical Association Journal* 19, no. 4 (1988): 121–32.

Glatthaar, Joseph T. "The 'New' Civil War History: An Overview." *Pennsylvania Magazine of History & Biography* 115 (July 1991): 339–69.

Hale, Douglas. "Life and Death Among the Lone Star Defenders: Cherokee County Boys in the Civil War." *East Texas Historical Journal* 29, no. 2 (1991): 26–40.

———. "The Third Texas Cavalry: A Socioeconomic Profile of a Confederate Regiment." *Military History of the Southwest* 19 (spring 1989): 1–26.

Harris, Emily J. "Sons and Soldiers: Deerfield, Massachusetts and the Civil War." *Civil War History* 30 (June 1984): 151–71.

Hess, Earl J. "The 12th Missouri Infantry: A Socio-Military Profile of a Union Regiment." *Missouri Historical Review* 76 (October 1981): 53–77.

Johnson, Ludwell H. "The Red River Campaign." In *The Civil War Battlefield Guide,* edited by Frances H. Kennedy, 163–66. Boston: Houghton Mifflin, 1990.

Kemp, Thomas R. "Community and War: The Civil War Experience of Two New Hampshire Towns." In *Toward a Social History of the Civil War: Exploratory Essays,* edited by Maris A. Vinkovskis. New York: Cambridge University Press, 1990.

Marvel, William. "A Poor Man's Fight: Civil War Enlistment Patterns in Conway, New Hampshire." *Historical New Hampshire* 43, no. 1 (1988): 21–40.

Mitchell, Reid. "The Northern Soldier and His Community." In *Toward a Social History of the Civil War: Exploratory Essays,* edited by Maris A. Vinkovskis. New York: Cambridge University Press, 1990.

Riggs, David F. "Sailors of the U. S. S. *Cairo*: Anatomy of a Gunboat Crew." *Civil War History* 28 (September 1982): 266–73.

Rorabaugh, W. J. "Who Fought for the North in the Civil War? Concord, Massachusetts, Enlistments." *Journal of American History* 73 (December 1986): 695–701.

Ruffner, Kevin Conley. "Civil War Desertion from a Black Belt Regiment: An Examination of the 44th Virginia Infantry." In *The Edge of the South: Life in Nineteenth-Century Virginia,* edited by Edward L. Ayers and John C. Willis. Charlottesville: University Press of Virginia, 1991.

Savas, Theodore P. "A Death at Mansfield: Col. James Hamilton Beard and the Consolidated Crescent Regiment." *Civil War Regiments: A Journal of the American Civil War* 4, no. 2 (1994): 68–103.

Vinovskis, Maris A. "Have Social Historians Lost the Civil War? Some Preliminary Demographic Speculations." *Journal of American History* 76 (June 1989): 34–58.

Wilson, J. Woodfin, Jr. "Civil War Medicine in North Louisiana." *North Louisiana Historical Association Journal* 17, no. 2–3 (1986): 58–64.

———. "Some Aspects of Medical Services in the Trans-Mississippi Department of the Confederate States of America, 1862–1865." *North Louisiana Historical Association Journal* 12, no. 4 (1981): 123–46.

Winschel, Terrence J. "To Rescue Gibraltar: John G. Walker's Texas Division and the Relief of Fortress Vicksburg." *Civil War Regiments: A Journal of the American Civil War* 3, no. 3 (1993): 33–58.

Woodworth, Steven E. "'Dismembering the Confederacy': Jefferson Davis and the Trans-Mississippi West." *Military History of the Southwest* 20 (spring 1990): 1–22.

Wooster, Ralph A. and Robert Wooster. "'Rarin' for a Fight': Texans in the Confederate Army." *Southwestern Historical Quarterly* 84 (April 1981): 387–426.

UNPUBLISHED WORKS

Bailey, Lelia. "The Life and Public Career of O. M. Roberts, 1815–1883." Ph.D. diss., University of Texas at Austin, 1932.

Kiper, Richard Leslie. "Dead-End at the Crossroads: The Battles of Mansfield (Sabine Crossroads) and Pleasant Hill, Louisiana, 8 and 9 1864." Master's thesis, Rice University, 1976.

INDEX

Executions, 44–45, 83–84. *See also* 28th Texas Cavalry, execution

Fairfield, Tex., 9
Falls County, Tex., 148
Farrow, S. W., xiii, 47, 56, 71, 75, 87, 97, 128, 133
15th Texas Infantry, 29, 69, 82
5th United States Artillery, Battery G, 103
50th Indiana Infantry, 118
1st Arkansas Infantry [African descent], 56
1st Kansas Colored Infantry, 115
First Manassas, battle of, 43
1st Mississippi Infantry [African descent], 54
1st Texas Infantry, 14, 136–37
1st United States Dragoons, 7
Fitts, O. A., 86
Fitzpatrick, Rene, Jr., 25, 32, 85–86, 120, 146
Fleummons, George, 149
Flinn, J. J., 79
Florida, state of, 43
Flournoy, George, 74
Flournoy's brigade, 29, 82–83
Food supplies, 31, 39, 42, 44, 82, 86. *See also* 28th Texas Cavalry, food supplies
Ford, C. E., 18
Forney, John H., 131–32, 134–35
Forney's division, 131, 134–36
Fort Beauregard, La., 79–80, 87
Fort DeRussy, La., 51, 73, 87, 92–95; capture of, 91, 94, 145–46, 148
Fort Donelson, Tenn., battle of, 4, 92
Fort Humbug, La., 93
Fort Jesup, La., 97, 99
Fort Smith, Ark., 38, 92, 115
Fort Sumter, S.C., 3
48th Ohio Infantry, 103–4
43rd Illinois Infantry, 120
Foster, W. J., 19
Fountain Hill, Ark., 46
14th Texas Infantry, xiii, 29, 34, 77, 79, 86, 88, 97, 105, 109, 117–18, 121, 130, 141
4th Texas Mounted Volunteers, 21
France, 80, 92
Franklin, William B., 80–81, 83, 89, 92, 100, 104, 138

Freestone County, Tex., 8–9, 11, 16, 29, 147–48
Freestone Freemen. *See* Company H, 28th Texas Cavalry
Fuller, Jesse W., 64, 88

Galveston, Tex., 9, 62, 83, 136
Galveston Daily News, 135
Galveston Weekly News, 122, 143
Garner, John N., 28, 67
Garrett, R. M., 147
Gause's brigade, 108
Gay, W. T., 145
Gay, W. W., 147
Gee, James H., 64
George, G. W., 147
Georgia, state of, 9, 18
Gibbs, Archibald P., 149
Gifford, E. L., 144
Gilliam, W. H., 145
Givins, H. L., 17
Goodrich's Landing, La., skirmish at, 56, 63
Gould, Robert S., xiii, 29–30, 103, 109, 118, 125, 129–30, 136
Gould's Battalion, xiii, 29, 34, 77, 88, 105, 109, 117–18, 121, 125, 130, 136
Grandberry, Henry, 56
Grand Ecore, La., 74, 99, 106, 110
Grand Gulf, Miss., 51–52
Grant, Ulysses S., 37, 45–46, 49–51, 53, 80, 99
Gray's brigade, 103
Green, Henry J., 143
Green, Thomas, 101, 110, 113
Greene, Colton, 116
Greene's brigade, 116
Green's brigade (Thomas Green), 80–81, 83, 100, 106, 110–11
Gregg, John J., 18
Guttery, D., 145
Guynes, John, 133

Haldeman's (Horace) Texas Battery, 34, 44, 66, 141
Hall, Henry Gerard, xiii, 13–14, 17, 85, 113, 117–18, 120

INDEX

INDEX

INDEX